Fighting to Find Peace:
A Belfast Boxer's Journey

My Autobiography

Eamon McAuley

ORPEN PRESS

Published by
Orpen Press
Upper Floor, Unit B3
Hume Centre
Hume Avenue
Park West Industrial Estate
Dublin 12

email: info@orpenpress.com
www.orpenpress.com

Paperback ISBN 978-1-78605-124-0
ePub ISBN 978-1-78605-125-7

Printed in Dublin by SPRINTprint Ltd

Fighting to Find Peace

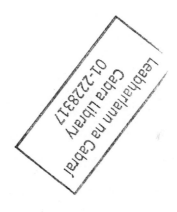

About the Author

Eamon McAuley grew up in the Ardoyne area of North Belfast. He boxed as an amateur since the age of twelve, having a very successful boxing career in both Ireland and England, winning many national titles. McAuley went on to have twelve professional fights. Since his boxing career ended he has been involved in boxing as a coach and a commentator, and is widely regarded as a local boxing expert and historian. McAuley was instrumental in getting three boxing statues erected in Belfast and in setting up the Belfast Boxers Facebook page, which has over 9,000 followers. He now has a growing online presence with his YouTube channel having over 1,000 subscribers.

The Boxer's Prayer

I ask you not for victory, for somehow that seems wrong, but only for protection and courage to be strong. Strength not to conquer but just that I fight well, and prove myself a sportsman at the final bell. I ask you Christ of suffering, that should I suffer pain, I'll offer it for all my sins so that it won't be in vain. And if perhaps he cuts me and the bright red blood I see, I ask that I remember the blood you shed for me.

Dedicated to the people of Ardoyne

Foreword by Barry McGuigan

I remember watching Eamon McAuley winning the Amateur Boxing Association (the ABA) title in 1985, against a man I later shared the ring with in sparring, the very clever Carl Crook. It was a tremendous fight and Eamon won it with a spectacular overhand right in round two. Then I got to meet Eamon when he joined the great stable of boxers we had at the time in the Castle Street Gym in Belfast in 1985. I also had the pleasure of sparring with Eamon and starting a friendship with him, that is still ongoing today (33 years later). As a fighter, Eamon was a precocious talent and a very heavy puncher. Sadly, the stars just didn't align for him as a pro and he did not get the breaks. I remember some years later, when Eamon was in semi-retirement, I rang him and enquired as to what he was doing regarding his boxing career and I fixed him up with Barry Hearn, and I told Barry that Eamon had the ability to be a world champion. I always found Eamon to be a bright, articulate, straight-talking honest bloke; someone I could be relaxed around and trust implicitly. Eamon's knowledge of boxing is incredible, and he remains a real student of the game. I was fascinated to read about his dad, Coco, and many of his exploits on the streets of Belfast. Coco was, quite rightly known, as the hardest man in Belfast. I was also unaware that Eamon's great-uncle was former world flyweight boxing champion, the legendary Rinty Monaghan, whom I had met on a few memorable occasions.

Eamon is such an aficionado of the sport that he embarrassed me one day. Here's how it went: we were chatting about my fourth professional fight in the Ulster Hall against the late great Jean Marc Renard from Belgium, and I told Eamon that Renard hit me with a fantastic left hook in the seventh round that dropped me to my knees for the first time in my career. Eamon interrupted me to say that it was a right hand that decked me and I said, 'With respect Eamon I took the punch and I will always remember that punch and believe me it was a sweet left hook,' and Eamon (like a dog with a bone) wouldn't let go and said, 'Well Barry, I got hold of a very rare private video of that fight from a collector, and I was watching it for the umpteenth time less than a week ago and I am telling you it was a right swing that brought you to your knees.' In the end, we agreed to disagree and we moved on (or so I thought).

Less than a week later, a video of the Renard fight arrived in the post, sent by Eamon, and I watched it for the first time ever and lo and behold, Eamon was correct – it was a right that put me down. Renard must have hit me harder than I thought. I have never argued with Eamon about fight facts again.

In finishing, I would like to say how delighted I am to be asked by Eamon to write a few words about him and his inspiring, engrossing, honest, witty and sometimes heart-breaking autobiography, which he himself wrote every word of. I loved it and I hope you do too.

Barry McGuigan

Acknowledgements

I have often asked myself, why do I want to write a book about me? Why do I want people knowing my business? I suppose I have always been an open book anyway. I wrote most of this book during a very difficult and challenging period in my life. I found writing very therapeutic. I never intended to release to the public what I was writing. When I started writing stories about Ardoyne, I just couldn't stop. People have always told me there should be a book written about my Dad. Maybe one day, there will be. I wrote most of this book about eight years ago and then parked it for a few years. I came back to it two to three years later and did some more work on it. Then as I was on the verge of looking for a publisher, a book came out about another Ardoyne character, Eamon Magee (another product of our environment), and this was a big setback for me. It would have been silly to release a book about a boxer from Ardoyne called Eamon when a book about a boxer from Ardoyne called Eamon had just been released. I put my book on hold again. I have waited a couple of years to give Eamon's book some space, and I think now is as good a time as any to get my story out there. I can't wait forever. As a practising Christian, I have sought to be honest and truthful. Regarding stories of my Dad, 'Coco', I have to take people at face value. Believe me when I say, that I have been around some bullshitters in my time. As I'm getting older (and hopefully wiser), I can better discern them. Some friends said, 'Juice the book up'. Believe me when I say, that I wouldn't be dishonest and deceitful and simply put there's no need! Some people's names have been omitted for obvious reasons, as I wouldn't want to cause any hurt or embarrassment to anyone. Special thanks to Orpen Press, to Trevor Gordon and his wife, Sarah, and to all the Ardoyne library staff. Thank you also to Dr Anthony McKeown for helping with the spelling, grammar, formatting, etc. and for helping to put the story together in a coherent way. In addition, I want to thank them for their encouragement and support. I could not have done it without you. I hope you all enjoy reading it.

Eamon McAuley

List of Abbreviations

ABA	Amateur Boxing Association
ABC	Amateur Boxing Club
ABH	Actual Bodily Harm
BBC	British Broadcasting Corporation
DAAD	Direct Action Against Drugs
EBU	European Boxing Union
FC	Football Club
GAA	Gaelic Athletic Association
GB	Great Britain
GBH	Grievous Bodily Harm
HAF	Hard as Fuck
HTF	Harder than Fuck
IBC	International Boxing Council
IBF	International Boxing Federation
IBO	International Boxing Organisation
IPLO	Irish People's Liberation Organisation
IRA	Irish Republican Army
ITV	Independent Television
KO	Knockout
LA	Los Angeles
LOL	Laugh out Loud
MLA	Member of the Legislative Assembly
MP	Member of Parliament
NABC	National Association of Boys Clubs
PIPS	Public Initiative for Prevention of Suicide and Self-Harm
RIP	Rest in Peace

RUC	Royal Ulster Constabulary
SDLP	Social, Democratic and Labour Party
SJB	St John Bosco
UDA	Ulster Defence Association
USA	United States of America
UTV	Ulster Television
UVF	Ulster Volunteer Force
VOL	Volunteer
WBA	World Boxing Association
WBC	World Boxing Council
WBO	World Boxing Organisation
WBU	World Boxing Union
YTP	Youth Training Programme

Table of Contents

1

Growing Up in Violent Times

I was born on the 4 January 1966 in Butler Street in the Ardoyne area of North Belfast, the middle of three siblings born to Patrick (Patsy) McAuley and Roseleen O'Kane. My sister, Tanya, was the eldest of the three and Paul was the youngest. Mum and dad married in Holy Cross Church on the Crumlin Road in 1964, hence they celebrated their fiftieth wedding anniversary in 2014. My grandparents on my dad's side, were Harry and Sarah McAuley, of 158 Brompton Park and on my mum's side, Edward and Bridget O'Kane, from 111 Butler Street.

I was born with my fists closed tight and they couldn't get them opened. They thought there was a problem and there were some worrying moments, but a special nurse was sent for and she eventually prized my hands opened. Then Peggy O'Rourke from Ardoyne, who was on the same ward, and had also given birth to a daughter that day shouted, 'He's going to be a boxer!' I do not have many memories of Butler Street where my mum and dad lived with my granny Bridget until we got a house up in Ligoniel (my granda Edward 'Ned' died in 1963), but I do recall an incident when we moved to Ligoniel. Mum was telling a bedtime story to Tanya and me (Paul was not born yet), when a bat flew in through the open bedroom window. Tanya, mum and I were squealing our heads off when my dad entered the bedroom, with only a bath towel wrapped around him, and killed the bat. We moved to Fairfield Street in Ardoyne shortly after that. My first memory of Fairfield Street was when we moved there in 1969/1970, and watching in anticipation as my mother turned the key in the front door to enter the living room. I must have been two or three years of age and I am 54 now, but believe me, I can still close my eyes and relive that moment.

My brother, Paul, was born later that year on the 1 December. Fairfield Street was two small rows of houses that ran horizontal off Butler Street. We lived on the right-hand side in the second door (number 3), one of the fourteen houses on the block. The houses on the other side were much older and had seventeen dwellings. There were no gardens for these houses, but looking back I do think gardens were intended on our side, as the footpath was twice the width of any other in the district and had one half flagged, and the other half nearest the house cemented. These houses were three-bedroom dwellings – two up one down (the master bedroom), but most households had the lower bedroom as a dining room or an extended kitchen, which is what we had. This being the case, I shared a bedroom with my brother and sister in Fairfield Street until we moved to Estoril Park in 1981.

Tanya was sixteen and I was fifteen, before she had a bedroom of her own. Our side of Fairfield Street had hot running water, which made a big difference to the household. Unfortunately, like all streets in the area, except upper Elmfield Street, there were only outside toilets and no bathroom, just a big tin bath that was put out in the kitchen every Saturday night. We did have trips to the Falls Baths though, every now and then.

On 9–10 August 1971, when I was five years old, the British Army conducted Operation Demetrius, which was the introduction of internment (imprisonment without trial), which led to the mass arrest and internment of 342 people suspected of being involved with the Irish Republican Army (IRA). As the British Army enforced internment, many Republican areas, such as Ardoyne, were targeted. Homes were raided and many arrests were made. Like many other families in our street, such as the Donnelly's and Kennedy's, myself, my mother, my older sister, Tanya, and my younger brother, Paul, had to flee the area, while the men of Ardoyne stayed behind to defend the district as best as they could. We all ended up in the village of Gormanstown in County Meath in the Irish Republic, where we were welcomed and well-looked after at the local Irish army barracks. Overall, nearly 3000 refugees arrived in Gormanstown during August 1971. Many were forced to sleep in the hangars initially and then tents, while field kitchens were hastily created to ease the situation. The army medical corps were the doctors and nurses for the refugees over a two-year period from 1969 to 1971. It is estimated that up to 12,000 people came to Gormanstown from the North. Some of the refugees were born there and some families decided to stay there, and no doubt are well established now.

Four months after the introduction of internment on 20 December 1971, Margaret McCorry our neighbour at number one was shot dead in an exchange of gunfire between the IRA and the army. Margaret was on her way to Fusco's chippy when she got caught in the exchange. She was twenty years old and was due to get married to Michael McCarthy from America in a few months. Just two months later on the 19 February 1972, our neighbour on the other side David McAuley (no relation) of number 5 was shot and killed in an accidental discharge from an IRA weapon (he was just fifteen years old). David McAuley was older than me and was a member of Na Fianna Eireann (IRA Youth). I remember once he borrowed my football and on returning it, he explained that it had burst. I started to cry and, in an effort to console me, he gave me one of the green cloth hats worn in Vietnam at the time. The youths of Ardoyne were also wearing them, so I was happy enough.

A couple of months after interment was introduced, the British Army would often wreck homes, bully families and arrest young men, knowing that they would be subjected to inhumane treatment and in all probability torture, at the hands of special branch of the Royal Ulster Constabulary (RUC). I remember the British Army raiding our house and digging up our concrete steps in the backyard and waking us up and getting Tanya, Paul (who was just two), and me out of bed. I remember my dad being livid that the Brits got his children out of bed. He was one of the lucky ones who was not dragged out of his house and forcefully put into the back of a British Army Saracen.

A vivid memory I have of this time, were the brutal murders by the British Army on 23 October 1971, of my mother's cousins, sisters Dorothy Maguire and Maura Meehan. On this particular day, Dorothy and Maura were travelling in a car to warn the people of the Lower Falls that the British Army were on their way and that a raid on people's homes was imminent. They had been sitting in the back of a car (there was four in the car), and while they were warning the people of the Lower Falls (with horns), shots rang out and the sisters were killed. This was one of the first shoot-to-kill incidents of the Troubles. I went to their funerals with my mum, and I can still remember it. Tragically, Dorothy was only nineteen and Maura, who was just 30, was married with four children. Dorothy was shot through the back of her head as the shots came through the back windscreen. Because her face had been completely blown away, the coffin remained closed during the wake. Their mother, Bridget, had three daughters, and as well as losing

Dorothy and Maura, she also lost another daughter, Madge, who died at sixteen from knee sarcoma (blood poison).

There was a court case regarding Dorothy and Maura's murders. The findings proved beyond all reasonable doubt that they were completely innocent people. The soldiers, however, were cleared of any involvement in their deaths, even though they were the ones who riddled the car. They knew that they were immune to prosecution and were able to lie about killing Irish people, then lie about it in court and then get off, scot-free. Only three soldiers ever did time for killing Catholics, but they got released early, were let back into the British Army and then promoted! Many legacy cases of killings by armed forces during the Troubles remain a contentious and unresolved issue to this day. Gerry Adams knew the Maguire family well and he wrote about them in his book *Selected Writings* (Adams, 1994). Their dad, Ned Maguire, was a Republican legend who had once escaped from the Crumlin Road prison in the 1940s. The family were from the Whiterock/Ballymurphy area in West Belfast. Ned and Bridget also had five sons and the youngest, Edward (also called Ned), joined the IRA shortly after his sisters' deaths and was sentenced to life imprisonment (and went to Long Kesh) for murdering a judge. A female witness identified Ned as the person running away from the scene, but the witness had earlier picked out two other people who had cast iron alibis and they were released, so where was her credibility? I remember in 1985–1986, Ned sent word to me to come up and visit him (I would have been on TV and in the papers all the time then), so my mum and I went up to Long Kesh to meet him and I can still remember it vividly. Ned was a man-mountain and was both feared and revered by the screws (prison warders). I remember he winked to me and said, 'Watch this', and he threw his box of matches on the floor and whistled to the screw. He looked down at the matches and the screw walked over, lifted them, put them on our table and smiled. I was astounded

In these violent times that I grew up in, I encountered various deaths of innocent people in my area by both the British Army and Loyalists. For instance, another neighbour at number 19 on our side of the street, Tommy 'Tucker' McAuley (again no relation), was shot twice in the head while standing outside his own backyard door. Though Tucker somehow survived the ordeal, he was left badly brain damaged. Tragically, I also had two childhood mates who were murdered during the conflict. Danny Barrett was murdered by the British Army as he sat outside his front door; he was only fifteen years old. This happened during the hunger strikes on 9 July 1981. The other childhood friend killed, was John Todd. John was murdered by

Loyalists as he stood in for someone at his brother's taxi depot in Ligoniel. My sister, Tanya, also witnessed the murder of Seán McKee outside our front window on 18 May 1973, by the British Army.

During the Troubles, my dad, Patsy McAuley, was shot three times in two separate shooting incidents. The first time was when he was shot in the stomach and foot by the IRA as he came out of a bar in Pilot Street near Belfast's city centre. During the writing of this book, I was approached in Ardoyne library by a man who knew I was writing about my dad. He claimed he knew who shot my dad. The guy he named was a notorious killer who died in Shannon in 2009. I don't know if it's true. I didn't previously know the guy who told me this, but I recognised his face and knew he was from Ardoyne. He was in the library most days. We think it could have been a personal vendetta and this guy had done this off his own bat and it might not have been sanctioned by the IRA, but we do not know for sure. He was shot again in 1988 by Loyalists in the Avenue Bar in Belfast city centre; the bullet went through his shoulder. Three men were shot dead in this cowardly attack on innocent Catholics out having a drink on a sunny Sunday afternoon. In between these two shootings, my dad was caught up in a bomb explosion in Etna Drive in Ardoyne in 1977.

Loyalists attacked the funeral of Trevor McKibbin, an outrage that claimed the lives of two Ardoyne men, Seán Campbell and Seán McBride, and left my dad badly injured and very lucky to be alive. Seán Campbell was leaning against the car with the bomb in it and when it exploded it blew his head clean off and it landed in a nearby garden. It was the first Loyalist bomb to explode at a Republican funeral. I was at school that day in Holy Cross Boys and was sitting next to Danny Barrett (I always sat next to Danny Barrett) in Mr Hicks' classroom, which is two floors up, when the bomb went off. The whole school seemed to shake and windows came in (though not in my class). A boy in my class started squealing and he went into convulsions and Mr Hicks had to restrain him. His name was Frankie Carville, and four weeks earlier, he was in a car with his dad, Danny Carville, when it was stopped at a ramp in Cambria Street by Loyalists who had watched it come out of the Nationalist/Catholic Flax Street, and as the car slowed down to go over the ramps, two Loyalists ran over and shot Danny Carville dead right in front of his son. Incidentally, Mr Cyril Murray was a teacher in the next classroom to Mr Hicks and he was shot dead by Loyalists in his own home in July 1992, aged 51.

Around this time my brother, Paul, and his mate, Paddy Gormley, decided (for reasons only known to themselves) to sellotape AA batteries to the lampposts in Fairfield Street. They did such a great job, that the army evacuated the area and people were out of their homes for hours before it was declared a hoax, Paul was about eight at the time. Another incident involving Paul was when he landed in trouble at the corner of Fairfield/ Butler Street in Lena and Joe Hughes' old derelict house where there was a loose brick in the gable wall where the IRA had the odd rattle at the army. My brother, Paul, and Paul Mallon were aware of this, and went to the house and were playing cowboys and Indians, or should I say IRA and Brits. Anyway, they removed the loose brick and poked their plastic toy gun out of the hole. The army opened fire from their observation post in Flax Street and followed up with a raid. After a standoff and much mediation from neighbours and relatives, the two little shooters were brought out of the house, how lucky they were, this could have been another major tragedy.

During the Troubles, there was a lot of tragedy, but there was always fun ways to amuse ourselves. I have always had an interest in sport and I was naturally athletic. I was football mad during the mid/late 1970s and my favourite team was Celtic, my dad brought me over a few times to see them. While living in Fairfield Street, I was constantly kicking a ball about against cable walls or playing on the Holy Cross School pitch with Una Smith, Tricia McClafferty, Martin Cahoon, Billy Begley, Gerard Kelly and Paddy McKenna. Paddy was murdered by Loyalists on 2 September 1989.

Another boy in my street had the same name as me, Eamon McAuley. He lived at 4 Fairfield Street and I lived at 3 Fairfield Street. He moved to 72 Estoril Park and my family moved to 73 Estoril Park. We were in the same class all through primary and secondary school. Teachers called us Eamon P. for Patrick and Eamon G. for Gerald, I was Eamon Patrick. On top of that, we were two excellent footballers and our lives were so synonymous.

Our playground was the monkey bars at Butler/Hooker Street and my regular playmates were Danny Barrett, Robert, Harry and Malachy McErlean, Mickey and Paddywack Holland and Monkey McBride. Monkey McBride got his nickname because his dad kept a live monkey in a cage in the backyard. Incidentally, John 'Topper' Deeds from Brookfield Street kept live snakes, Jigger McConville and Hatchet McGuinness were characters in the district also. Where on earth did they get those nicknames? Other pals of mine were Gerry McKeown of Crumlin Street, Danny Loughran of Oakfield Street and John Todd, whose dad, Jimmy, had a shop at the bottom of Butler Street. I helped and got paid to deliver the **Belfast Telegraph** and the Sunday papers for Jimmy. John Todd was murdered by Loyalists on 5 December 1993, after his brother Brian asked him if he would step in for a guy who didn't come into work in Brian's taxi depot in Ligoniel. I was talking to John Todd in the Shamrock social club shortly before he was killed. I knew John worked in Shorts making airplane parts (he had brains to burn), but he told me he was offered a job in London for much better money (and he was already earning a good wage in Shorts), and he was going to take it. John was also soon to be married and he had the world at his feet before his life was brutally ended. What sort of abnormal society was I being brought up in? While playing at the monkey bars or when I was making my way to my granny, Bridget's house, I made sure to avoid the Fosters, the McCarthy's and Chucky Holland as they didn't like me. I remember there were card schools on nearly every street corner. There were plenty of card sharks about, Bap Travers and Hughie 'Golden Balls' McGahan, being two of them.

Young and old would play handball against the gable walls at Fairfield Street, Crumlin Street and Brookfield Street at Toby's Hall. Pitch and toss would be quite common in the area, and kids would also be playing with their football cards against the cable walls. Does anybody remember 'standers' or when you placed a football card down on the ground and you then tossed cards to try to land on it or touch it? If I wasn't at school, then I would go out in the morning, come home for dinner then go back out again. Our parents never saw us. I remember being in Wales in 1977. Elvis Presley died when I was in Wales (that's how I remember the year). Anyway, when I came home from Wales, I arrived at Fairfield Street and as I opened the living room door, I saw my dad lying on the settee (as usual). I had woken him up and he shouted at me, 'For fuck sake, will you stop running in and out?' I had been in Wales for two weeks, did he not know?

I remember the army kicking in doors and raiding houses, they dug up the steps in our backyard. I remember the Donnelly family who lived across the street from us; six of them went to Long Kesh. I remember my mum and I going up to visit Michael Donnelly. Life was strange for everyone then, people didn't have much. My Granny O'Kane helped us out a lot as she was receiving her late husband, Edward's, war pension. My mother told us that when she was growing up, her parents were among the first family to own a TV. Children used to crowd around my granny's front window to watch the TV, which was permitted by my granny. I would have gone regularly to Toby's Hall to pray the rosary with my granny and others for peace in Ireland. My mum was an only child and my granny doted on her and when Tanya and Paul and I came along, we got the same treatment and it was like having two mums. I got a little more of this treatment because I was her 'blue eye'. I was a regular visitor to my granny's and stayed over on a Saturday night. I actually stored most of my toys down in Granny's (action men, marbles, football cards, etc.) well away from my brother, Paul, and also from my sister, Tanya, who was a tomboy. TV was always great on a Saturday night. *Starsky and Hutch* or *Kojak*, *Match of the Day* and *Parkinson*. What have you got now? *X Factor*, *Britain's Got Talent*, *Strictly Come Dancing*. Oh please.

I remember the youth workers would show films in the big hall at Butler Street which used to be a dinner hall for Holy Cross, but was now Ardoyne Youth Club. There would be standing room only and they would show mostly Hammer horror films or martial arts films. After the *Kung Fu* movies, everyone poured out and there would be a mass brawl outside as everybody would be acting out Bruce Lee moves. You had to watch out for a big kick in the back at any time.

When I was ten years old, my granny bought me a Dawes bicycle and I still remember the cost, £52 a good wage in those days. It was gold coloured and I was the envy of every young boy in Ardoyne. One clear memory of that time was when 'Paddywack' Holland offered me 10p for a ride on my bike. The deal was that he could cycle from Greasy Nellies at the bottom of Butler Street to Reid's shop and back. That was at about 1 p.m. and I didn't see him again until about 8 p.m. when, with a big smile on his face, he brought the bike back, intact may I add. I had spent the whole day searching for him and crying my eyes out. He must have gone through the gap into Glenard, a place I rarely went unless to visit my granny, Sarah, in Brompton Park.

We lived in Fairfield Street for eleven years (1969–1980) and strangely enough, my mum said that they were the happiest of her life. We moved to Estoril Park, Glenard in late 1980 or early 1981, as all the houses in old Ardoyne were pulled down and new ones built, but streets like Fairfield Street, Butler Street etc. disappeared forever. Another memory of Fairfield Street, was of my friend Danny Wilde, who died aged seven in a tragic accident in the park up on the Bone hills; he fell off the slide and hit his head on the concrete ground (no astroturf then). Rest in peace Danny.

Two very dangerous games that most kids would have played were hopping lorries and chasing rubber bullets. At the age of nine or ten, I would have got my kicks by waiting on a lorry going down Butler Street and I would have run out from Fairfield Street (or even Oakfield Street) and hopped onto the back of the lorry for a ride down to Flax Street. The easiest lorries were the beer lorries, who would be on their way back from delivering beer to the local bars, the Saunders and the League. The driver wouldn't see you hop on with all the barrels and kegs of beer in the back of the lorry. The dangerous thing was, that if the lorry needed to brake suddenly then you were in big trouble, as your head would have whiplashed into the back of the lorry and this could have killed us. It was death-defying, but we never thought about the consequences.

The other very dangerous game we played, was chasing after rubber bullets during a riot to keep as souvenirs or to sell to the British or American reporters who would frequently be in the area during the Troubles. I can clearly remember rubber bullets bouncing off the walls at Butler Street/ Oakfield Street (at McNab's chippie) and us kids would be chasing after the rubber bullets and fighting with each other to get a hold of one. When the rioting was over, and the army left, then we would be up where they had been shooting from, to look for the rubber bullet shells that had been dispensed. When you had the rubber bullet and the shell you had the full set and all you needed then was a gullible Brit (or Yank) to sell it to. When the deadly plastic bullets were introduced and seventeen people were killed (mostly children and nearly all Catholics), we did the same with the plastic bullets (chasing after them for ourselves, tourists and reporters). Sadly, we didn't put a lot of value on our own lives at that time. I remember my good Protestant friend, former boxing Commonwealth gold medallist at welterweight and British Lonsdale belt outright winner, Neil Sinclair, saying to me a couple of years ago that he never seen one British Army soldier in his area (Carnmoney) when he was growing up. I said to him, 'That's because they were all in Ardoyne.'

One positive aspect about the Troubles was that, despite all the horror, they brought communities together, a strong will and community spirit existed, and neighbours genuinely helped each other. People huddled together during gun battles in the 1970s and through the night swapped stories. People left their front doors open then and neighbours, at times, would rap your door to borrow milk, sugar or teabags. I salute the people of Ardoyne for their courage and resilience as we carried on regardless, trying to get by under extraordinary circumstances. Getting to school and getting to work safely, and constantly fearing for the safety of our loved ones when they were at school or work, was always a worry.

Thank God my kids do not remember the Troubles and are not psychologically scarred by them, unlike us. Now come with me on an amazing journey as I put some meat on the bones of some of these stories and tell you others of glory, despair, love, hope and faith.

Childhood Fun and Games

As I mentioned earlier, my brother Paul was born on 1 December 1969 in the Mater Hospital. Belfast had erupted into widespread violence four months previously and the streets were not safe. Consequently, it was an ordeal for my dad to get down to the hospital to see his second son, but Paul came home to Fairfield Street a week later. We had not long moved into Fairfield Street. Paul was always my mum's blue eye, probably because he was the youngest and perhaps because Paul was a wee bit wayward. He got that little more attention. Tanya was nuts, a real tomboy, she was brave and fearless; I was a bit more reticent. Tanya wouldn't stop to think too long about things, she would act on impulse. She could beat Jimmy Gormley in a fight, I couldn't. A boy called Paddy Grimley used to call regularly to his granny's in Fairfield Street (I think Paddy lived in West Belfast). Tanya cut part of his ear off when she threw a roof slate at him.

Tanya and I did this amazing feat that even today, brings a shiver to my spine. We would climb up the drainpipes (spouts) in Holy Cross Boys School and we did something that day that could have and by logic, should have cost us our lives. Tanya jumped from the school down onto a mobile hut which was absolutely death-defying. The hut was maybe two feet below us, but more importantly, there was about a ten foot gap, so I guess we would have been about twenty feet off the concrete ground and if Tanya had missed, she would have been dead – pure and simple. She took a run and jumped across and when I think about it now, I think, not only what courage she had, but also, what stupidity. When Tanya did it then, I knew it was doable, although I think it was a few days later when I did it. We kept coming back, I would say to Tanya, 'Do it again,' and she did, so I eventually did it and without doubt, it was the bravest thing I have ever done, but Tanya was braver. I would say I would have been around twelve or thirteen years old then. That mobile hut would still have been there up until a few years ago, and when I would have gone round to collect my son, Shea, I would always look at the gap between the school and the mobile hut and think to myself, 'How did we ever make it?' Amazing, absolutely amazing, I don't want to understate the magnitude of this amazing feat, we should be dead!

Another death-defying thing that Tanya and I did, was jump from our bedroom window onto a mattress, which was placed in our backyard. The McCorry's next door thought we were nuts, having said that they were a bit older than us, and perhaps a bit more sensible! Their youngest son, Lawrence was two years older than me. He was a great guy, but I think he was warned by his parents to be wary of Tanya and me.

One time, beside Tom's shop in Butler Street, Tanya hit me smack in the face with a snowball (ice ball more like it). She had snuck up on me and smacked me with the ice ball at point black range. It really hurt and I think I ended up with a thick lip, such was the force put into her throw. I was out for revenge and was waiting all day for the opportunity. Tanya was walking up Butler Street towards our house in Fairfield Street. She must have been down in my granny's. My granny dreaded to see her coming as she said Tanya always started murder. I, like all the kids in Ardoyne, were great throwers and deadly accurate as we got plenty of practice throwing stones, bricks and bottles at the army. Putting these skills into practice, I made a snowball, but put a stone in it and hit Tanya smack on the head. Well, the blood started to gush out of Tanya's head onto the white snow and it was like something out of a horror movie. Well, I ran and ran all the time shouting, 'Fuck, fuck, fuck.' I was scared, I really was, but what did I expect putting a stone in the snowball? I stayed away for hours. Tanya was brought to hospital and got stitches. My dad was really angry with me, but I gave him time to cool down by staying away.

My dad very rarely hit us, but Tanya and I got a beating from him after nearly blowing the whole street up. Tanya and I woke up early one Sunday and went downstairs; my mum was still in bed, but my dad was out. He could have been out drinking or playing cards, I don't know. We had a co-hole (cubbyhole), where the gas meter was and we used it to hang coats, so there were lots of coats as well as the gas meter in this confined space. We were always up to something, so we ended up in the co-hole and we lit a wee tiny fire. It was an 'I dare you thing'. Unsurprisingly, one thing led to another and before we knew it the fire was getting out of control as the coats had started to go on fire (I kid you not). Tanya and I froze with fear. I do not think Paul was with us, and as God is my witness (I would not tell a lie), my dad just walked in at that moment. We could have blown the whole street up if the gas meter reacted. My dad acted quickly and put the fire out with buckets of water, but he was really shaken up, then the anger came. Tanya and I both got the belt and grounded for a week.

We had a po (a blue bucket) in our bedroom (like the 1970s TV show **Little House on the Prairie**) in case any of us got caught short in the middle of the night, most young families had one. We had an outside toilet and it would have been freezing in the middle of winter, and our parents would not have wanted us running up and down the stairs and waking them in the middle of the night (we were only small children). Well, one morning Tanya and I were awake and we had hatched a plan to annoy Paul. Our parents were asleep in the other room and we woke Paul up and Tanya lifted the po and swung it around and around, but the contents did not come out because of the speed she was swinging it. She said, 'Paul, you can do that,' and Paul still half asleep said, 'I don't think so.' So I said, 'Paul, it's easy – look,' and I swung the po around and around and I said, 'Paul, it's all in the speed that you swing it.' Well, it took a wee bit of persuasion, but eventually he said, 'Ok, I'll try it,' God bless him. So, Paul got up and was swinging it like a good 'un until Tanya stuck her foot out which collided with the po and the contents went all over Paul. He started squealing which got our parents up. Tanya and I ended up getting the belt and grounded for a week again, but our plan was executed to perfection, we just never thought of the consequences. Tanya blamed me and I blamed her.

When Tanya was nine or ten years old, our neighbour in Fairfield Street, named Grace Henry, asked Tanya to run up to Cassidy's shop on the Crumlin Road facing Holy Cross Church to buy the **Irish News**. In those days, us kids loved to run to the shops, as we would be given a few pence or a bob or two (5p-10p). Paddy Cassidy's was a two-minute run from Fairfield Street. I always liked to count when I went to the shop and I liked to shave a second or two off my previous time. Tanya was very near when a bomb exploded in the shop. Luckily, no one was in the shop at the time. I don't think it was Loyalists who planted the bomb, perhaps it was a warning to

Paddy Cassidy to pay protection money? I don't know. Tanya was thirty seconds from the shop when it exploded.

I remember the toyshop at Twaddell Avenue, beside Ardoyne round-about. Tanya and I used to sneak over all the time just to gaze in the window and dream. I was big into action man toys and this shop called the Cabin had plenty of them. They also had toy soldiers and they came in many different colours, the Brits were green, the Japanese were yellow, the Yanks were grey, the Germans were blue etc. They were plastic and came in bags and boxes and I got a kick going over and looking in the window at all these wonderful, but expensive toys. We had been well warned by our parents not to cross that road, as it brought us into a Protestant area and Protestant kids could have attacked us, but sure, we never listened to our parents. The Cabin is still there today (although not a toyshop) and I would pass it regularly and think back to those wonderful memories. Tanya and I used to torture our mother to go to Mr and Mrs Rice in Fairfield Street and ask them for a lend of their Christmas catalogue. We would spend hours looking at the toys, and when I was on my own with the catalogue, I would look at the photos of the women with the see-through bras, as my burgeoning sexuality was awakening.

Sometime, around 1973–1975, I nearly drowned on the Mourne Mountains in Newcastle, County Down. I was with a crowd of adults and children from Ardoyne. One of the children was my best friend at the time and next-door neighbour, Lawrence McCorry. What I can remember from this incident was a pool of water on the mountains like a lagoon. I was unaware that it was very deep and there were a few people swimming in the water, and I rolled my trousers up to stand in the shallow bit. There were also a few children in the water, but they could swim, I couldn't! There were rocks like steps clearly visible under the water. I remember gradually taking one step that brought me about six inches into the water and a further step that brought me about twelve inches into the water. I went to take a third step, but there was no third step and I went down right under the water, and you know what? I can still remember being under the water for the amount of time it took Gerard Davidson to bravely jump in and rescue me. Gerard lives in California now and is Lawrence McCorry's cousin.

Not too long after the near drowning incident, my dad taught Tanya and I how to swim. He would have brought us to the Falls leisure centre, as the nearby leisure centre up in Ballysillan was staunchly Protestant and in the mid-1970s was a no-go area. In addition, a bus left from Ardoyne to go to the Falls Baths and Tanya and I would have been on that bus, me with my football shorts and goggles rolled up in a towel and also some money to pay for the trip. The downside to going on the bus, and not with my dad, was a lot of rough kids and bullies would have been on that bus. This would have been around the time of the *Jaws* movie hysteria and you would have had some kid shout 'Shark!', and the pool would have emptied in seconds. Or you would have been swimming along and some bully would have grabbed your leg from under the water, scaring the life clean out of you. I was always worried about a great white shark getting into the pool at the Falls Baths in Belfast. It was scary enough living in Belfast in the mid-1970s and worrying about shootings and bombings without having to worry about a man-eating shark. What imagination I had.

I can recall the whole phenomenon with the first *Jaws* film in 1975. Everybody was talking about it and busting to see it. I remember my parents promising us that they would take us down to see it. Well, Lawrence McCorry had seen it before us and talk about a spoiler! He must have told Tanya and Paul and me every part of the movie. Another thing I remember about that day in 1975 at the ABC movie house in Belfast, was the part in *Jaws* when Richard Dreyfuss persuades Roy Schneider to go out at night in a boat to look for the shark and when they are in the water they see Ben Gardner's banged-up boat. Dreyfuss dives into the water and goes under where he sees a hole at the bottom of the boat where the shark has hit it. And, as he's inspecting the hole, he finds a shark's tooth and as he's inspecting the shark's tooth, Ben Gardner's head comes rolling out! Well, my mother let a loud scream out of her which frightened the life out of my dad. My dad lost it and started shouting at my mum. My dad's nerves weren't good with the shootings and bombings he had come through. There they were having a row in the middle of a film in Belfast city centre, with people around them going, 'Ssshhhh.' After the film, my dad drove us to 'provie' Charlie's, the nickname given to a Chinese takeaway at the top of the New Lodge on the Antrim Road, where he and my mum shared a mixed grill, and Tanya, Paul and I got chips. Chinese chips tasted beautiful then; they tasted different. Now all chips taste the same. I can still taste those Chinese chips.

I also remember the fear I had of Protestants. I was very aware then of the Shankill Butcher killings (1975–1977), which created great fear and hysteria in Catholic areas as men would be snatched off the streets, bundled into a black taxi (or car) and their bodies would be mutilated and dumped in Loyalist estates such as Glencairn, just off the Shankill Road. I remember being in my friend, Gerard McKeown's, house in Crumlin Street, and his mother, Mary, telling us a story of two Catholic boys being cut up into pieces at the Grove baths on the Shore Road in North Belfast. This story absolutely scared me senseless and I was petrified of Protestants, as I thought they were all slashers to a man. That story about the Grove was made up by Mary McKeown, but she never told me that she had made it up. It put the fear of God in me of Protestants, but thankfully when I started boxing, I boxed Protestants, mixed with Protestants and went into Protestant areas to box, but it took some time for that fear to subside. Praise the Lord for boxing, a sport which has always brought the two communities together. Today, I walk up and down the Shankill Road on my way into town and back, and on a good day I might get at least five people who will shout, 'Alright Eamon', or stop and have a chat with me. Furthermore, I worked over two years as a youth leader and I brought kids down to the Shankill (stadium) on a regular basis. Through boxing, I forged many friendships across the religious divide.

My mother would have allowed me to watch the horror double bill on BBC2 on a Saturday night. The deal was that Tanya and Paul would have to be asleep, then I could sneak down. The films would start at around 10 or 10.30 p.m. and sometimes I would miss most of the first movie before Tanya fell asleep (Paul would be in the land of nod as soon as his head hit the pillow). Normally when we went to bed, Tanya and I would be up to something or other or we would be having a game of 'Keep it up' where whoever said the last word before we fell asleep would be the winner (Tanya always won). Sometimes the game would go on for hours. I would be very quiet on a Saturday night though and wouldn't engage Tanya in conversation and when I thought Tanya was asleep, I would whisper, 'Tanya, are you awake?' And, if there was no reply, I would repeat it and if I didn't get a reply a second time, then I would be up out of my bunk bed (Paul slept underneath me) and down in the living room in a flash.

My dad was always out, but my mum would have made me a drink and some toast and I would have been so content and happy. The first movie was always an old Universal horror film in black and white, and it could have been *Frankenstein*, *Dracula*, *The Wolfman*, etc. and then it would have been followed by a Hammer horror movie in glorious colour. Believe it or not, the best and most exciting part of the night was at the end, when it would show you trailers of the two films that would be on the following Saturday and I would then go to bed counting the seconds until next week. Quite often, I would wake up in the middle of the night after having a bad nightmare and I can still remember standing at the top of the stairs whispering, 'Mummy, can I sleep with you and Daddy?'

Many a time before my dad would go on a drinking binge, he would go mad in the house and be shouting and bawling and would storm out threatening to come back and wreck the house later. He would just be looking for an excuse to go on the drink, and he needed to blame my mum for something and that would be his justification for his behaviour. Or he might have blamed the IRA or the British Army for making him drink, anybody but himself. It affected me deeply and I would have stayed awake waiting on my dad to return from the pub to see if he was going to start on my mum and wreck the house. Tanya and Paul would have been fast asleep. Mostly, when he was drunk he was a happy drunk and he would have come home laughing and joking. Then, when I knew my mum was safe I fell fast asleep very quickly.

I remember being forced to go to a cousin's birthday party in Havana Street on the same day as the 1974 World Cup final between West Germany and Holland. It was my uncle, Gerard's, daughter, Donna's, second birthday party, and after showing my face and staying a wee while, I eventually booted round to my Granny O'Kane in Butler Street just in time to see the whole second half of the match (West Germany won 2–1). My favourite song of 1974, and probably my favourite song of the 1970s, was the Rubettes number 'Sugar Baby Love' and I used to try and hit the high notes in that song, but my voice would break somewhere in the middle of the chorus. My mum worked in Grainger's sewing factory up in Ligoniel in the mid-seventies, and I remember she brought me up to Graingers to spend a whole working day at it. All the female workers made a big fuss of me and at the end of the day, I got a brown pay slip with a shiny, crisp one pound note in it. I was on cloud nine. Then sometime in the mid/late seventies, my mum would have worked in a sewing factory in the town, and I would have cleaned the house for her Monday-Friday and on Friday, she would have bought me a pop record that she would have bought at Premier records in Smithfield on her way home, one that I had specifically requested. I had my own wee record player and later, my granny, Bridget, bought me an electric guitar and an amp and I joined a three-piece mod band with two hairdressers – Jimmy Weir and Ciarán Liggett. We called ourselves 'The Clean Cuts'. It was a mod band as I say, and I was hired because I was a mod and had an electric guitar, but I was fired three weeks later, as I couldn't play the electric guitar and was too slow in learning how to play it. I was replaced by Seán Kearney and I had to stand and watch them make their debut in Ardoyne Youth Club (Brookfield Mill) and I must admit they were brilliant.

There was a family that lived across the street from us and the parents (Hughie and Mary Burns) had a young boy around two years old called Patrick and Tanya and I doted on him (this would have been around 1976). One night in Fairfield Street when our parents were out Tanya and I had this blanket, and we were tossing our dog Rory up and down in it. One of us then suggested going over to get Patrick, to toss him up and down in the blanket. Well, everything was going great and Patrick, Tanya and I were having a great old laugh, when as we were moving around the living room we chucked Patrick up in the air, but before we caught him in the blanket, he came down and his head hit the corner of our wall cabinet and the blood just started spurting out of his head. We started squealing and shouting for help and Patrick's parents were quickly over as Tanya had a towel wrapped around Patrick's head, but the blood was seeping through it. It was a bloodbath and a scary sight for his parents to witness. The fear in me that night was palpable and it's hard to remember all the facts, but I think Hughie drove his son to the hospital to get stitched up and no doubt my parents were not too happy with Tanya and I when they heard.

We lost contact with the Burns family after that (nothing to do with this incident I think), but about eight years ago I bumped into Hughie Burns up in St Gabriel's Secondary School, as the school was closing down and this was the last chance for past pupils to walk round before the demolition men tore it down. I am sure Hughie was standing behind me and I brought up that incident with his son Patrick all those years ago and Hughie said, 'This is Patrick here with me,' and this young man turned around and smiled at me, and we spoke about that night and he showed me the scar on his head that he will have for the rest of his life. It was not an uncomfortable moment, we laughed and shared stories of Fairfield Street and I said to Hughie, 'What possessed you to send your son over to Tanya and I? He would have been safer with the Moors murderers Ian Brady and Myra Hindley.'

There was a wee shop at the bottom of Fairfield Street, known locally as Jimmy and Minnie Blacks, and I remember this one time my mum sent me up to buy two eggs for my dad's breakfast. I guess I would have been around ten or eleven years old at the time. When I entered the shop I can remember Jimmy being in a jovial mood and when he lifted the two eggs he started to juggle them before he put them in a paper bag and I was totally mesmerised by his juggling act.

When I got outside I lifted the eggs out and tried to replicate what Jimmy had done, but the two eggs smashed on the footpath. I was horrified.

I casually walked back into the shop and told Jimmy that there was a hole in the paper bag and the eggs slipped out through the hole and smashed on the ground. Jimmy wasn't buying it so I thought 'Well screw you Jimmy' so I went back to the house and my mum said, 'Where's the two eggs?' and I told my mum and dad that Jimmy broke the eggs while doing a juggling act with them. My dad then said, 'And he still charged you for the eggs that he broke?' and I said, 'Yeah' so my dad said, 'Roseleen get my shoes, I am going up there now to see him.' Looking back now, over forty years later, this was a chance for my dad to wind me up. They knew that Jimmy didn't break the eggs and charge me for them. They knew I was lying through my teeth. Just before my dad left the house he turned to me and said, 'I am gonna give you one more chance to tell the truth.' But I had gone too far now with this lie to turn back, and it didn't bother my conscience if my dad went up and throttled 60-year-old Jimmy while walking behind the counter to get his two eggs (God he must have been starving). My mum and I watched my dad walk up the street and into Jimmy's shop and that's when I broke. I screamed at my mum, 'Okay, it was me that broke the eggs.' and I started to cry. I then saw my dad coming out of the shop with a paper bag in his hand and I thought, 'Hold on, what's going on here?' But when my dad entered the house, and saw that I was a broken and remorseful man, he burst out laughing and couldn't stop. He told me that when I do something wrong, then put your hands up and tell the truth because when you lie and blame someone else, then the lie is even worse than the wrong you have done. Looking back all those years ago, I must admit that my dad handled the situation very well. Me, well I was prepared to sacrifice poor old Jimmy Black to save my own skin. I couldn't look Jimmy in the face for weeks…

In the mid-1970s, at the height of the violence, some adults decided to start a summer soccer league involving teams from Ardoyne, the Bone and the New Lodge. The reason for this was to try to give the youth a focus and take them off the streets and away from rioting and anti-social activities. Holy Cross and St Gabriel's boys school were very supportive of this as at the time high numbers of young people were getting locked up in jail, sent to youth detention centres or they were joining paramilitaries. If my memory serves me right. there was under nine (years) right up to under eighteen (years) and I played for Hookerville (Hooker Street) under nine's. The matches were played in both the Holy Cross Boys School pitch and the Bone hills pitch (both gravel). Jimmy Glennon and Jimmy Barrett were in charge of Hookerville and were also involved in organising the whole tournament, as were two other fellas I would like to give credit to Gerry Graham and Bunion Toal.

Hookerville wore yellow tops, white shorts and blue or white socks (just like Brazil) and I lived for these matches, as for a child of eight or nine years of age it was like playing in the World Cup as there were good crowds who went to watch these games and support their street. I remember Hookerville won the under nine's league that first year, and the organisers had a presentation day at Toby's Hall in Butler Street which was attended by hordes of children (many of them didn't even play football), as prizes were handed out to all the winning teams in their respective age groups. Local soccer legend Danny Hale was on hand to present the prizes and crisps and juice were handed out as we watched a re-run of Celtic winning the 1967 European Cup Final against Inter Milan. Then there were special awards handed out to the boys voted to be the best player in their respective age groups, and Danny Hale announced that the under-nine player of the tournament was Eamon McAuley! There was some confusion as I looked round to the other Eamon McAuley and I said to him, 'Is it you or me they are calling for?' He gave me a look as if to say, 'Catch yourself on.' And as I looked around, everyone was looking, pointing and shouting to me, 'It's you.' The other Eamon had moved to Estoril Park and he had played for them, but they hadn't won the league. I was stunned as I walked up to receive my first ever trophy (a silver foot-baller with a ball at his feet on a black plinth). My legs were shaky as everybody was screaming, 'Speech, speech.' It was like an Oscars night for a boy of my age, and I can still remember walking home to Fairfield Street in a euphoric daze.

I was lucky enough to play for one of the greatest teams to come out of Ardoyne (and there were many good ones). The 1976 Holy Cross Primary School team swept all before them going through a whole season unbeaten. That year, Holy Cross won the Northern Ireland Primary School Cup, the Belfast Telegraph Cup and were the best P7 team in Northern Ireland. In fact, three players on that team were only in P6 – Eddie Flood, Tom Austin and me. Many a time we were photographed and appeared in the *Irish News* and *Belfast Telegraph* (which was a big deal then). As God as my witness, sometimes I would dribble the ball around all the opposing team and score as it seemed I had the ball stuck to my feet. I was untouchable.

Ardoyne Youth Club won the Northern Ireland Cup, beating Red Star Derry 3–1 at Solitude, the home of Cliftonville Football Club, in 1979–1980. Danny Trainor got two goals, and I got the other. I remember it was a huge occasion at the time. Later that season, there was a trial match arranged at the Clarendon Park playing fields in the Somerdale Park area, to pick a team to represent Northern Ireland. Tom Austin and Eddie Flood and me were chosen from St Gabriel's. I remember they split the players into two teams, and we played off against each other. My team won 4–2 and I scored two goals and featured heavily in the game and was confident of selection. On the way home, Tom and Eddie added to my confidence by saying that they thought I was a cert to get picked, but I never was. The teachers thought it might be because I was from a Catholic school. I was thirteen-years-old and took it very badly. I was absolutely and totally disgusted and appalled. I made up my mind then and there that was me finished with football and I took up boxing (I could have been the next Georgie Best, who knows).

My dad was not happy with my decision, as his dad had died very young (58) from pugilistic dementia brought on by the many blows he took in the ring. My dad spoke privately to youth club workers, Mickey Brennan and Hugo Magee, in an effort to get them to change my mind and go back to the football, but it was to no avail. I am sure my mum was not over the moon either with my decision.

Throughout my childhood, I loved most sports. I loved watching *Grandstand* or *World of Sport* on a Saturday at my granny's or *Sportsnight* on a Tuesday night. The only sports I didn't like, were cricket and horse racing. My heroes were Jimmy Connors (I always rooted for Jimmy against Borg or McEnroe), Seb Coe, Muhammad Ali and Kenny Dalglish (when he was with Celtic). In my own wee imagination, I played tennis with Jimmy Connors regularly against Toby's gable wall, and always beat him. I raced Seb Coe and Steve Ovett all the time. The race would be from my granny's in Butler Street, up to my mum's house in Fairfield Street I always won. I would be doing the David Coleman commentary, 'It's Coe in the lead and Ovett is right on his shoulder as we approach the final bend, but here comes McAuley with a late kick. Coe responds, so does Ovett. It's Coe, it's McAuley and McAuley wins and breaks the world record, the fastest 800m. in history.' I would be saying this out loud. People must have thought that I was not right in the head. It reminds me of the great Undertones song Teenage Kicks (teenage dreams so hard to beat…). If you're gonna dream, then dream big, and I did.

I excelled in sports and always did well on the school sports day, but there was a lad in my year that I could never beat as he was physically bigger and stronger. His name was Emmanuel McFarland. I was never a sprinter, but more of an endurance runner. I was also an exceptional high jumper. There was once this big event involving loads of schools at the Mary Peter's track and I was picked to represent my school. My race was running around the track several times and there must have been twenty or 30 in the race and I finished second and you know what, the winner didn't beat me by much. I remember my mum being delighted and she bought me some clothes as a present. The next day in school, Mr Doors made a point of calling into my teacher Mr Hicks' class, and he proceeded to tell the class that I did really well and brought a lot of pride to the school and the whole class (including Mr Doors and Mr Hicks) gave me a round of applause and I felt ten foot tall. Then later, when I went to St Gabriel's secondary school, I couldn't beat this one other boy called Jim Docherty. I remember the fourth-year presentations in the big assembly hall a few days after sports day, I got one gold (high jump) and 4–5 silvers and Jim won 4–5 golds. The large crowd cheered for me every time I went up to get my silver medals and booed every time Jim went up to get his gold medals. Jim was a nice well-mannered boy who used to live in Butler Street and then moved to the more upmarket Mountainview. Jim was polite and quietly spoken and went on in life to become an architect and I haven't seen him since 1982. It would be lovely to meet up with him again. I always bump into Emmanuel McFarland, as he lives in Ardoyne and Emmanuel is a big lump of a lad who 20–25 years ago regularly won the Ardoyne strongest man event at the local Ardoyne Fleadh.

POSTSCRIPT

I bumped into Mr Hicks about ten years ago in St Gemma's girls school, which was being used for the local elections, and he clearly remembered me and was delighted to see me, and we chatted for a while. He was very busy that day, but still made time for me. I saw Mr Hicks on TV one day, and he won a quiz show. My friend Gerard McNulty told me that Mr Hicks lived in Glengormley and was a regular visitor to the St Enda's quiz night, which, going by Gerard, he always won. Gerard said that Mr Hicks was an intellectual genius. Sadly, I heard from Gerard the other day that Mr Hicks died from an illness (cancer I think) in 2018. Sweet Jesus have mercy on his soul.

Teenage Kicks

From 1978/1979, up until I went to England in August 1982 at the age of sixteen, I ran the streets of Ardoyne and rarely ventured anywhere else except to the town to buy records. I was a mod and loved the music and the clothes. Being a mod kept me tidy and clean. I washed my own clothes. Being a mod was all about clothes and style. There was a wee woman called Betty Power who lived in Hooker Street; she was brillant at turning my trousers in if they were too wide. Betty would do this on her sewing machine. She was the mother of Billy Power, who was one of the Birmingham Six. Betty would charge next to nothing for the work she did, God bless her. I can't remember ever giving her a tip, but what I did do was give her plenty of work.

I bleached my Levi's, ironed my own clothes and spit-polished my shoes. I couldn't afford some of the more expensive clothes, but my mum got me a pair of Hush Puppies and desert boots. I remember my mum getting me a pair of loafer shoes, but she didn't buy me the more expensive leather loafers. As I went to school, I was proud as punch with my new loafers, Fred Perry grey jumper and three button black blazer with narrow lapels and turned in trousers. Well, it didn't take Danny Barrett long to realise that my loafers were not the real McCoy 'leather ones'. He started calling me, 'Plastic loafers,' and soon the whole class did. I never wore them again, but the nickname still stuck. He also used to call me 'Ace face' after a character in the 1979 film *Quadrophenia*.

I was a mod for about three or four years, but I was on a one-man crusade. A bit of a loner. On my green Parka coat I had a red, white and blue target and when I passed the Sinn Féin incident centre at the bottom of Brompton Park, the crowd outside it used to throw stones and bricks at me. They were trying to hit the target, which was on the back of my coat. My mum also knitted me a big chunky red, white and blue jumper, that also didn't go down well with the local Republican youth. Looking back, I can see their point as it was in the middle of the 1981 hunger strikes and the British were seen in Republican areas as oppressors, the Brits were *the* enemy. The British were loathed and here's me walking about with the British colours red, white and blue. Naive or what? My mum and I didn't think politically then, and we just thought that these were the mod colours, simple as that. Eventually, some clever spiv started selling green, white and orange targets.

I missed the first week of attending school at St Gabriel's Secondary School (nicknamed St Gabs) in 1977, due to being in Wales playing football. On my first day in school as a first year pupil, I got into a row with Mickey Thompson. He hit me a three or four punch combination in the gob for being cheeky to him. As I went to respond, people got in between us and I shouted that I would see him after school round the back beside the sand pits. He shouted back that he would be there, and the fight was on. I didn't previously know Mickey Thompson, as he didn't go to my primary school. St Gabriel's was made up of kids from Ardoyne, Ligoniel and the Bone. Round at the sand pit, after school, about ten or fifteen boys turned up to see the big dig. My next-door neighbour and mate, Lawrence McCorry, who was two years older than me, was there to watch my back in case anyone jumped on. It was a fair fight and I got the better of it. Afterwards, we both shook hands and became friends from that moment on.

While we were first year pupils (twelve years old), we went to Armagh Planetarium on a bus run and before we came back home, we were allowed a short break to stretch our legs, or go to the toilet, or have a smoke! I remember we parked the bus facing a public toilet and I would imagine the teacher, Mr Gormley, would have told us to be back at the bus for a certain time. We all broke away in groups and my group found a sports shop and we decided to pop in to see if they had any soccer badges. When we entered the shop, there was just this woman on her own and we inquired about the badges and she went out the back of the shop and came back with a box full of soccer badges. The shop was starting to fill up as more and more of the St Gabriel's pupils entered and the boys were asking her all sorts of questions and she started to get nervous and agitated. Over the course of the next five minutes, there was a few hundred pounds of sports equipment stolen and as we were getting on the bus, police cars with their sirens blasting surrounded our bus. Obviously, the woman had rang them and we panicked. When we saw the cops, we tried to hide the stolen goods including badges, scarves, woolly hats, jerseys, golf clubs, tennis rackets. You name it, we tried to steal it. We all had them well hidden from Mr Gormley, who was unaware of what was going on. There was a mad panic as we were all rushing off the bus and going to the public toilets to get rid of the stuff. We even tried to flush things down the toilets. The game was up though and nearly all the stolen goods were retrieved and no serious harm was done, but the shame, embarrassment and indignation done to St Gabriel's reputation was immense.

When the dust had settled, Mr Gormley got us into his classroom one by one and interrogated us, but we had gotten together and made a pact that no one would rat on each other. When Mr Gormley got me into his room, I denied being in the shop and told him I had played no part in it whatsoever. Mr Gormley said, 'Oh, is that right? Well, such and such said you were there and so and so said you stole goods' (naming names), and I said, 'Well did they? Well, he stole, he stole and he stole.' Mr Gormley had tricked us into naming people and I squealed the place down because I thought they had grassed on me. We were only twelve and not fully sane. Our parents were sent for within days and it took years for the shame to subside. The school I am talking about. I had no shame.

In 1981, when we were fourth year pupils, we went on another trip (our first since Armagh) to Crossgar monastery. Mr McCafferty was in charge. The pupils had planned this out in advance, and we stocked up on alcohol and glue and our behaviour that day was shameful and disgusting and looking back now, I am deeply ashamed. There was a feeling of despair and hopelessness in 1981, and the stench of defeat was everywhere. The hunger strikes were in full flow and our mate Danny Barrett was shot dead that year. It was devastating to think that someone our own age was dead. We were all waiting for full-scale civil war to break out. Danny Barrett was one of my best mates and I sat beside him everyday in school. Every time I hear the Madness song 'It Must Be Love', I fondly think of my friend, Danny Barrett. It was his favourite song at the time of his death.

Back to the trip, and we knew that Mr McCafferty was a soft teacher, so we could take advantage at every opportunity. I remember we were glue-sniffing in the toilets and he came in and took our bags of glue off us and

I slapped him on the top of the head (bald spot) like Benny Hill did with Belfast's Jackie Magee on **The Benny Hill Show** and I took my glue back and he walked on outside as I was in fits of laughter. God forgive me.

Other pupils were drinking and shouting abuse at the priests during talks and going into the confessional boxes drunk or high as a kite. Shameful stuff, but as I said at fifteen, you're not fully sane. It's not what you were, but it's what you are now that's important. Or it's not how you start the journey in life, but rather it's how you end it and what you have learned on the journey. I have been back to Crossgar on many occasions as a Christian and when I am there, I always think back to the madness of us on that trip in 1981.

One day in 1981, Barney Hughes and Thomas (Ta) Cosgrove and I decided to get the bus up to school (St Gabriel's). I would have been fifteen at this time. It would have been unusual for us to get the bus to school as St Gabriel's was a five minute walk up the Crumlin Road. Only thing with walking was, that we had to pass a Protestant area (Hesketh Gardens), but there were always stewards to watch that everyone got to school safety. The stewards patrolled the area, but we must have been late or something that day to get the bus.

No one really paid for buses in those days. What you did was, you bought your bus ticket in the shop and it would have lasted forever. There would have been eight journeys on the ticket (eight dings) and you would have put your ticket into this machine and it would ding and print a black ink message that gave you the date etc. that you used the bus. There was a way around this though. If you put candle wax on the ticket and put it into the machine then it would print onto the wax. You could then wipe the candle wax away and there would be no ink on the ticket and you could do this again and again. Well anyway, Barney and I sat together and Ta Cosgrove sat behind us. As soon as we sat down, we realised that a man was staring at us. We had our uniforms on and that would have given our religion away. He would have known that we were Catholics. We just ignored him and chatted away to each other for the two-minute journey. As we got up to get off the bus at our destination, Barney and I walked down the middle of the bus to get off, but as Ta walked past the guy who had been staring at us, he put his foot out and tripped up Ta. Ta didn't say anything, but I just couldn't let it go. I said to the man (for he was a man), 'What did you do that for?' But Ta said, 'Eamon, just leave it,' but the guy got up and came right at me in an aggressive way and as he got to within touching distance of me (striking distance), I threw a right hand that connected to his chin and he went down like a bag of shite (I have never understood that expression).

Fair play to the bus driver, he had kept the doors open for us to get off and as the bus was driving off the guy leaned out waving his fist and telling me what he was going to do to me if he ever caught up with me again. And you know what, he could easily have jumped off the bus as it was only starting to pull away from the St Gabriel's stop. He must have been cut to the bone with embarrassment that some schoolboy had decked him on a bus full of people. It must have been a long journey home for him. But he deserved it, bitter old fucker. I often wonder was he a Loyalist killer? Did that incident make him even more bitter that he took it out on innocent Catholics? Loyalist killer and leader of the notorious Shankill Butchers gang, Lenny Murphy, was persecuted as a boy for having the misfortune of having a Catholic name and he took that persecution out on innocent Catholics. Did this guy do the same because of me? Who knows?

In fifth year, some of my classmates would steal cars and drive them into the school grounds and do handbrakes etc. We would be hanging out the windows screaming encouragement at them, as the teachers would be screaming at us to close the windows and get back to our seats. Then the lads would have driven out knowing that the school would ring the cops. They would have been there and gone in five minutes and this would happen quite often. I finished school halfway through my fifth year. I just didn't go back (and no one from the school inquired as to why I was not coming into school). I hung around street corners until I could get unemployment benefit. I was not on the dole for long though, and I joined a local youth training programme (YTP) in July. Then I packed my bags for Manchester in August 1982.

Starting the Boxing

*T*started boxing in 1979, at the age of twelve at the Sacred Heart Boxing Club in the Oldpark, North Belfast. The Sacred Heart Boxing Club opened in 1963, in the big building in Gracehill Street. Gerry Smith was the first coach, followed by a brief stint by Mickey Ferrin. The club then folded for a few years and in the late 1960s, Eric McCullough got the boxing club up and running again. Big Anthony Maguire won the Irish senior title shortly after the club got going again and represented his country against Germany. In fact, all of the Maguire family boxed with the exception of oldest brother Rab (the barber). Rab could have talked his way out of anything so he didn't need to learn how to fight. The Maguire's cousin, Chris Mahony, won an Irish juvenile title and Charlie Mawhinney and Stan 'the man' Corbett were two other notable boxers.

Another great boxer from the Oldpark area, was a fella called Barney Burns, who lived in Parkview Street. Barney boxed for the Crown ABC (in the crown entry in Belfast city centre) as the Sacred Heart ABC hadn't opened yet. Barney won an Irish senior title at middleweight and boxed for Ulster and Ireland many times. Barney then moved to Birmingham, England, and boxed for Small Heath ABC and won two more Irish senior titles while coming back to Ireland for short stays. Barney also got to two ABA semi-finals (beaten by Chris Finnegan in one) and got to an ABA final in the early 1960s and a crowd from the Oldpark travelled over to Wembley to watch him lose a split decision to Peter McCann. Eamon Maguire was one of the crowd that went over, and he thought the decision was close and could have went either way. Barney boxed the great Chris Finnegan three times (once in an ABA semi and twice in Ireland v. England international matches) and lost all three, but they were close contests and Barneys brother, Pat, told me that he thought Barney won one of those contests for sure. Chris Finnegan went on to win the Olympic gold in Mexico in 1968 and was a British, Empire and European light heavyweight boxing champion and boxed Bob Foster for the world light heavyweight title as a professional.

A lad in my classroom, called Anthony 'Monkey' McBride, got me started with boxing. He told me that maybe I would do him in a street fight, but he would do me in a boxing ring and he challenged me to a spar over in the Sacred Heart ABC. He said this in front of a crowd of school mates, so I accepted his challenge on the spot not really expecting to stand by it. It was just bullshit talk in front of my peers. It played on my mind for a while though and for a few days I did nothing, all the while listening to Monkey boasting (in school) that while I had accepted his challenge, I hadn't backed up his challenge yet. Eventually, curiosity got the better of me and one night I ventured over to the gym to check this boxing thing out.

Eamon Maguire, who was the head coach and the main man, was not there that night, but I got what I came over for (a spar with Monkey) and I will tell you what, he was on the receiving end of a vicious beating, that I must admit gave me a real buzz. I had now backed up my challenge. The other coach, Eric McCullough (and others), were impressed and Eric asked me would I come back again to meet the head coach, Eamon Maguire (my dad beat Eamon in a boxing contest when they were ten years old), and that's what I did. I had my first boxing contest in the old St John Bosco club (beside St Patrick's chapel in Donegal Street, Belfast). I got a bye, and I was straight into a County Antrim final against a boy called Fleming. It was a wild and woolly fight. A slugging contest with very little style or finesse. I won by a unanimous decision and could proudly call myself the 7st. 7lb. champion of County Antrim (for my age and weight). From that moment on, I lived and breathed boxing for the next ten years of my life.

There were some great lads in my school year (form) and some tough nuts. I remember Danny Loughlin was tall, wiry and confident, Steven Arbuckle was tough and brave, Martin 'Walter' Kearney was fearless and Noel Magee was an Irish boxing champion and was very tall, quiet and well built, everyone knew not to mess with him. We used to rank the hard lads one out of ten and until I started boxing, I was not even on the radar. I remember being on the roof of the old Ardoyne Youth Club/Holy Cross Boys dinner hall in Butler Street with Danny Loughlin, and we were carving our names into the tar roof with a knife, when Steven Arbuckle walked up Butler Street on his own. Danny Loughlin started to convince me that I could do Arbuckle now that I was a boxer and was a County Antrim champion. We then started to shout abuse at Arbuckle and he shouted at me to come down off the roof and face him for a fair dig. I thought to myself, 'Yeah I am a boxer and I am a champion', and I was off that roof and squaring up to Arbuckle in ten seconds flat. We got stuck into each other, and I was throwing punches with blinding speed and deadly accuracy and absolutely punching the head clean off him. I was awesome. Then something strange happened. Some adults broke the fight up and it gave me too much time to think (as I had acted on impulse) and I started to lose courage and started to doubt myself, as a crowd had formed out of nowhere and they were baying for blood. When the people who had broken the fight up passed on by, the crowd tried to get the fight started again; Arbuckle was a bit reticent, but willing to continue, but my balls had dropped and I said that I didn't want to fight no more. The more reluctant I became then the more confident Arbuckle became, and him and the crowd followed me as I beat a hasty retreat to 3 Fairfield Street.

The crowd were shouting to Arbuckle, 'Just get into him', but he was very wary and I think I shook his hand and said, 'You win' (he never landed a blow). He accepted my surrender, but I felt ashamed and humiliated. I was taught a lesson that day, and I thought to myself that even if I had just got into him and taken a beating, then it wouldn't have felt as bad with the shame and indignation I was now feeling. I knew that I had to work on the mental side and toughen that up. I must never quit again. About two or three years later, I picked a fight with Steven Arbuckle. I started slabbering to him at the top of Estoril Park (where the yellow security gate and the dragon's teeth were). Once again, Steven was up for it and was slabbering back. This time I was really up for it, however, people got in between us to break it up. Unfortunately, Steven and his brother Paul ended up alcoholics and both died in their thirties. May they rest in paradise.

Incidentally, my dad had a run-in with Steven Arbuckle's brother, Paul, in John Magee's house in Holmdene Gardens. John Magee's daughter, Tracey Magee, is a deputy political editor with UTV Live and is on TV five or six days a week. John Magee was an alcoholic, and his house was used as a drinking den as John was single. One night, Paul Arbuckle overstepped the mark by hitting my dad while they were in the middle of a session, my dad hit him back (knocking him out) and Paul's wife, who was also at the session, hit my dad over the head with an empty bottle of vodka splitting his head open and my dad knocked her out also. My dad was banned for a while from John's house over this incident as John had a code of ethics, 'No fighting!' My dad's best friend around this time was Terence 'Doc' Magee (dad of boxer Eamonn Magee), but they had a love/hate relationship as Doc was also an alcoholic, but they were two characters. A friend of mine who I did the door with, Jim McDonald, said he was having a drink one time with my dad and Doc in the Crumlin Star and Jim said to me, that when Doc went to the toilets, my dad would rip the back out of Doc telling Jim that Doc was one mean, miserable, lousy bastard and when Doc came back, my dad would be all smiles and when my dad went to the toilets, Doc would rip the back out of my dad saying something similar. Jim said this went on all day and he was stuck in the middle.

My mum and dad, and Doc and his wife Isobel, went away together for a week to the Isle of Man. When they all turned up to get the ferry, Doc was blocked and my dad became self-righteous saying to my mum it was an absolute disgrace Doc turning up blocked and had Doc no shame etc. However, when they came back a week later it was my dad who was blocked and Doc was sober and this time it was Doc who got on his high horse saying Patsy was a disgrace. My mum and Isobel are two best mates to this day and would be confiding with each other. They just let their husband's get on with it (drinking), while they spent the week being together and enjoying themselves (and they had a great time). My mum said that it was like something straight out of **Rab. C. Nesbitt** as my dad reminded her of Rab, and Doc was a bit like Jamesy. Steven and Paul Arbuckle, John Magee, Doc and my dad are all dead now for many years. Alcohol, indirectly or otherwise, killed them all.

I loved boxing. It was in my blood. I enjoyed the training from the skipping to punching the bags. I also liked trips to other boxing clubs for fights. I remember our boxing club, the Sacred Heart ABC, would have gone up to Ballyclare ABC most Tuesdays for boxing contests. They were wee novice shows, but there were decisions, so they were not spars or exhibitions. Having said that, there was no weigh-in, no medical and the result didn't go on your medical card so it was sort of unofficial (if you know what I mean). I had some great wins up there; in fact, I was never beaten. Sometimes you got a trophy and, on some occasions, you got a tin of coke or a bag of crisps instead of a trophy. One fight that sticks out, was when I boxed this lad called John Lowry (not to be confused with East Belfast's John Lowey, who boxed Mexican legend Eric Morales for the world title). John was a year younger than me and he was a very bright prospect. His coach wanted him to box that night, but was very wary of putting him in with me. He was from a Belfast club, and his coach brought him up to get him fights and experience as it was hard to get anyone his own age and weight to box him. Eamon Maguire told this kid's coach that he can have the fight if he wants it, but warned the coach that I was very good and a full year older than this kid (I was 14). The coach made a big mistake and said yes to taking the fight, and I stopped the kid in two rounds giving him a bad beating in the process. I heard the kid (who was an outstanding prospect) never boxed again.

We all loved and respected Eamon Maguire. He was like a dad figure to me, as my own dad would have been in London for long spells. I remember when we boxed in Dundalk, Dublin or wherever and Eamon would stress to us to look neat and tidy and behave responsibly, that we were representing the club and our parish. Many a time before we set off, he would cut our hair. He was (and is) a proud man and would have been straight as a die with us (if not blunt) and would have taken no nonsense. The Sacred Heart had shows all the time and we were busy boxers (which I loved). Most of our shows would be in Ardoyne and I boxed in most of the social clubs. I boxed in the Glenpark, the Shamrock and the GAA quite a few times. I remember my mum, my granny, Sarah, and my aunt Peggy being at a show in the GAA and I knocked out the Irish champion, Michael McAllister from Clonard ABC, in the last round. It must be over twenty years since there was a boxing show in Ardoyne that was run by Ardoyne ABC or Sacred Heart ABC. Why is that? Especially in an area with a strong boxing heritage. It was the boxing club that created a strong sense of community and pride.

One time Eamon Maguire and I went over to Beechmount ABC to spar Irish senior champion, Alex O'Neill. This would have been 1981. Alex was a light flyweight, I was fifteen and a featherweight and I had sparred with Alex before and it had been a competitive spar. For one reason or another, he didn't come to the gym that night even though it had been arranged between the two clubs. The head coach at Beechmount was furious as we had ventured over for a spar during very dangerous times in Belfast. One of the other coaches said, 'What about wee Billy? (not his real name) I saw him at the rear of the club with some friends as I came in.' The head coach said, 'Yeah, that's a good idea, go round and get Billy.' When Billy came round he was well up for the spar, but his behaviour was a bit irregular and when I was in sparring with him, I could smell the glue off him (he stank of it). He was wearing a t-shirt and a pair of jeans and was as high as a kite on glue, but he gave me one hell of a spar. I had sniffed glue before and it wears off you very quickly (you have to keep sniffing your bag of glue to maintain the high). His coaches must have known that he was sniffing glue, as he stank of it, but I will tell you something – he was one tough wee bastard. I would imagine it would have been 'highly' dangerous (no pun intended) and irresponsible to put this young lad into the ring to spar with me. I could have killed him or done permanent damage to him.

Boxing gave me a great life and an escape from the shootings and bombings and the madness that was all around me. It would affect you daily, as there wouldn't be a day that passed that I didn't have a rifle pointed at me during British Army patrols of the area. I would be stopped, searched and questioned on a regular basis. I remember being lifted and driven about for a while, then being asked by the army if I would be a tout for them and keep them up to date with IRA activities. I am sure this happened to many young lads in the area and unfortunately, some succumbed to British Army or RUC pressure to inform, and it was to cost many young lads in the area their lives. I personally knew over a hundred people who were murdered during the conflict. I had my dream though, an ideal that got me out of bed in the morning. It was boxing, which gave a lot of people a focus, kept them off the streets at night and, importantly, out of trouble.

I had a wonderful time boxing and it lasted over ten years. I boxed in some amazing places and met some amazing people. I boxed in Windsor Park, Maine Road (Manchester City Football Ground), Wembley Arena, Royal Albert Hall, King's Hall, Ulster Hall, York Hall, Grosvenor House Hotel, Hilton Hotel, Preston Guild Hall, Los Angeles, Panama, Colombia and many many more. In England, you always got well fed after a fight and I was always treated with a lot of respect. People seemed to have a lot of respect for boxers.

Between 1979 and 1982, I would have had around 55 boxing contests and I only lost four. I have a photographic memory regarding my boxing contests, and I used to keep a record of my fights like a statistician would. I might not have remembered all the names, but I would remember some-thing about the fight and I would mark it down in a notebook, as not all our contests were marked down in our medical cards. It could be a venue, a defeat, a stoppage or knockout win, hospitality etc., something.

I had a rivalry with a lad from East Belfast called Bill Nicholson. The first time we boxed was at Windsor Park in 1981, and I lost a close decision. A few months later, I boxed Bill at a club on the Newtownards Road in East Belfast. Incidentally, it was during Ian Paisley's 'Day of Action'. The Ulster Defence Association (UDA) stood around the ringside wearing armbands, and here I was, Eamon McAuley, from Sacred Heart ABC. I had one of the bravest coaches ever. I remember as I was in the ring, my coach, Eamon Maguire, told me not to be kneeling down to bless myself (I sometimes did this). And you know what? I got robbed. Even my opponent told me that I won clearly. Bill was cut badly and the fight should have been stopped on the cut, so it was a double whammy when the decision went against me. They were not going to let him lose on his own club show (Ledley Hall). My team were not going to kick up too much of a rumpus though. We were just glad to get out of there – alive. That made it one win each, in my eyes at least, between Bill and I. The next time I boxed Bill was in the National Stadium in Dublin in an All-Ireland youth final at 9st. Previous to this All Irelands, I had won the Ulster title at 9st. 7lb. I had moved up in weight to avoid Bill. I didn't want to box him in Ulster, I wanted him down in Dublin where I might get a fair decision. I was still seething from that bad decision against Bill. In the Ulster's, I won my final with an impressive second round stoppage and I remember my dad and my Uncle, Brian Woods (who was married to my dad's sister, Peggy), being in the hall. The last time my dad had come to watch me was the previous year when I made my international debut at the young Ulster v. young Wales tournament in the Recy club off North Queen Street in Belfast, and I won convincingly. But a year on, I was much bigger and stronger and I was proud to put on a great display for him and my uncle. Bill won by stoppage that night also at 9st.

In the All Irelands, I moved back down to 9st. and I won two fights to get to the final. In the quarter-final, I chinned the guy with a left hook and in the semis, I beat Chris Graham from Ards, who had a win over Bill. Bill had two stoppage wins to get to the final. He had been the aggressor in our first two fights, just charging at me, but I would catch him coming in with lovely counterpunches. I would wait for him to lead and I would make him miss and make him pay. In the final though, Bill changed tactics which I didn't expect or prepare for. I must give Bill and his coaches full credit for employing the perfect tactics in the final. In the first two rounds, Bill didn't come rushing at me. He waited on me to lead. There was very little to talk about in those first two rounds as it was like a Mexican standoff. Coming out for the final round it was anybody's fight. My corner told me that if I wanted the title, then I would have to go out and earn it. I thought that sounded okay and I upped the tempo and started to go forward, which I never did previous to this fight. This was just what Bill was waiting on. I had ended the Mexican standoff. Sometime during the final round, I had rushed in and Bill countered with a massive haymaker right hand which landed flush on my chin and put me on my arse for the first time in my boxing career! The *Rocky* films have got the knockdown part correct. You can hear the noise of the crowd, then silence, apart from the sound of your heart beating, and then when you hit the canvas the noise returns. It feels like going down in slow motion.

I picked myself off the canvas, but the referee wouldn't let me continue. I was furious at him for stopping it and was shouting at him and pushing him. In 130 amateur contests, I was only ever knocked down twice, once by Bill and I was knocked down by Ben McGarrigle in Strabane, but I got up to stop Ben in the same round, and put him in hospital. The fight with McGarrigle is on YouTube – check it out. I really thought that Billy Nicholson would have gone far in the boxing world, but he didn't. I had a few more contests for the Sacred Heart after the Irish final, and I remember beating Seán McCormick twice and in the second contest, we both went through the ropes and fell out of the ring and, as God as my witness, he made a funny remark to me. I can't remember what it was, but it was not, 'Last one up's a sissy.' Seán's dad was the legendary Spike McCormick and, in former world lightweight boxing champion Ken Buchanan's book *The Tartan Legend: The Autobiography* (Buchanan 2000), he pays Spike a huge compliment by saying Spike give him one of his hardest fights as a pro.

I moved to England later that year and that's when I really came to the fore. I tried to keep my eye on Bill, but he never really did anything at junior or senior grade. He was a multi-titled juvenile and youth and had got to an Irish junior final where he was beaten by a guy who boxed me in England, and I easily beat him. I sparred Bill when I was back in Belfast in the late 1980s, but he was really easy. I had too much respect for Bill in that Irish final, but it was a lesson learned, and when I went to England in 1982, I had respect for no one. The only other guys to beat me before I went to England, were Hugh McGuinness (St Agnes) on a close, but fair decision and I was robbed blind in the National Association of Boys Clubs (NABC) in Derry by a lad called Rafferty from Pennyburn. Bill Nicholson stopped him in one round in the final.

One other night, 27 March 1981, Gerry Stafford, Noel and Terry Magee and I were making our way home from the Sacred Heart boxing club. Along the way, we said cheerio to Noel and Terry as they lived at the top of Holmdene Gardens and at the bottom of Estoril Park, I bid farewell to Gerry Stafford as I lived in Estoril Park and Gerry lived on the next street, Cranbrook Gardens. As Gerry made his way to Cranbrook Gardens, he passed a fella named Paul Blake and they both nodded to each other and as Gerry was walking up his path, he noticed a car approaching Paul Blake. As Gerry put his key in the lock shots rang out and Paul Blake was shot dead. I had just walked into my house and put my training bag down when the shooting started. It came to light afterwards that UDA commander, Jimmy Craig, had sent out two young lads from a Loyalist club in the Shankill to go up to Ardoyne and shoot the first Catholic they saw and when they returned job done, they were rewarded with a few pounds each. My dad knew Jimmy Craig well. Craig was an ex-boxer who, although a Protestant, had boxed for a club called the Star which was a Catholic club in the Nationalist New Lodge area. Within six months of this incident, all four of us had packed our bags and headed overseas to further our boxing skills, but more importantly for a better quality of life.

In closing this chapter about the Sacred Heart Boxing Club, I would just like to mention that there were some great boxers around me in the Sacred Heart gym. The Magee brothers from Holmdene Gardens (Terry, Noel, Patrick and Eamonn) won titles for the club; Darren Corbett and his brother Eamonn won Irish titles. Other great boxers that I remember were Martin Hamill, Laurence Marley, Colin Magill, Hugo Wilkinson, Colin McGarrity (RIP), Tucker O'Neil, Brian Corrigan (RIP), Tommy Scott, Mark Savage, Dermot and Dominic Gilmore, John Noble, Jude Brennan, Tony McNulty, Norman Heagney and this list could go on and on. Today, there is an unbreakable bond between all the boxers and coaches who passed through the club. It is such a shame that the club has been closed for so many years. Sadly, it lies barren and defunct. Every time I walk past the building, the great memories come flowing back. I would like to take this opportunity to thank the men who looked after me in the Sacred Heart ABC. Eamon Maguire, Eric McCullough (RIP), Patsy McKenna and Jimmy Boyle. Also big Gerry Dunleavy (RIP) and also Trevor 'Dandy' Close (RIP), who was murdered by so-called Loyalists in 1983 (when I was in England).

Coco

My dad, Patrick 'Coco' McAuley, was a hard man. He was one of the hardest that ever came out of Belfast. He sits up there comfortably with other legendary hard men from Belfast, Silver McKee from the Markets and Stormy Weatherall from the Shankill. My dad had the reputation of being one of the toughest and hardest men ever to come out of Belfast, but he was from good stock. His dad, Harry McAuley, from Portrush, was a Northern Ireland professional boxing champion. His mother Sarah, was Rinty Monaghan's eldest sister. In horse racing terms, my dad would have been a thoroughbred.

As an amateur boxer, my grandad was Ulster junior champion, Ulster senior finalist and boxed for Ireland on a few occasions including, a good win against an English opponent. As a professional boxer, he was coached and managed by Frank McAloran in the Hardinge Street gym in North Queen street, where he trained with notable boxers Gerry McAllister (who boxed as Patsy Quinn) and Northern Ireland, Irish, British, Empire, European and undisputed world flyweight boxing champion, Rinty Monaghan (his brother-in-law). Tommy Monaghan (Rinty's brother), told me that he witnessed many a spar between my grandad and Rinty and he said that they were sizzling hot. Rinty was a flyweight and my grandad was a featherweight, but Rinty was at world class level (there were also tales that Rinty wore 6 oz. gloves and my grandad wore 16 oz. gloves). Great-uncle Tommy told me that they had no water in the New Lodge gym, and they had to go next door with jugs to get them filled with water, and Tommy told me that is how he met his wife. My grandad won the Northern Ireland area title by beating Billy Donnelly over fifteen rounds and he lost his title to Jim McCann, whom he had a great rivalry with. One of my grandad's best wins was against Dublin's John Ingle, who was the brother of legendary Sheffield coach, Brendan Ingle. John was knocking everybody out, and no one wanted to box him. Frank McAloran went up to Rinty Monaghan's mum and dad's house in Highbury Gardens, Ardoyne to offer my grandad a fight against John Ingle in the Ulster Hall for £10 or £15.

My grandad (who would fight anyone) accepted the offer to fight John Ingle and in the first round, Ingle hurt my grandad with a right, which landed just under my grandad's heart, but my grandad came back and decked Ingle in the second round, Ingle got up and my grandad decked him again and the ref stopped the fight. It was a massive upset and everyone who previously did not want to box Ingle now wanted to box him, as they now thought he had a glass jaw. My grandad boxed all over Britain and Ireland and took many late notice jobs against area champions and even some Empire champions. Also, many of his stoppage losses were cut eye losses, as he had very sharp features and high cheekbones. By all accounts, my grandad was a quiet man and would have gone to the Wheatfield social club. I would see him regularly at Toby's for bingo nights, where he would be with my granny, Sarah, and I would be with my granny, Bridget. I would call to my granny, Sarah's, regularly and my grandad would always be there, but he was not in good health and couldn't talk.

My grandad would go out sometimes and forget where he lived and he would be roaming about North Belfast in very dangerous times. My dad and my uncle, Seán, would be out in their cars looking for him and sometimes they picked him up on the Shankill Road (during the Shankill Butchers' murder campaign) and the family reckoned he was looking for his old boxing mate, Tommy Armour, who lived in the Shankill. My grandad died in 1978 from pugilistic dementia, he was only 58. The blows to the head that he took in the ring put him in an early grave.

My dad's street fighting prowess was legendary. He had knife and bottle scars on his body from brawls in bars before the Troubles broke out.

In Ardoyne in the early 1970s, he was well known for fighting with the British Army, especially the paras. They couldn't get one to beat him. They even flew in an army boxing champion who had been serving in Germany (you just couldn't make this up), and my dad filled him in after the boxing champion judased my dad with a knuckle duster. My dad fell to the ground, but rose and gave the para a beating. When my dad left him lying in a heap, that's when they discovered the knuckle duster. After that the Brits respected him, revered him even, and they never bothered him again. Having said that, the stories about my dad's street fighting skills are incredible. I have heard so many Coco stories about him fighting. They can't all be true. If they are, then he must have been fighting ten times a day, seven days a week. When other people start telling lies and making up stories about someone, then it takes on mythological proportions and they become a legend. And without doubt, in North Belfast, my dad was a legend. In North Belfast among the older generation, I will always be known as 'Coco's son.' That's how one old guy introduces me to another old guy, 'That's Coco's son.' I am used to it, I have it all my life. No matter where I am in North Belfast (and beyond), if I say to an older man, 'Have you heard of Coco from Ardoyne?' nearly all of them will say, 'Yes', and tell me a story about him. In fact, people's faces light up when I mention Coco.

My dad was given a bravery award from the Royal Humane Society in 1973 for jumping into the water and saving the life of a woman who was drowning at Queen's Bridge in the docks area (I still have the bravery award). It was one of the coldest days on record. A few weeks later, my dad bumped into the woman in Belfast city centre and instead of showing her gratitude, she beat my dad over the head with an umbrella. She had been trying to kill herself and sadly, we heard that she eventually did. This incident just sums up my dad's life.

Also, a guy got knee capped (shot through the back of the legs to blow the knee caps off) in Fairfield Street/Oakfield Street entry and my dad brought the guy to the hospital in his car. There was blood all over my dad's car. So there was also a compassionate side to Coco.

Let me tell you how my dad got his nickname. My dad was very young at the time, when a truck overturned in Brompton Park/Etna Drive and I'm not sure if the truck was specifically delivering cocoa powder, or there just happened to be boxes of cocoa powder among other products. Anyway, my dad's mates ran to the truck to raid it of its goodies, and as they reached the truck, my dad was already inside the truck with his face covered in cocoa powder as he was eating it as fast as he could. It was as a result of this that a lad called Patsy Gillespie, started to call him 'Cocoa' which was shortened to Coco.

In 1980–1981 he tried to rescue two children who were trapped in the bedroom of a house which was on fire. As my dad tried to get up the stairs to the children, the stairwell collapsed in front of him. There was no way now for him to get to the children, who were squealing from the bedroom, and sadly they died. My mum said that my dad came home that night and cried his eyes out, and this haunted him for a long time. The thing was, that if my dad had taken a few more steps then he would have been on the wrong side of the stairs when they collapsed in the middle. My dad cheated death so many times.

There were rumours that my dad killed a guy in Camden Town in London. The story goes that this guy and my dad had an altercation in a bar and the guy followed my dad into the toilets, where my dad is alleged to have chinned him, walked out of the toilets and out of the bar. I heard the newspapers covered the story and reported that the police were looking for a man with a Scottish or Northern Irish accent, with massive arms. Did the guy hit his head on the toilet floor? Did he choke on his own vomit? Did he have a heart attack? So many unanswered questions. My dad had to leave Belfast to go to London as he was receiving death threats. One time we got a St Patrick's day card in the post and when we opened it, it had a live bullet sellotaped to it. There was a coffin drawn around the bullet in black eye liner and it said, 'RIP Coco Bully Boy.'

The Irish People's Liberation Organisation (IPLO) also had a go at my dad in September 1989. I remember the date, as I had my eighth professional fight a few days after the attack and my family hid the details and the damage to my dad's face from me. I didn't find out until after my fight in London. The attack happened in Monaghan's Bar down in the docks. What happened was that Martin 'Rook' O'Prey and his gang, came into the bar and saw my dad sitting over in the corner on his own. My dad was drunk and past his prime and there were less than a handful in the bar, but my cousin Michael Monaghan was there, and he told me what happened. They knew my dad, they also knew of my dad's reputation and they singled him out. They went over and picked a fight with him. A fight broke out and Michael said that my dad was knocking them about like ten pins. He said that my dad put about three of them out of the game, but there was too many of them. Again, he got warned that he would be shot dead. They ended up kicking my dad on the ground, then they left. Michael said that my dad just got straight up, didn't moan or complain and just carried on drinking. There was blood gushing out of his wounds and he eventually had to go to hospital (after he finished his drink of course). He got stitched up in hospital.

A few weeks later, my dad was drinking, this time in the Dockers Club, when Rook O'Prey, Geek Donnelly and their gang entered. Rook walked over to my dad and offered him to a fair go outside. My dad (drunk again) looked around at all Rook's backings and said, 'I am getting too old for this son.' Rook replied, 'Well shake my hand and we will just forget about all this then.' My dad shook his hand. My dad was not stupid. He knew they would all gang up on him again. Martin 'Rook' O'Prey was shot dead in 1991 as he sat, with his daughter on his knee, at their house in Ardmoulin Terrace (facing Divis Tower). The Ulster Volunteer Force (UVF) came in the back entrance and there was no doubt the UVF were kept up to date with Rook's movements on the day. There were high tech cameras on the top of Divis Tower facing the front of Rooks house, but the UVF came in and went out the back.

In 1997, my dad had an altercation with a Republican's wife in the Jamaica Inn pub in Ardoyne. It was a silly row over a seat and she attacked my dad. My dad fended her off, but she went and rang her husband and told him, 'Coco McAuley just attacked me!' My dad left the Jamaica Inn to go home with a friend of his (Midget McClafferty) and as he was going up Brompton Park, a car pulled over and it was the girl's husband and he shouted, 'Did you fucking hit my wife?' My dad said, 'No, I didn't, your wife was attacking me and I was fending her off.' The Republican then said, 'I will see you tomorrow,' and my dad said, 'See me now, what's wrong with now?' The Republican then drove off.

About two or three weeks later my dad, who by then was a full blown alcoholic, was drinking in a house opposite the Glenpark club, when a car pulled up and four or five guys got out and went straight to the house (owned by an alcoholic by the name of Millar). It was my dad they were after. It was very strange they knew where he was. They told him if he lifts his hands, then they will shoot him dead. They made him lie on his belly with his arms out in front of him and one guy put his foot on one arm and another guy did the same with the other arm. Then a guy came forward with a hammer, and he beat the fuck out of my dad's two hands causing multiple fractures and lacerations. I was told that my dad made no noise at all. He wouldn't scream for those bastards. He was rushed to Dundonald specialised unit and he was there for weeks.

Legendary Republican, Martin Meehan, a lifelong friend of my dad, came to see him and he brought a guy from Connolly House, Sinn Féin's main office on the Falls Road, Belfast. Meehan, a Republican hard man from Ardoyne, cried when he seen my dad. I witnessed this myself while they were visiting. Many Republicans stopped me and said that it was a disgrace what happened to my dad, but nothing was done. No action was taken. If this guy did this off his own bat, without it being sanctioned, then he would have got done. So was it sanctioned? When my dad died in 2014, he was laid out in a coffin in the living room for the wake, but O'Kane's funeral directors couldn't close his hands to wrap the rosary beads around due to the damage done by the IRA. O'Kane's just decided then to hide his hands.

Apparently, my dad put a fella from Ligoniel's eye out in a street fight. That I do know. As a matter of fact, I am friends with the fella's son. A girl who worked in a local shop used to be a bit ignorant towards me. I know her name. Turns out my dad had a row with her dad and her dad's head hit the cribby when he was knocked to the ground by my dad. A few years later, the fella died from a brain haemorrhage and the family blamed my dad for his death.

I only ever saw him fighting once and it was in the summer of 1982. I remember it well because I was on my way back from sparring Olympic bronze medallist and future British champion at two weights, Hugh Russell, in the Holy Family gym. Hugh was a pro boxer at this point. On our way home, as my dad and I were driving up the New Lodge Road, a guy tried to overtake him. It was a dangerous and reckless act on the guy's behalf. My dad gave way, but beeped his horn at the guy. The guy beeped back and indicated to the right at Felons club (Lepper Street) and he then put his arm out the window and motioned for my dad to pull in to the right, which my dad did willingly. The two of them got out of their cars and squared up. The other guy was a big guy, and he was quicker off the mark and kicked my dad in the balls. Well, in the excitement it had no effect on my dad. My dad threw a flurry of punches, like a young Mike Tyson, and the last one caught the guy a glancing blow to the head and the guy went down. As he went down my dad put the boot in (he later said that was the first time in his life he ever done that). The guy got up, but he was very unsteady and didn't want to know. My dad said later that the guy was drunk and he could smell it off him. He accepted the guys unconditional surrender because there was a little girl squealing in the guy's car. On our journey home, my dad complained the whole way about the pain in his balls.

I remember being in bed one night in the mid-seventies when my dad came back from the Saunders club with a friend called Jimmy Hill (no, not the football presenter). My dad had knocked two or three guys out and Jimmy was very excited and being very loud and hyper (he couldn't contain himself). Jimmy was describing to my mum what had happened and he was shouting things like, 'Roseleen, Coco chinned three of them and all I saw was bang, bang, bang.' And I then heard my dad say. 'Jimmy, will you fuck up. My kids are in bed sleeping.' But Jimmy couldn't shut up. We used to enjoy Jimmy calling to our house in Fairfield Street, as sometimes he would bring a present for us, or my mum, but I clearly remember that he always used to have a boxing question for my dad to try and answer.

A friend of mine, and my dad's, called Sam 'Foot' McClenaghan told me that he once worked as a barman in the Hemisphere in Belfast city centre, and he said he witnessed my dad knock out four guys from Sandy Row. Sam said that he would have been about nineteen at the time (around 1970). In Sam's words, my dad, 'Owned the town at that time.' Sam who is 66 now, told me that my dad put the four of them down in under ten seconds. In Sam's words again, it was, 'Bang, bang, bang, bang.' Sam is a Christian and has credibility with me, so I do believe him. The more stories I hear about my dad. the more I believe that he was as hard as they all say.

When my dad worked on the door in the late seventies, early eighties, he hit and hurt one of UDA leaders, Tommy 'Tucker' Lyttle's bodyguards, and considering who it was, it was a very big deal. I remember a series of phone calls between my dad and another UDA commander, Jimmy Craig, to try and get things sorted out. Craig had known my dad since the sixties when they both boxed. Craig had boxed for the Star boxing club in the Nationalist New Lodge area. Shortly after this series of phone calls with Craig, my dad was having a drink in one of the clubs he worked in called Shadows and my friend, Bobby McCabe, who was doing the door that night told me that my dad was off duty and was drinking quite heavily, when members of the UDA turned up and gave my dad quite a kicking. Bobby told me that my dad was too drunk to fight back, and they left him on the ground bleeding from cuts and bruises to the head and body. Bobby told me that when the UDA left, my dad picked himself up and left the club. He told me that my dad later told him that he went up the Shankill Road looking for Jimmy Craig. So, you can draw your own conclusions. Was the beating arranged to pay the price for hurting Lyttle's bodyguard? If so, why was he looking for Craig? No doubt Craig would have said, 'Patsy they wanted to shoot you and I talked them into just giving you a kicking.' Did Craig tell them where my dad would be at a certain place at a certain time? The Shankill Road was a very dangerous place to be for a Catholic then, and I can imagine my dad going into Loyalist clubs, while drunk and in a bad way asking for the whereabouts of Jimmy Craig.

When my dad lived in London, he worked as a minder for a Newry businessman called Ally Morgan. We liked Ally. He died in Poland a few years ago as he owned a bar out there. My dad had a love\hate relationship with Ally and eventually fell out with him, chinning Ally before he came home to Belfast. He used to laugh about it when he was drunk, as he claimed he chinned Ally in the toilets of a bar as Ally was sitting on the toilet (he said it was fitting, as Ally was full of shit). In London in January 1985, long after my dad fell out with him, I met up with Ally as he attended one of my fights at the Grosvenor House Hotel where I boxed for London against Tel Aviv. I chinned the guy in the first (one punch knockout) and Ally was delighted. He said, 'Forget about your dad, you're my new minder,' and he gave me a few quid. My dad's uncle, Rinty Monaghan (undisputed, undefeated world boxing champion), said that my dad was the biggest waste of talent that he had ever seen. He also said my dad was the hardest puncher he ever saw. Rinty said my dad should have been a millionaire. My uncle Seán said to me that one time a guy hit Rinty (Rinty was old then). My dad went and saw the guy and chinned him. My uncle Seán also said that he saw my dad hit a guy in a boxing contest in Dungannon, and the guy was out cold and was covered in horsehair, the glove had exploded such was the force of the blow. I know this to be 100 per cent true as my dad had a scrapbook with newspaper cuttings of him boxing or playing darts or snooker, and I clearly remember reading that story of the glove exploding in Dungannon. It's amazing the number of people my dad chinned in the district.

Ardoyne was quite a bit smaller then. When you went through the gap in Brompton Park towards the school, then you were entering the real Ardoyne. Now Glenard is called Ardoyne, but I was born and reared in the real Ardoyne. All that's left of old Ardoyne now is the Holy Cross boys primary school and the League club. Old Ardoyne was full of drinking clubs. There were the Wheatfield (Crumlin Road), Star (Butler Street), League (Chatham Street), Hibs (Herbert Street), GAA club (Butler Street), and the Saunders club (Elmfield Street), where my dad brought me over to see the great darts player, John Lowe, in the mid-seventies. In Glenard, you had the Shamrock club (Brompton Park), and the Highfield in Etna Drive. All these drinking clubs in an area with a population of around five to eight thousand. My dad fought in them all! I know a lot of guys that my dad chinned and they are fine with me. They almost wear it as a badge of honour. Two friends of mine whom my dad chinned (Phillip 'Buster' Larkin and Henry McBride) told me that my dad was their hero. Of the hundreds of stories I have heard about my dad's fighting prowess, I only ever heard of him getting beaten once and my dad disputes it.

Marty McCartan, a guy who once lived across the street from me in Cranbrook Gardens, told me that his dad (who was from the Ormeau Road) did my dad in the Brew (dole/unemployment benefit offices) in Corporation

Street when they were eighteen. I remember asking my dad about it, and to my surprise, he remembered the guy and the incident. He said the guy was a cheeky slabber and had accused my dad of bunking him in the line to sign on, they had words and McCartan banged my dad and left him with a swollen eye, but my dad said, 'Make no mistake about it, I gave him a vicious beating.' I don't know Marty's dad, but I do know that Marty is a bit of a Jack the lad character and he is very lucky to be alive, as he escaped an assassination attempt on his life a few years ago and he was also the victim of a punishment shooting. I liked Marty, and when I lived beside him in Cranbrook Gardens, he had Sky TV (early 1990s) and would record all the big fights onto a video tape for me. I remember he was involved in a fight in Cranbrook Gardens and he got stabbed, and it was me that drove him to the hospital. He squealed the whole way.

My dad's old mate, Stanley Corbett, rang me the other day. Stanley was drunk but sounded very annoyed. He said 'Eamon, it's a disgrace what they are doing' and I replied, 'What's that Stanley?' and he said, 'They are trying to destroy your dad's character and reputation just like they did to Silver McKee' (another legendary hard man from Belfast). He went on. 'Eamon, that's the second time in a matter of months that I heard somebody claim they had a relative that did your dad. It's lies Eamon, all lies', said Stanley. 'Eamon, I was one of your dad's best mates and knew him all his life and when he was alive, I never heard one person ever claim they, or a relative, did him and that's because no one did him. But they are coming out of the woodwork with their lies as he isn't around to defend himself.' I told Stanley not to worry, as long as we are alive, we will defend him. He then spoke for twenty minutes about my dad and how great he was. He told me about the time Coco knocked out Nailer Clark (another hard man), in the Joe Saunders club. He then started to get emotional so I made up the excuse that I had to get ready for work and we said our goodbyes. About two years ago, when I worked in the Beechlawn Hotel, a guy called Ciarán McLaughlin called me over to his table where he was having a debate with his mates. He said in front of them, 'Eamon, these guys are claiming that Stanley Corbett did your dad in a street fight.' I tried to explain that my dad was Stanley's hero and they had been lifelong friends. They 100 per cent had never fought each other. That's how ridiculous it's getting. One of the guys said, 'Well I heard different', or such and such told me, etc. One eejit can tell a lie and other eejits will add to it. That's life, that can't be stopped and will go on forever.

My dad hit quite a few Republicans in Ardoyne in the 1970s. Maybe that's why they tried to wipe him out that time when he came out of the Dockers club in Pilot Street in 1973. He was shot in the stomach and the foot. We know who did it. He's dead now, but he was a Republican. It was dangerous stuff in dangerous times. One day, my dad was in a card school beside the League club and he was doing quite well. My dad's brother, Harry, was in the card school also, but he got skinned and my dad handed Harry a few quid to go about his business. Harry went against the code of ethics and got back into the card school again, and ended up skinning everyone including my dad. This caused my dad and Harry to exchange bitter words. Harry pulled a knife on my dad, but my dad gave him a bad beating. Harry was known to be a hard man and was in and out of borstals in his youth. In the early 1970s, Harry was working with a number of Protestants and decided to go for a drink with them after work. They left him for dead and he received the last rights from a priest, but he pulled through, but he was left with damage to his brain. As I am writing this, I believe Harry is alive and well and living in Dublin, but I haven't seen him in over twenty years and he was not at my dad's funeral. I don't even know if he knows my dad has died. We have no address or phone number for him, but my dad and him did make up and he would have come up to Belfast from time to time.

My dad was the oldest male sibling, but he had two older sisters, Ann and Peggy. Ann (the oldest) went to America in her teens and lives in Los Angeles with her husband Tony and kids. She is a millionaire, and I believe that she was a very driven woman. I have only met her a few times. Good luck to them and I wish them well, but I don't really know them. Peggy, the other sister moved to Los Angeles in 1984 after the death of her husband, Brian. We all loved Peggy and Brian. When I was in Los Angeles in 1987, I met up with Ann and Peggy, and also my granny, Sarah, who was out there living with Peggy. As I write this, my dad is the only sibling that has died. My dad had three brothers, Harry, Seán and Gerard. Seán lives in Ligoniel (about a mile away from Ardoyne) and has been the head coach at the Ligoniel boxing club ever since the previous coach, Terry McCafferty, was shot dead on 31 January 1974 by Loyalists while out doing a day's work. He was simply murdered because he was a Catholic and an easy target. Seán got an award from the Belfast city council for the great work he has done, not just for the boxing club, but also his work for the community. I had written a letter to Belfast city council telling them about all the great work Seán had done for many decades, as they had appealed (via TV and the press) to the public for feedback on unsung heroes. I am not sure if my letter had any impact, but that's not important.

I remember an old friend, Bobby McCabe, telling me a few stories about my dad. Bobby (from the Pound Loney in the Lower Falls) and my dad were working at a Queen concert at Slane Castle. Bobby was my dad's boss that day. My dad brought his friend Terence 'Doc' Magee along, and there must have been 30–60,000 people at the concert that day. During the course of the day, my dad came looking for Bobby and by the look on my dad's face, Bobby knew that this was serious. 'What's wrong Coco?' Bobby asked, 'I think I've killed someone', my dad said, 'Fuck sake, Patsy', Bobby said, 'Where did this happen?' 'Come on and I will show you', my dad replied. Bobby went with my dad expecting to find some poor fella lying unconscious. When my dad brought Bobby to where this happened, there were three guys still lying on the ground just coming round after being knocked out five minutes earlier by my dad. Other people told me my dad knocked out a massive bodybuilder that day. Frankie Donnelly said that my dad knocked a big 6ft guy clean out at one of the big concerts in Slane in the early/mid-eighties. Frankie says he was standing right beside my dad when this happened, as the mob just tried to push on through without tickets. This big giant guy was one of the ringleaders as they tried to push the security out of the way, but after the leader was chinned, they decided that discretion is the better part of valour and they paid the doormen in cash to go on through to the concert. The security boys from Belfast made a fortune that day letting people in with no tickets in exchange for cash, no questions asked.

A big giant man-mountain known by all the locals as 'Big Ray' used to work in the amusement arcade at the bottom of Brompton Park. Big Ray would have been 6ft. 2in. in height and about fifteen or sixteen stone. He stood very upright and was very muscular. He used to sleg with the youths in the arcade that he was the hardest man in Ardoyne, but the kids would have said, 'No, Coco is,' and Big Ray's catchphrase was, 'No way, Big Ray' in a very deep voice. This went on for months, if not longer. The kids would even shout in the street at him 'You're not as hard as Coco.' Unbeknown to anyone, this must have started to get to Big Ray and one night when he was drunk, he picked a fight with my dad in the Highfield club off Etna Drive. My dad knocked him cold. From when Big Ray hit the deck until he was helped to his feet twenty minutes had passed, and my dad was only about 5 ft. 6 in. However, he was very powerfully built. There were many other men (and I know their names) who challenged my dad and got knocked clean out, and they were hard men, but they just were not in my dad's league. It must have been just like the Wild West in Ardoyne in the 1970s, and my dad was a gunslinger, the fastest gun in the west (or north). There is a well know Republican family in Ardoyne, and there are lots of brothers in this family. They were known as hard men and this particular brother was known as the toughest and hardest. He started on my dad in the Highfield, but my dad left the club. Maybe he was worried about comebacks, but sometime later my dad was again in the Highfield and this guy once again tried to start a row with my dad. This time, the fella was knocked cold and there were no comebacks.

My mate, Tony McNulty, once told me that when he did the milk round in 1982 with his boss Derek, they called to our house in Holmdene Gardens to complain to my dad that I had stolen milk off the van and threatened Derek with the IRA. My dad came out in his bare belly and when Derek told his story, my dad defended me and said that I was a quiet boy. He said to Derek, 'If you're right then I will sort him out, but see if your wrong!' Tony said that Derek was terrified and when they got back to the van, Derek said to Tony, 'Did you see the size of his fucking arms?' When my dad confronted me, I said that I never stole milk and it was Kevin McClenaghan that said, 'We are the IRA' (we most certainly were not). I am not sure if he believed me or not.

My dad was both loved and loathed in equal measure. I didn't have a good relationship with him, as he didn't treat my mum too well. To be honest, I hated him for years. When he got sick and was bedbound, I began to feel pity and compassion for him. God was also coming more and more to the forefront in my life at that time also. I looked at this big hard strong man having to be looked after and fed by my mum and carers. He had to be fed liquid stuff through a tube (he couldn't swallow). He just lay in a bed in the living room dependant on those around him. I thought of the things he had gone through in his life; the death threats, the shootings, the bombings. Nearly every time he went into a bar, he had people torturing him or challenging him. They would never leave him alone. I realised that I had never walked a mile in his shoes, I had never gone through the horrific things that he did. Who was I to judge him? The last six years of his life, I talked to him every day, he couldn't talk back, but I would bring a smile to his face. I would feed him by injecting food (and water) through the tube that went into his stomach. When my mother and sister went to Florida (twice), I looked after my dad for the fortnight they were gone and moved into my mother's house for the duration of their holiday.

Our dog, Rory was a black Labrador and my dad loved him. Rory was an honorary member of the League club and would lie under the snooker table when my dad was playing. No one dared to tell my dad that dogs were not allowed in. One time during the early 1970s, my dad and Rory were pictured in the front page of the newspaper. There was rioting going on and the photo showed my dad throwing a hammer at the police with Rory at his side, as always. The headline was, 'A Lone Rioter and His Dog.'

In the Crumlin Star club, they had a pseudonym for my dad. They called him 'Harry Lime' (behind his back of course). The reason for this, I was told, was in case anyone was running him down behind his back and my dad overheard them or if he had just come into the room and was not noticed. Or if a friend of my dad heard someone running him down and told my dad. When my dad came into the room, word normally went around so instead of saying 'there's that bastard Coco', they would say, 'Harry Lime's just entered.' Anybody who used that pseudonym was not a friend of my dad's. They were not daft, and this shows the fear he instilled. There was a rule in the Star that anyone playing snooker was not allowed to climb up on the tables to play a long shot, they had to use the rest (or long rest). My good friend Brendan Toal told me that people were always getting pulled regarding this and were annoyed that the management never ever warned my dad. This was inconsistent and there was even a sign to let people know (no climbing on the tables). Brendan said it caused resentment that the management hadn't the balls to warn Coco, and were always looking the other way when my dad climbed up on the tables. He said quite a lot of people called my dad 'thicky' on account of the size of his arms. Many times in late 1985, my dad and I would have gone to the Star for a game of snooker after my early morning run, and as we appeared at 9.50 a.m. with ten minutes to spare until opening time, there would be a line of people who were also going in for a game of snooker and my dad would say that he was at the front of the line, but had just dandered around to Delaney's shop to get the paper and they would say, 'Yeah that's no problem Patsy, you go on ahead' (there were only two tables). I blushed with embarrass-ment when he did this.

Only certain people were allowed to call him 'Coco' and he would say, 'Just say hello' to people that were melters or whom he didn't really like. Friends of mine loved that one and they would use it to me. My dad did a bit of boxing as a kid and won a few Irish titles. He drifted away, but his brother, Seán, coaxed him back to the Holy Family and he had one year in the senior grade. I mentioned earlier that my dad knocked a guy out in

Dungannon and the glove exploded. Well that fight was prior to entering the Ulster Senior Championships and he got a bit carried away with his power, and in the Ulster's he came up against one of the clever boxing 'Sempy' brothers and my dad told me that he was loading up on all his punches trying to go for the spectacular knockout, as he wanted to please the crowd. He wanted to give them what they had come to see, but Sempy moved and jabbed his way to a points win. My dad said that this taught him a lesson and he wanted to pass it on to me. He told me that if you go looking for the knockout, you neglect your jab (points scorer) and the knockout very rarely comes, so don't neglect your jab.

My dad worked in Shadows nightclub as a doorman and in 1984, he hit a guy and there was a court case over it and my dad nearly ended up going to jail. The guy he hit was a black guy and was one of ex-world boxing champion, Cornelius 'Boza' Edwards, sparring partners. Boza was over to fight in Belfast as the main supporting bout to Barry McGuigan's fight against Felippe Orozgo, who was a southpaw. Barney Eastwood brought in southpaw, Edwards as a sparring partner for McGuigan, and then decided to feature him on the bill against Charlie 'Cho Cho' Brown. My dad was supposed to have taken a lot of verbal abuse from this guy (he could have possibly been American), and ended up hitting the guy, cutting a lump out of the guy's eye. This court case dragged on into 1985 and my dad couldn't go to my ABA boxing final at Wembley, as the verdict was to be heard and he couldn't miss it as he could have ended up going to jail. My dad was found guilty, but escaped going to jail. For the record both Barry and Boza won their fights with stoppage wins for both.

A local guy and friend of mine, Henry McBride, hero-worshipped my dad and quite often they would have a drink together. One night, again in the Highfield club, my dad was with company and enjoying himself and Henry tried to enter the company, but he was very drunk and my dad told him not to join. Henry persisted and started becoming a nuisance. My dad was the only one in the company that he knew, but to get rid of Henry, my dad suggested to his friends that they leave to go to another bar nearby. As they were standing outside, Henry followed them and him and my dad had words. Henry was feeling belligerent and by all accounts my dad had warned Henry of the consequences a few times and tried to get away, but Henry was in one of those moods and after one thing or another, my dad lowered the boom on poor Henry, knocking him out and breaking his cheekbone. Worst still, Henry dislocated his shoulder as he hit the ground. It just was not his night. The story goes that Henry put in for a claim, saying he had tripped on the potholes coming out of the Highfield and fell (indeed there were many potholes). His claim was successful and Henry got quite a few quid. When my dad heard this he made it his business to go and see Henry and he told him that he would never have got the claim, but for my dad hitting him and he was entitled to half. To be fair to Henry, I asked him this and he denied that he ever put in for a claim.

Incidentally, Henry had two brothers who were killed in the troubles. One brother, Seán, was killed in the Etna Drive Bombing in 1977, where my dad very nearly lost his life, and another brother, Paul, was shot dead in the Avenue Bar in Belfast city centre in 1988, where my dad was shot and wounded that day in a cowardly attack by Loyalists. A remarkable co-incidence.

Stan 'the man' Corbett (dad of former Commonwealth Cruiserweight boxing champion, Darren Corbett) used to joke that one time he was fighting four or five Brits over in the Bone area (beside Ardoyne) and just as he was coming under some pressure, my dad just happened to walk around the corner and rushed over to help Stan and an ungrateful Stan shouted, 'Fuck off Coco and get your own paras.' He was happy enough. My dad was one of Stan's heroes and when my dad was bedbound for five or six years. Stan would call over and see my dad at least once a week and he would bring a lolly for my dad to suck on (as my dad couldn't eat anything solid). Stan would tell my dad at least ten new jokes each time (had my dad not suffered enough). Thank you Stan. You're our hero. There were guys who were in my mum's house drinking with my dad when my mother would have been in work, but when my dad was sick and bedbound, they never once called to see him. Sometimes, they would stop me and inquire after him and I would say why don't you call and see him, but they never did. My dad had outgrown his usefulness for them.

Stanley told me that my dad knocked out that many in Kilpatrick's club in Ardoyne in the early 1960s that they had to ring for two ambalances.

One night (before my dad met my mum) my dad and Stanley were in the Houston Bar and two other men were trying to touch for these two attractive girls. The girls weren't interested in the fellas but they were interested in my dad and big Stanley. At the end of the night my dad and Stanley left the bar with the girls and the two other guys who were rejected earlier followed them outside. The two guys jumped my dad as he was lagging behind but they were both badly beat up by my dad. As my dad and Big Stanley dandered on with the girls one of the guys lying on the ground said to the other guy, 'Fuck if the wee fat guy [my dad] was able to beat us up so badly then it's just as well we didn't jump the big guy.'

These are stories about Coco that I know are true. I am not getting into the lies, the rumours and the half-truths. There are so many stories about my dad and people have been telling me for years that someone should write a book about his life. There were rumours that he had a run-in with another hard man, Lenny 'the guv'nor' McLean, when he was in London. There were also rumours he did former wrestler and actor, Pat Roach. When he was sick I asked him did he have a run-in with these two hard men and he shook his head to say no. Another story was that Richard Branson's bodyguard (or former bodyguard), while serving in the British Army in Belfast, said that there was only ever one guy who did him in a fair fight and he was from Belfast and his name was Coco (maybe that was the para who was flown in from Germany). These are just some of the rumours that I have heard, but there are thousands. By the way, there used to be graffiti up on a wall in Herbert Street in the early 70s and it said 'Coco rules the paras.' I wish someone would have taken a photo of it.

My dad didn't have a good relationship with his own dad who, as I mentioned earlier, was an ex-professional boxing champion. When my dad got drunk, he would talk about his dad and sometimes he would be crying. He would say that he was a great man and I could see that he loved him and missed him. My dad could never show affection or love, he just couldn't. I think his dad was like that also. I know he didn't go to my mum and dad's wedding. My granda suffered from pugilistic dementia for many years, and I don't remember him ever talking, he just made noises. I remember going out for walks with my dad, and one time he put his hand on my shoulder and I shrugged him off, it hurt him and I regret that I did that. He did play games with us when we were small children. In Fairfield Street, we played this one game called 'stiff' and he would be lying on the settee and we would stand on his stomach and we had to be stiff as he would lift us up with his hands around our ankles. He also brought me over to Scotland a few times to watch my favourite team Celtic.

My dad's uncle, Joseph Morrissey, was brutally murdered by the notorious Shankill Butchers gang in 1977. Joe was making his way home from the National Club in Queen Street and was abducted as he passed St Patrick's Chapel in Donegal Street. His mutilated body was found outside a community centre in Glencairn the next morning. His head was nearly decapitated. Martin Dillon, the author of the book *The Shankill Butchers: A Case Study of Mass Murder* (Dillon, 1990), states that he had to think long and hard if he should publish the grim pathologist report on the brutality meted out to an innocent man. Joe was married to Rinty Monaghan's sister, Martha. My mum and dad both liked Joe very much and my mum said he was a bit like the character 'Del Boy' from *Only Fools and Horses*. A bit of a happy-go-lucky sort of character.

A few years ago, I was standing at the door in the Hercules Bar in Castle Street one night, when well-known author Brian Madden was about to enter. We got talking about the excellent boxing book he had written about local boxers called *Yesterday's Glovemen: The Golden Days of Ulster Boxing* (2006), which is part of my own personal collection. Brian knew me and knew that I was a grand-nephew of Rinty Monaghan. As we were standing chatting, Brian tells me that he is writing a follow-up book and I quickly seized this opportunity and I told him that I had won the senior British ABAs in 1985, becoming only the second Belfast man to ever win them, after Jack Gartland in 1928 (the same year he went to the Olympic Games). Brian showed little interest. I then told him that I had turned professional at nineteen and had won twelve out of thirteen pro fights, and my only loss was a retirement injury after I had my opponent down and nearly out in the previous round and I had packed the boxing in at the tender age of 22. Again, Brian showed little interest. I then moved on to my grandad, Harry McAuley, and I told Brian that my granda was an ex-Irish international as an amateur and that as a professional he had won the Northern Ireland feather-weight title and was one of Rinty Monaghan's main sparring partners. This didn't cut any ice with Brian either, and Brian said, 'Right Eamon, I am going to go on in now for a drink.' I thought to myself, 'Well screw you Brian, and your book', and Brian entered the bar. About two minutes later, Brian comes bursting out the door shouting 'Eamon, you never told me that your dad's Coco.' Someone must have told him in the bar. Well, Brian stood there in front of the Hercules with me for another twenty minutes telling me all sorts of stories about my dad (and he took my phone number). Later as Brian was leaving he shouted, 'Eamon I will give you a ring regarding that new book I'm writing.' And he did you know.

Former World Boxing Union (WBU) champion Eamonn Magee mentions my dad in his book, *The Lost Soul of Eamonn Magee* (Magee, 2018). Magee states in his book that he wanted to be just like my dad and become an Ardoyne legend. He also states in his book that my dad was the hardest man in Belfast. In his biography, Magee recalls how he was once in a card school with my dad and a few other men in the Highfield club on Etna Drive. Eamonn was wearing his school uniform and a fella sitting next to my dad was annoying him. My dad dealt with the fella without looking up from his five card hand, with a swift, stinging backhander which knocked the guy unconscious. I can only assume that this fella has been annoying my dad (which happened often) and after my dad had warned him a few times, he had run out of patience.

On another occasion, Karen's (the mother of my two children) dad started on my dad one night in the Highfield club. Jimmy Crossan was having a row with his wife and turned nasty on my dad (probably hoping my dad would hit him), but my dad turned away and walked out of the bar. My mum told me this when I just started to go out with Karen. My mum thinks that Jimmy Crossan wanted my dad to hit him to get sympathy from his wife. I clearly remember this one time, a drunk woman from Labrooke Drive calling to our house in Holmdene Gardens to ask my dad would he go up and sort her husband out as they had been having a drunken row. This would have been in 1985–1986 and I was in the house when she called. My dad chased her. Nearly everyone in Ardoyne from my dad's time and era have stories to tell about him, and I am still hearing new stories all the time.

There was an incident regarding my dad's fighting abilities and it happened in Letterkenny in County Donegal in the mid-seventies. I can clearly remember my dad bragging that he knocked a few out in an incident up there, but I can't remember the details. I asked my mum but she can't remember either, but as god is my witness, there was a big brawl and people got knocked out. You may think I am exaggerating these stories, but it is important to me that the readers of this book believe me and trust that I am not making up stories, and if I was then. I could make up a better one than this. So trust me, when I say that Coco chinned a few guys one night in Letterkenny in the mid-seventies.

My dad died on 12 December 2014. I had been to a meeting that morning regarding getting a statue of Ireland's only home based undisputed world boxing champion Rinty Monaghan. Davy Larmour (who was also at the meeting) gave me a lift up to the City Hospital as my dad was getting a camera put into his mouth and down into his stomach that day. I met my mother and my sister at the hospital, and we went up into the ward to see my dad before this tricky, but not life threatening procedure. I had known my mum and sister were coming up to the hospital but I had no intention of going that day because of the meeting, but the meeting finished early and on a whim, I asked Davy could he drop me up and Davy, being Davy said, 'No problem.' When I was in the ward with my dad, I explained everything to him and told him not to worry as we were here and we will be in the ward when he comes back up. He came up dead. In fact, they actually let us come down and put us in a room beside where this procedure was taking place. What I remember is Tanya and my mum and I were talking away in this room and were not unduly worried, when suddenly a doctor walked in and said that my dad had had a heart attack during the procedure and his organs were closing down and to be ready and start preparing for the worst. This came out of nowhere. The doctor had tears in his eyes. Why? He didn't know my dad. The doctor went away and maybe ten minutes later came back to say my dad had passed away. He was fine when he was up in the ward twenty minutes earlier and was acknowledging me when I talked to him and now he's dead.

I would like to finish this chapter dedicated to my dad with a funny story about him. We used to have a white budgie called Joey and my dad used to love to talk to him, and when my dad was drunk (which was quite often) he would open a box of matches and Joey would throw the matches out of the box. My dad loved Joey and talked to him all the time. One day, when Joey was out of the cage, someone opened the front door and Joey flew out. My mum panicked and her and my sister looked all around the district for Joey. My mum was worried sick about what would happen when my dad came home from a drinking session to find out his beloved budgie was gone forever. They didn't know what to do, so Tanya suggested going down to Gresham Street in Belfast city centre to get a new budgie. So that's what they did and by luck there was a similar white one so they bought it, brought it home and put it in Joey's cage, hoping and praying that my dad wouldn't know the difference. I know this sounds just like that episode of *Only Fools and Horses*, but with God as my witness, I swear this is true. When my dad came home (drunk as usual) he eventually started talking to Joey (or so he thought) and went over and opened the cage door, but Joey wouldn't come out. My dad continued saying, 'Come on Joey,' but the bird wouldn't come out. My dad thought this was very strange so he went over to the cage and said, 'Come on Joey, come on Joey' (we were all holding our breath) then we heard him say, 'That's not fucking Joey!'

Just at that moment there was a knock on the door and it was our neighbour across the street, Patricia McAuley. Patricia had called to inform us that a budgie had flown into a garden in Eskdale Gardens and the young lad in the house had captured it and it was now safely in their house (the whole district knew that we had lost Joey). Patricia's boyfriend, Seamus McErlean, had told Patricia as it was Seamus's sisters house where Joey was now. Well they all rushed round to Pat Cosgrove's house and there was Joey, but the young lad who had rescued Joey had taken quite a liking to him and was crying when he was asked to hand Joey over to his rightful owners. Mr Cosgrove asked my dad, 'Are you 100 per cent sure that is Joey?' So my dad said to my mother, 'Quick Roseleen, go over to Joey's dentist and get his dental records' (only joking, that was in **Only Fools and Horses**). My dad put the box of matches down and, true to form, Joey flew over and started throwing them out of the box. This was final confirmation that this was indeed Joey, and my mum gave the other budgie to the young lad and everyone lived happily ever after. This was not the only incident with my dad and one of his beloved pets. The next incident was with my dad's beloved dog Rory and it would land me in England for three years. That's the time it took for my dad to calm down. And this happened on Friday the 13th.

Friday the 13th

On Friday 13 July 1982, I was living with my mum, dad, sister and brother. I was sixteen. We were living in Holmdene Gardens after moving from Estoril Park about six months previously. My dad was also back home after spells in London. The previous month my dad, my friend Noel Magee and I had watched (on TV live from Las Vegas) Larry Holmes retain his heavyweight title against great white hope, Gerry Cooney. I remember it was shown on RTE at 4 a.m. I bet £10 on Holmes. I had quit being a mod and became a skinhead. I was on a one-man crusade as a mod, as I didn't have any other mod friends. But I had loads of skinhead friends at school like Mickey Holland, Ta Cosgrove, Tony Lynch and many more. I didn't bother with them outside of school, as it was not cool for a mod to be seen with a skinhead (and vice versa). I gave in, and gave up being a mod to have some friends and a better social life. I got my head shaved and became a skinhead. To be honest, I had more fun in the few months I was a skinhead than in the three or four years that I was a mod, but the thing was, I was trying to impress and fit in, which meant I started to drink alcohol, get into fights, steal, joyride. You name it, I was doing it. I even started to beat mods up in an effort to impress my skinhead friends. Belfast then was something like the film of that time *The Wanderers*, as there were gangs everywhere, mods, punks, skinheads, rockers, rude boys. I was just trying to fit in. I became a hitman for the Ardoyne skins and I did some stuff which I am truly ashamed of.

I remember in the summer of 1982, just hanging around street corners trying to relieve the boredom, when two mods walked past, one of whom I knew, his name was Billy O'Halloran. Billy was a decent bloke and was just going about his business, but there had been tension lately between the Bone Hard as Fuck (HAF) mods and the Ardoyne Harder than Fuck (HTF) skins and we wore t-shirts with HTF on them. I was the man that day who caused the spark that lit the match, that ignited the fire that nearly burnt relations between the two factions, causing a very tense standoff as both groups gathered on the Oldpark Road and had to be dispersed by the police. What happened was a few of my skinhead mates and me stopped Billy O'Halloran and his friend as they were walking from the Bone into Ardoyne and I said to Billy, 'You are now entering skinhead Ardoyne', take your parka (coat) off. To be fair to Billy, he told me to fuck off and I just banged him and he fell to the ground and as he was on the ground, I bent over him and landed three or four more punches as my mate Jokey Brown was beating up the other mod. When Billy eventually got up, he stormed off with his mate telling me this isn't over

That night my skinhead cronies and I headed over to the youth disco in the Parochial hall in Gracehill Street in the Bone. We had been consuming alcohol and were feeling belligerent as we were looking for a few mods to beat up and as we turned into Gracehill Street (about five of us), Billy O'Halloran just happened to walk out of the disco with about twenty mods and Billy said, 'Right McAuley, me and you now in a fair fight.' Billy was two years older than me (and a big lad). I wouldn't say I was shitting myself, but I was concerned to say the least. I said, 'Ok', but we will fight on down the street as I don't want anyone jumping on or putting the boot in.' We walked down a bit and he said, 'Right let's fight' and I replied, 'No, on down another bit,' as I knew the rest of my skinhead mates would be turning up very soon as there were about twenty of us, with me and four others walking a wee bit in front of the rest of them. When we walked down another bit, my skinhead friends walked around the corner. I breathed a huge sigh of relief, and I said to Billy, 'Ok. Let's go, right here, right now,' but Billy started to lose courage and he beat a hasty retreat back to his mob as I was with mine. There was about twenty of them and twenty of us. Then suddenly the police sirens wailed out as somebody must have rang them, and everybody panicked and the mods ran down the Oldpark Road towards Harcourt Drive and the skins retreated back to Ardoyne.

Billy O'Halloran started to do bodybuilding shortly after this, and was built like a brick shithouse (according to his cousin Frankie Maguire), but

I headed off to England and when I came back to Belfast three years later, Billy went to live in England and I haven't seen him since that night in the summer of 1982. Billy, if you ever read this, I just want to say sorry for my cowardly actions that night, I can't possibly defend myself and I won't, as there was no justification for what I did. It was just cowardly bullying and nothing less. If you're ever back home visiting relatives or whatever, please look me up and I will take you out for a few beers.

Back to 13 Friday 1982, and I arrived home that night with a black eye and the smell of alcohol on my breath. It was a good thing that my dad was home in Belfast at the time because I would have got up to much worse if there were no authority (boundaries) in my life. I feared my dad. Well, my dad pinned me up against the wall by the throat. My mum started to squeal (which always made my dad worse, as she has a high pitched voice) and Rory bolted out the open front door in fear of my dad's shouting and mum's squealing. Unfortunately, Rory bolted out onto an on-coming car. Rory was hit by the car and was badly injured. With all the shouting in the house we didn't hear anything. Rory was unconscious, but still breathing and there was blood everywhere. By a strange co-incidence it was my Karen's dad, Jimmy Crossan, that did the humane thing and he put Rory out of his misery (I wouldn't have known Karen then, we were four years away from meeting). It was a hit and run. It was my dad's friend Patsy Martin's wife, Roisin, who hit Rory and she sent two men back to find out who she had hit. She had been drunk, and was not sure if she hit a dog or a human. I had known Patsy Martin, as he was a popular butcher who worked in a shop up the road. He was well known to locals and I still remember him, as he knew I was Coco's son and he was always pleasant and was always smiling. Ardoyne was much closer and tighter then and everybody knew everybody. Patsy was murdered by Loyalists as he lay in his bed the previous year on 16 May 1981. His wife was brought in and questioned about his death by the police as it was a strange killing, but she was released unconditionally.

Patsy was a Catholic who had recently moved into a Protestant area in Abbeydale Parade, off the Crumlin Road, but he was an innocent man who was involved in nothing. His wife had slept in a spare room the previous night as she was up for work very early and she didn't want to disturb Patsy. That was their arrangement and Roisin went on out to work the next morning, not even realising Patsy was lying dead in his bed in the next room. Whoever had killed Patsy had cut the telephone wires in that area and a silencer had been used. It was a really professional hit, which was strange. The police hadn't a clue. Loyalist paramilitaries didn't work like that. If they would have wanted to have him killed their 'modus operandi' would have been just to come and shoot him, smashing the front door in with a sledgehammer. It was really strange. Anyway, Patsy's poor wife had started to drink heavily after this terrible ordeal. Further details of Patsy Martin's murder can be found in the book ***Ardoyne: The Untold Truth*** (Ardoyne Commemoration Project, 2003).

Getting back to Friday 13th, and we eventually heard the commotion and my dad went out to see what all the noise was about. I went up to my bedroom. It was my mum shouting, 'Rory's dead' that alerted me to what was going on outside. Tanya and I ran to the front bedroom window as the drama outside was unfolding, and the realisation of what had happened was sinking in. Tanya just looked and said to me, 'You're dead,' and I remember saying quietly, 'My life is over.' We had a big giant pillar/ stone in the middle of the garden, it weighed a ton and my dad lifted it like it was a twig and he buried Rory then and there. To be honest, my dad took it very well once he had a few hours or a few days to let it sink in. Rory was very old and coming to an end anyway and was going blind. My dad held no grudges against Roisin and he never held any grudges against Karen's dad (who sadly died of a heart attack aged 43). I didn't hang around to see if he was going to hold any grudges against me. I was living with my uncle Gerard in Manchester within a week.

Quite a number of years after the incident involving our beloved dog Rory and Roisin Martin, my dad was talking to her in a bar and she was with this fella. The subject of Rory came up and Roisin's friend said, 'Sure it was only an aul fuckin' dog anyway.' Yeah you know what's coming don't you? Unfortunately, Rosin's friend didn't see what was coming. A big right hand that put him to sleep.

Manchester

I lived in England for three years from 1982 to 1985. The first eighteen months were spent in Manchester with my uncle Gerard, his wife Barbara and their three children. Things were a bit cramped in the two-bedroom house. I joined Cavendish ABC after seeing a write up in the *Manchester Evening News* about England U19 European bronze medallist, Peter English. What appealed to me was that he was a featherweight, same as me, and I knew I would get great sparring and I would learn from him. Initially, I was happy in Manchester and that joy showed in my boxing contests as I ran up a string of wins, many of them inside the distance, many of them one punch knockouts. I became the scourge of the north-west counties' featherweights at my age and weight. My confidence was sky high. I remember one contest in Warley (beside Birmingham), and I remember I boxed a man of 26 (Kenny Rudge was his name and I still have the write up in my scrapbook to prove it). I was seventeen. I told all my coaching team that I was going to knock this guy out with the first punch I threw and I told them it was going to be a left hook, and I did just that. The *Manchester Evening News* sports editor, Ed Barry, started to call me 'the Belfast Bomber', but the IRA had planted bombs in the Arndale Centre in Manchester that year and IRA bombs were going off in other parts of England causing death and destruction. My uncle Gerard and I ended up having to go down to see Ed Barry and we asked him would he desist from calling me 'the Belfast Bomber'. I told him that I had come to Manchester from Belfast to get away from all that (and I have some write ups in my scrapbooks to prove this).

I remember Gerard would bring me to the Manchester United games at Old Trafford on a Saturday. I had fallen out of love with football at this time, but it was still a novelty to go to this amazing stadium with 40,000 people to watch this great team. Former Northern Ireland international Norman Whiteside, who still holds the record for being the youngest player to play in the World Cup, was born and reared a ten-minute walk away from where I was born and reared. He was from the Shankill and he was a big star at Manchester United in 1982–1984. I also got to see one of my football heroes from the 1978 World Cup, Mario Kempes, and his team, Valencia, play Man Utd in the European Cup Winners Cup. My uncle Gerard was ten years older than me and was a good man (how he stuck me and my spoiled tantrums I will never know). Gerard and I used to spar in the living room when the kids were in bed and many a time we woke them up with the sound of the blows landing as we wailed into each other. Gerard was my dad's youngest brother and was a half-decent boxer when he boxed for Ardoyne ABC in Belfast. My dad was the head coach then (Ardoyne ABCs first ever coach). I remember Gerard was a tea addict and very soon I was also.

There was a dartboard on the back of his front door at 45 Goulden Street, Salford, and Gerard and I would regularly play darts to see who would make the tea. I remember Gerard (or Ged as the locals called him) would go to the university during the day and sit and read books in the house for hours on end at night. He had a blue Cortina that many a night before training I would have to push down the street to get it started and Gerard would be bump-starting it. The light was always on, indicating that it needed petrol. Gerard always put the bare minimum of petrol in the car and it was always touch and go if we would make it to the gym and back.

I remember the first night I arrived in Manchester. There were a crowd of girls standing around beside Gerard's door as I got out of the car, and I remember they said hello and I looked at them and smiled and said hello back. Within five minutes of arriving, there was a rap at the front door and Gerard went to answer it. He said, 'Eamon, it's for you', and I got up thinking no one knows me, but it was the girls and one said, 'We all fancy you so you can take your pick.' I blushed as I would have been very shy around pretty girls, but I was thinking, 'How forward are they?' Belfast girls certainly were not like this.

Gerard got me a place in a YTP and, as I remember, we made concrete flags. I distinctly remember going to the chippie one lunchtime with my workmates and when it was my turn to order I said, 'Could I have a chip please?' Well the whole chippie burst out laughing and I was puzzled and the women behind the counter said, 'Just one chip?' In Belfast that's what you say. One of my workmates then said to me that I had to ask for one lot of chips or one portion of chips. I had been asking for only one single chip. I was in Manchester now and not Belfast. My face was bright red. In Belfast even today (35 years later), when I order chips I still would ask for a portion of chips and not a chip and that's because of that incident.

Talking of chips, I know that some people can use alcohol as an excuse for their behaviour, my own dad used to, but I am very wary with myself when I have alcohol in me. I very rarely drink alcohol in public now as I don't trust myself, but when I do, I am very careful not to go over four pints. Four pints gets me drunk and feeling good. I am what they call in Belfast a soup drinker, which means I get drunk very easily. I remember one night in 1984, when Gerard and I went out for a drink and I was way over the limit of four pints. I had come up from London to see him. We had a good night and a good laugh and on our way home we decided to get some Chinese takeaway food for us and Gerard's wife, Barbara. As we turned into the street where the food outlet was, this guy walked across the road very slowly as he stared at us. We had to slow down to let him cross the road. When he got to the other side he continued to stare so I wound my window down and shouted to him, 'What the fuck are you staring at?' Gerard said to me, 'Shut up Eamon, just ignore him' and we parked the car and got out and went into the shop to order food. As we were looking at the menu, four guys came walking in and one walked up to me (we were the only customers) and said, 'What are you fucking shouting about?' and before I could react, Gerard knocked this guy out with a left hook. Then I loaded up on a massive left hook which missed one of the other guys and ended up on the floor. I used my hands to climb up the guy's trousers and thumped him and he went down. We did the four of them. A crowd started to gather, and I had to pull Gerard off the guy he had pinned to the ground outside the shop. Gerard was shouting, 'Who are you calling an Irish bastard?' while he was punching him on the ground; the guy was screaming. I shouted, 'Gerard we have to get the fuck out of here!'

As we drove away (in the nick of time), people were running after the car shouting and screaming, 'Irish bastards!' Salford is a hard, tough area with close family ties. There was no glory to be gained. This all started because of me. I just couldn't ignore the guy and let him go on about his business. The alcohol had brought out the ego in me. I feel ashamed now as I write this, but I didn't at the time and Gerard and I went home and laughed ourselves silly. I remember at the time, the fellas seemed to be a lot older than me. I saw them then as really old men, but they were probably in their 40's, but oh they were so slow. Maybe they froze after Gerard threw that devastating left hook. Maybe they were in shock. I don't really think they fought back so there's no glory at all. God forgive me. Regarding my behaviour, it was so wrong. It was provocative and cowardly. I feel ashamed and don't want anyone to think I am revelling in it. In my opinion, this was all down to my drunken immaturity and ego. I know that if I had been sober then, I would have ignored the guy, who seemed drunk himself. I went back down to London the next morning, but later that day Gerard was arrested and charged with assault and GBH. He ended up having to pay a large fine. I got off scot-free. Gerard rang me when he got released and I can't print what he said, as there could be children reading this. Gerard was also banned from the Chinese food outlet and he said this hurt the most as he really loved their grub.

In December 1982, Cavendish ABC made a trip over to Edenderry ABC in the south of Ireland and I boxed a lad called Dermott McDermott, and stopped him in two rounds, hurting my left hand in the process. I had qualified for the finals of the NABC class B finals in January by knocking out Northampton's Paul Allen with one punch (a left hook) and I remember after I stopped McDermott, I had a massive swelling on my left hand, but we got a bucket of ice, which was swiftly ordered from the bar and I sat with my hand in it until the swelling reduced. Edenderry fielded a strong team with many Irish internationals like Martin Brereton (who went to the 1980 Moscow Olympics), Tommy Tobin and Noel Hickey (among others).

The thing I remember about Dermot McDermott (Irish Ropes boxing club), was when I jumped into the ring to face him he looked massive. There was no weigh in and even though I was not scared of anyone, I was concerned that if McDermott was to stop me or knockout me, then it would be an automatic twenty-eight-day suspension and I wouldn't be able to box in the NABC national finals in London in January, and that worried me. I was shouting to my coaches outside the ropes and also to Bill Nedley, 'This guy isn't a featherweight, he's massive.' No doubt McDermott and his coaches heard me and this must have given them confidence, but after I made my justifiable point, I let it slide and focused on the task in hand as I thought about my tactics and strategy. I also realised that maybe my opponent thought that I was scared, but I knew he was going to be in for a big shock when the first round bell rang.

I remember a similar thing happening in Drogheda in 1980–1981, when a Sacred Heart boxing team travelled down. I had stomach cramps just before my fight and Eamon Maguire asked me did I really want to fight and that he was going to pull me out. But I said, 'Let me see how the first round goes and if it gets any worse then you can pull me out.' My opponent was aware of my problem as he seen me doubled over in pain as we were warming up. No doubt it gave him confidence and lulled him into a false state of security, but when the bell went, I immediately forgot the pain (and it was much more than a touch of nerves), and I gave the boy a vicious beating stopping him in two rounds. Well, against McDermott I did the same thing, stopping him in two rounds. Thirty-six years later, Dermot and I became Facebook friends and we met up again for the first time since we boxed each other in the Ulster Hall in Belfast at the Ulster elite finals in January 2019. I was on duty as one of our lads from St John Bosco was in the light heavyweight final and I was in the corner. After our man Paul McCullough Jr won by a first round knockout, I went over and introduced myself to Dermot and I brought him up to the dressing room and amongst the cheering and screaming for our new champion, Dermot and I had a chat and got some photos taken. Dermot told me he won five Irish titles and represented his country and he is now a top official with the Irish Amateur Boxing Association. He and another old opponent of mine, Ben McCarrigle, were both voted ref/judge of 2018 and this was the first time that there had ever been a tie in its history. I always remembered Dermot McDermott's name as not only am I a statistician, but it is a bit of a weird name. I told him this and he laughed and said to me, 'You will never believe who's sitting down at ringside beside me', and I said, 'No, who?' and he said 'my good friend Brian O'Brien'. It could only happen in Ireland.

I remember I represented a County Antrim team against Drogheda in 1981, and I remember two of the County Antrim boxers were Paul 'Sharkey' Brady and Gerry 'Chip' McKenna. I stopped my opponent in two rounds and the County Antrim coach, Gus McCluskey, was glowing in his praise for me and let my club coach, Eamon Maguire, know that I was some prospect.

I became friends with Gus's son, Seamus, in the late 1990s and he was tragically killed outside the Chester Bar on the Antrim Road, when he was punched and died, more as a result of his head hitting the concrete than the actual punch. This happened on Mother's Day 2000 and the amazing irony was, that in Seamus's coat pocket was a betting slip for a horse that was running the following day and it was called 'Betty's Boy' (Seamus' mother is called Betty and Seamus was her boy) and the horse fell and died that day (two Betty's boys). Seamus, who was also known to many by his very original nickname SBO, was a great fella, very popular and his dad is a cracker also. I am still very close to the family. Rest in paradise Seamus my friend.

It had been a good trip to Edenderry in County Offaly, and a good performance from me as McDermott would go on to win five Irish titles and when the Manchester team got the ferry home, I got the train home to Belfast to relax and spend time with my family and enjoy Christmas. Did I say relax? Not according to my dad who had me lined up to top the bill on a Sacred Heart show in the local GAA, where I beat Joe O'Neil on points (hardly throwing my left hand in the process), but there was not much time for relaxation as my dad had me running around the waterworks in the mornings, and sparring Spike McCormick in the evenings. I had beat southpaw Spike twice earlier in the year, but I must admit it was great sparring for me as I was to face a southpaw (Gary Andrews) in the NABC finals in London. Spike was an amazing talent in the gym, but when he boxed, he couldn't reproduce that form on Fight Night when it mattered. Nevertheless, Spike got to the Irish senior final a few months after this sparring, losing a points decision to the brilliant Tommy Tobin (who boxed and won on the Edenderry show).

Also just before Christmas, my dad brought me down to see his uncle, Rinty Monaghan, and Rinty, being the character he was, would throw combinations in my face, which missed by a mere fraction, as he was giving me advice. I had met Rinty a few times and they were always memorable occasions, but this would be the last time, as he died just over a year later. Me getting to the NABC finals (which covered England, Scotland and Wales) was a big deal in the local papers and the **Irish News** interviewed my old coach, Eamon Maguire, who said that I was a great kid inside and outside the ring and I had never gave him any trouble in the three years I had boxed for him. When I beat Andrews in the final, Eamon Maguire sent a wee message to the boxing trade paper, **Boxing News**, congratulating me on my great victory and wishing me well for the future.

In 1983 when I was living in Manchester, I asked my boxing club, Cavendish, if they would send me over to the Irish senior championships in Dublin, as I thought that I had a very good chance of winning. I had won a national junior title (NABC class B) for Cavendish and they let me enter the ABA senior championships at regional level, where I knocked out Brendan Connolly in three rounds in the East Lancs and Cheshire semi. I had to pull out of the East Lancs and Cheshire final against Kevin Taylor as I went down with a bad flu. I was bitterly disappointed, as I really fancied my chances against Taylor, whom I thought was made for me. Taylor ended up getting to the national final in 1983, won the ABAs the following year and went to the Olympic games in Los Angeles. I would later spar Taylor down at Crystal Palace in 1984, while he was preparing for the Olympics and I absolutely battered him. Another boost to my confidence came, when an Irish team travelled over to Manchester and not only did I beat Irish junior champion, Chris Halley, but my club mate, Peter English, easily beat Irish international, Noel Hickey. I got the better of Peter in sparring. Anyway, Cavendish agreed to send me over to Dublin for the Irish seniors at featherweight and in April, coach, Arthur Danaher, and I headed to Dublin with high hopes. It was a disaster from start to finish.

Cavendish could just about afford to send me to Dublin (so Bill Nedley said), but when we got there we soon realised that if I was to get to the final, then the final was a week later and I would have to fly back to Manchester and back to Dublin, then back to Manchester (we didn't know that). Then I weighed in and I was three pounds too heavy, which I couldn't understand. The draw and the prelims were starting shortly so what do I do? I had to make up my mind fast. Should I go a run and try to take the three pounds off or should I enter as a lightweight (a weight I had never boxed at), plus the fearsome Roy Webb was a featherweight, I had forgotten about him. Decisions, decisions. Arthur told to me that even if I got to the finals, then we couldn't afford to come back for it. It was a shambles. I decided to go for a run and I got my training gear on and went jogging up and down the South Circular Road. I also did some shadow boxing but when I stepped back on the scales, I was still two pounds too heavy. I then entered as a lightweight and I got drawn against Seán Barnes from County Wexford in the quarter-finals with the winner to face Belfast's Tony Dunlop.

What I remember about this guy Barnes, was him trying to intimidate me by hitting the pads right in front of me. He looked fearsome on the pads. They knew I was just a kid who seemed lost or in too deep (way over my head). He did look rough and strong, but I just laughed at him, I knew what his coach and him were up to. I was from good stock, coming from my dad, my granda and great-uncle Rinty, and I saw this as an exciting adventure. I was not scared, I had nothing to lose. All I remember from that fight in 1983, was that I fought a good fight and I gave it my best and the better man won on the night. I remember catching him a beautiful uppercut which drew gasps from the crowd. At the end of the fight I said to Arthur, 'Do you think I won?' (I wasn't sure), but Arthur said, 'No, but you can feel very proud of yourself.' I had impressed many observers and would come again and I was not even a lightweight. Barnes lost to Tony Dunlop in a bad tempered, foul filled semi and Dunlop went on to beat Paul Larkin in the final.

Years later, Gerry Storey said that he remembered me at the National Stadium in 1983 and said that I looked lost and was ill-advised to come over. Two years later, I was the No. 1 senior boxer in Britain and Ireland. Sometimes you learn more from the losses and the experience, they toughen your mental side and that's what happened. When I returned to Manchester, I continued to box as a featherweight for another year before moving up to lightweight, as my body grew bigger.

I had a rivalry with Neil Foran from Liverpool who was from a famous boxing family (same as me). Neil's younger brother, Steven, was a multi-titled schoolboy and youth and their grandad was Ginger Foran, who was a famous professional boxer way back in the day. In the north-west counties region of the NABCs, I had two good wins to put me into the final and I watched Neil win his two fights by stoppage. He boxed like a pro, was very strong, aggressive and punched a lot to the body. I knew I would have to be at my very best to run him close, never-mind beating him. The final was held over and went ahead on a club show in front of a capacity crowd, and after a half dozen or so wins inside the distance since arriving in Manchester, I knew this kid was going to push me very hard, but I was ready. I used to be a lovely boxer before I got my punching power, but I then became aggressive as I went looking for the big one, but on this night I reverted back to my boxing and counter-punching skills as, well, I had no choice. Foran scored heavily to the body, but my hooks and work-rate won the day in the best performance of my career so far, but Neil pushed me very hard. The *Manchester Evening News* was brilliant in covering local boxing then and I was the new kid on the block and was getting all the headlines and the sports editor, Ed Barry, said the win had established me as the favourite for the National title and he was correct, as I did go on to win the National title. The following year, Neil moved up to lightweight and won the prestigious NABCs, while I was robbed in the featherweight semi against Robert Smyth, who would go on to beat Arthur Messer in the final. I would get my revenge against Smyth a year later. Neil and I had become good friends, as we would bump into each other at various shows and I would be at squad training with him in Bolton or Wigan. Neil and I would box again, and this one would be watched by four or five million people on television. It was the final of Channel Four's

Henry Cooper's golden belt between Liverpool and Manchester, and it was up in Liverpool.

I had just recently moved up to lightweight and, as my uncle, Gerard, and I were about to walk out the front door to leave for the venue, the phone rang and it was my granny to say that her brother, former world flyweight boxing champion Rinty Monaghan had died. The date was 3 March 1984. Did that news affect my performance? Of course it bloody did! Neil won a decision that the TV commentator said was too close to call, but I was not too fussed.

To be honest, my heart was not into boxing at that time as I was very homesick (this was the fight before the Brian Roach fight) and I had lost a bit of form. I moved down to London shortly after this and was happy again. My form and love for boxing came back, as I won nineteen fights in a row (including two national titles) before I turned professional.

In my third fight in London, I was to box for London U19s against the north-west counties and I was to box Neil. I remember receiving the news, and getting my training gear on to go for a run as I really welcomed the chance of a rubber match with Neil, and I was very confident this time that I would win. It ended up Neil pulled out and I had a hard scrap with C. O'Brien and won on points. Neil represented England at senior level and would turn professional, winning his first six fights (four knockouts).

I entered the preliminary round of the NABC class C championships in 1983. It was the East Lancs and Cheshire stage which included Bolton, Wigan, Chorley etc. There were eight boxers on the list for my weight (57kg.), including a big name from America who had won the New York golden gloves called Tunde Foster, and he was getting all the headlines in the local papers. Foster was originally from Manchester and my dad was coming up from London to see what all the fuss was about. I knew that I would have to really be on my game against Foster, but I relished this kind of challenge and with my dad coming to watch me live for the first time in a couple of years, I was determent not to let him or myself down. I remember my dad ringing me after the weigh in and having to break the bad news to him that I had won the title on a walkover, as all the other boxers moved up, moved down or pulled out.

The New York boxer moved up in weight, but I am sure it was not because of my fearsome reputation for brutal knockout wins, and I will give him the benefit of the doubt on that one but regarding the other six, I also have no doubt that it was because of my fearsome reputation that they avoided me (why take a risk I suppose). I was very disappointed as my dad and his brother Gerard and I sat down and watched Tunde Foster win on a points decision, and even though he was a classy boxer with sublime skills, I didn't feel that I would have been out of my depth against him. Tunde Foster would go on to turn professional and was a world class boxer, whom I later watched on TV a few times in the late eighties as he based his career in New York, and I remembered how close I came to boxing him. He retired with a record of three defeats in 26 professional fights (sixteen knockout wins). If you google his name on the internet, you will see that he was a world-class boxer in his day.

I won two NABC titles and got robbed blind in the semi-finals of another against Robert Smyth from Wales. I dropped to my knees in disbelief as the ref raised his arm. I was heartbroken, as the finals were going to be tele-vised. After a year or so in Manchester, the novelty started to wear off and I missed my friends and family back home. I started to get depressed and it started to affect my boxing. I lost to people I should never have lost to.

My amateur record was twelve losses in 130 fights, but I am still haunted by a few of those losses. I just gave up trying in Manchester. I must have been a real handful to my uncle who was trying to rear three kids (four if you count me). My mood swings got bad and I refused to work or wash and I was on sleeping tablets. I wanted to come home to Belfast, but my dad kept telling me to suck it up and stick it out and things will improve. He got me out of Belfast as he was getting death threats and thought that someone might try to take it out on me, as I was making a name for myself as a boxer. My dad saw potential in me and in Belfast in the summer of 1982, I was starting to drink alcohol, get into fights and was running with a bad crowd.

When I came back to Belfast for a break in the summer of 1983, I remember I had a row with the pop band Bananarama in Ann Street, Belfast city centre. Bananarama were in Belfast for the funeral of Thomas 'Kidso' Reilly, whose brother was dating Siobhan from the band at the time. Thomas 'Kidso' Reilly was shot dead by the British Army on 9 August (he was an entirely innocent young man). That day in Ann Street, two fellas who were with the girl band, accused us of stalking them, as my skinhead mates and I, eejits that we were, were walking behind them, shouting abuse at the girls. One of the minders turned around to us and clearly told us to, 'Fuck off.' He was cheeky and aggressive and it was me who foolishly got into an argument with him. We had to be pulled apart as it nearly came to blows just with this one guy. It was a really big scene, as shoppers looked on. The girls from the band and the other guy were telling my crew to grow up and catch ourselves on. It was not nasty abuse we had been shouting, as we were fans of the girl band. It was just banter as a few guys in my crew were very quick witted, but obviously not everyone shared our sense of humour and messing about.

Around April/May 1984, I travelled over to Strabane with a Manchester select team to face St Marys ABC in Strabane. The previous year, St Mary's had come over to Manchester and after ten wins in England, my unbeaten run came to an end, but it took an Irishman to defeat me. I lost a close majority decision to Ben McGarrigle in Manchester. Ben would go on to win an Ulster senior heavyweight title and would go to the Commonwealth games. He also won the world police and fireman games title. Well, the rematch between him and I was all set for me to avenge a loss that ate away at me (still does). There was no weigh in at the Manchester contest and there was no weigh in for the Strabane match. Why was that? I am convinced now that Ben was much heavier than me, and he looked it, but I never lost any sleep over it. Ben and I were the last bout of the evening (top of the bill) and in my corner was Ricky Hatton's old coach, Paul Dunne. I was really up for this fight and the place was jam-packed and they were hostile towards me, but ten seconds into the contest, McGarrigle was on the seat of his pants after I caught him with a massive left hook as I rushed straight out and caught him cold. After an eight count, I battered him around the ring and was close to giving him a second count, when he caught me with a huge right as I was rushing in to finish it. The right caught me flush, and I went down face first although I still had my wits about me and I rose straight away. But the ref had to give me the eight count and this time it was McGarrigle who had the initiative. I fought back furiously to let him know I was not hurt and that is when I walked into another right and to be honest, I was badly stunned and I nearly went down again, but my pride, courage and determination stopped me. I don't think McGarrigle knew how hurt I actually was as I sucked it up and I knew I had to come back with something, and I did. I got him on the ropes and threw a barrage of blows and wouldn't stop until the ref pulled me off him. Before the ref pulled me off, three or four off the blows landed flush and McGarrigle didn't know what planet he was on. When the ref asked him if he wanted to continue, he bravely nodded and the ref let him continue. I battered him some more until the ref finally stopped the contest, as the crowd were nearly in the ring screaming and shouting for the ref to stop it.

Years later, Ben told me that he spent the night in hospital as he had stomach pains and a concussion. I have a video of this fight, which is on

YouTube, and it is brutal. I think it is a better first round than Hagler/ Hearns, so watch it and draw your own conclusions. At that time, I had the pick of the local girls and later that night, I touched for the best-looking girl in the place. I asked could I walk her home and she agreed, and I thought to myself, 'Happy days.' When we got to her house she said, 'Oh well, that is me home now and give me a kiss on the cheek.' It took me a couple of hours to find the hotel we were staying in as I had gotten lost and was wandering about trying to find it. There were no mobile phones in those days.

When I went back to Manchester, I remember boxing a guy called, Brian Roach, in the East Lancs and Cheshire preliminary round of the 1984 ABAs. During the fight, I had some sort of meltdown that had never happened before (or after) in the ring. At this time, I was suffering from depression and was not sleeping. I was in a very dark place and I would be a liar to say that I didn't get suicidal thoughts (a lot of self-pity there also). I went into the ring that night and after a decent first round where I drew blood from Roach's nose, something happened in my mind. I came out for the second round and just gave up. I stopped punching. I covered up and let him swing away. When he backed off, I waved him in again. I let him pound on me, I had my hands up, but I had stopped punching. I just thought to myself in the middle of the contest, 'Ack, fuck this.' I did not plan to do this, it just happened. As a Christian and with God as my witness, I would not lie, I just stopped trying. I just wish I could go back in time and fight that fight again. It still haunts me even to this day. It was stopped in the second round. I remember walking the streets that night with suicidal thoughts and the worst headache I ever had.

Shortly after that, my dad fixed me up with distant relatives in London and I moved down south, but before I went, Brian Roach came down to our gym looking to spar Peter English. Peter was not at the gym that night, but I said, 'I will spar you.' Only thing was, I did not have my gumshield with me and they were not going to let me spar. I begged my uncle Gerard to drive back home to get my gumshield. He was pissed, but I said, 'Please Gerard do this for me and I will make it worthwhile.' Well, he drove the three miles or so distance and returned with my gumshield and I give Brian Roach a vicious beating. The strange thing was, that I also had a splitting headache after that spar, but I think that was more down to tension than anything else as he hardly landed a blow on me. I knew I was on my way to London and my spirits were lifted so I let it all hang out. Don't get me wrong, Brian Roach was a terrific boxer. He went far that year in the ABAs eventually losing to Carl Crook in the quarter-finals. I would beat Crook in the final at Wembley the following year. Roach also boxed Crook twice as a professional. First fight was a draw, the second was for the British and Commonwealth lightweight titles, and Crook stopped Roach in ten rounds. So Roach was no mug, and he had previously boxed for England as an amateur and had won a multi-nations gold medal. When I was in London, I beat a guy called Alan Keogh handy enough and a couple of months later, Keogh beat Roach in an Ireland/England senior international. Incidentally, when Chris Halley, featherweight (1983), and Alan Keogh, lightweight (1984), were Irish junior champions, I was the British junior champion at those weights and I boxed them both (at that time) and beat them both, clearly in what was unofficially the junior championship of Britain and Ireland. I am just as proud of being the best junior boxer in Britain and Ireland (1983–1984) than I am of winning the ABAs in 1985, as the ABAs do not include Ireland.

London

I left Manchester to go to London around August 1984. My dad had fixed me up to live with Frankie Woods and his family. Frankie's brother, Brian, was married to my dad's sister, Peggy, so we were kind of related through marriage. Frankie looked very like the actor Kirk Douglas. He was married to Carol and they had three kids around my age (a girl and two boys). I lived with Frankie and Carol for about three months. I remember we all went to the Notting Hill Carnival one time and got drunk. I very rarely drank, but it was Frankie who encouraged me to drink and after too many pints and a great day in the blazing sun, Frankie and I got into a heated row and had to be pulled apart. I cannot remember what the row was about, but I am willing to accept that I was probably to blame as I could not drink then and I cannot drink now. I was probably cheeky to him, and Frankie being Frankie, was not going to be disrespected.

That was the beginning of the end. A few weeks later, I packed my bags and left. After I walked out of Frankie's, I rang my mum to tell her that I was coming home and she said, 'Eamon, you can't come home as things are bad here with your dad and the Troubles. You have a better chance of a good life in London.' I told her that I had nowhere to live and my mum said, 'What about that guy from the boxing club, Harry? Why don't you give him a ring and he might help you?' So that is what I did. I rang Harry Holland and told him I had a row with Frankie and if I do not get somewhere to stay tonight, then I am going home. He asked where I was and I said, 'Heathrow Airport' (and I was). Harry said could I ring him back in an hour, as he would try to get me somewhere to stay. When I rang him back, he asked me if I could meet him at Hounslow West tube station in an hour (Hounslow is not too far away from Heathrow) as he had gotten me somewhere to stay. Before all this happened though, Frankie had brought me up to a boxing club in Chiswick and that is where I met Harry Holland for the first time. I am not sure how we ended up in Hogarth, maybe someone recommended it to Frankie and Frankie knew that I was looking for a good boxing club to join, but I will tell you what, it was a first class choice. I remember telling Harry that I was a national junior champion and he stuck me in to spar with pro Billy Hardy and a guy I knew of from Derry called Tony Strawbridge. I hammered both, dropping unbeaten pro Hardy with a body shot. I was awesome, and Harry's eyes lit up as he was a professional coach, manager and promoter. From that moment on, I was given first class treatment from everyone.

When Harry, who had been a long time amateur coach, ventured into the pro game, there was some conflict in the gym as it was an amateur club with amateur coaches. Even though I was an amateur with no interest in going pro, it was Harry who coached me and not so much the amateur coaches who were scared to stand up to Harry. Harry asked me would I be interested in going pro with him on the very first night I was there. Harry was great in the gym and treated the amateurs the same as the pros and whoever had a big fight coming up, got the star treatment from him. Frankie and Carol Woods are dead now, but I did call down once to see them, as my aunt, Peggy, and uncle, Brian, were over visiting them in Fulham, so there were no hard feelings on my part and I was grateful to them for opening the door of their home and sharing it with me for three months. May they rest in peace.

I sparred one of Harry Holland's pro boxers and he was a middleweight. I remember he had blond hair and was called McCarthy. He was only meant to take me around (which means he would be giving it maybe 70 per cent of his power and strength) and wallop. He found himself on the canvas looking up at me as I had exploded a huge left hook on his chin. He jumped up quickly and tore into me, but coach John Bloomfield jumped into the ring and stopped the spar. I remember John grabbing me, but smiling as he said to me, 'He's a fucking pro middleweight and you just chinned him with 14–16 oz. sparring gloves on!'

Another guy I sparred with was a very colourful fella called Abdul Kareem; he had about a dozen pro fights and had just joined Harry's stable of boxers. He would go on to win the southern area light welterweight title.

He was born in Trinidad and Tobago, he dressed like a stockbroker coming and going to the gym, as he wore the most expensive clothes and he also wore more gold than Mr T out of the **A-Team** and **Rocky 3**. He was a surly type of person and I held my own with him in sparring, but they were great spars. We also had the odd celebrity boxer train in our gym including Errol Christie and Dennis Andries, but I never got to spar them as they were much heavier, and much too good. The pop band Bananarama did a video for one of their hits, 'Na Na Hey Hey (Kiss Him Goodbye)' in the gym when I was a boxer at Hogarth, with the boxers and the girls shadow boxing and punching the bags, but much to my regret, I was not at the gym that day. It must have been the only day I missed, but they did use our young boxers. I had that run-in with Bananarama the previous year in Belfast and I wonder would they have remembered? I am sure I would have reminded them, I probably told Harry about the incident, and maybe he kept me away that day. I also saw one of my favourite TV programmes, **Minder**, being filmed in Chiswick once or twice as I was heading to the gym, which was just around the corner. Harry Holland had once managed pop legend Shakin' Stevens (before he became famous), but Harry let him go as he thought the Teddy Boy era was well and truly finished by the late seventies (big mistake).

Amateurs and professionals were not allowed to train together at this time going by the ABA rules, but it did go on in some gyms. I had sparred a few pros in Manchester, but now I was sparring them every day. Billy Hardy, who was coached by one of Harry's friends and was not one of Harry's fighters, would go on to become a British, Commonwealth and European champion and later boxed Prince Naseem Hamed for the world featherweight title. In addition, Hardy has a leisure centre named after him in his hometown, Sunderland. I will tell you what, after dropping Billy the first time I sparred him, I must admit that I had my hands full every time I sparred him after that. One tough wee bastard he was. I also had some great sparring with Harry's main boxer at the time, Rocky Kelly, and sparred well over a hundred rounds with him. I used to hold my own with Rocky and we had some wars in the gym. I loved sparring Rocky and would much rather spar him than Billy Hardy, and Rocky was a welterweight and was the No. 1 contender for the British title. Between Rocky and Billy, among others, I was really improving as a boxer and I lived and breathed boxing.

In 1984 (when I was living with Frankie Woods and his family), I spent a week at Crystal Palace helping out the Great Britain boxing squad prepare for the Olympic Games in Los Angeles. It was my second visit to

Crystal Palace. In 1983, When I won the NABC (class B) championships, all the winners were invited down to Crystal Palace to train with the young England squad. It was there that I sparred future World Boxing Council (WBC) featherweight boxing champion, Paul Hodkinson. I had been with Paul on the north-west counties squad training a few times, but never got to spar him.

Anyway, getting back to 1984, and I sparred with Kevin Taylor (featherweight) and Alex Dickson (lightweight). Crystal Palace was simply amazing. In the late 70s and early 80s Britain had some amazing athletes: Daley Thompson, Seb Coe, Steve Ovett, Alan Wells, Fatima Whitbread and many, many more. Crystal Palace was where most of the big TV track meets happened and they were shown regularly on TV. Back in the 1980s, there were only three channels – so they were household names. I always watched these events on TV at home in Ardoyne and I could only dream of being in the stadium and being a big sports star one day. Kevin Hickey and former Olympic gold medallist and outstanding boxer of the 1956 Olympics, Dick McTaggart, were the head coaches of the Great Britain boxing team.

It was an honour and a pleasure to spend a week with such great talent and I was a big fan of Kevin Hickey. In the NABC class C finals at the Grosvenor House Hotel, Kevin had picked my fight as the fight of the night and as the winner of this, I received £300 of stereo equipment and to be honest, I did not think I boxed especially well that night. I had a feeling that Mr Hickey liked me (or felt sorry for me). We trained hard that week. It was summer and the boxing season had ended about April/May, but for that week I trained hard, I sparred hard and I ran with the Olympic boxers. I only sparred Kevin Taylor once, as I was much too good for him and gave him a bit of a beating. They quickly moved me up to spar lightweight Alex Dickson (Dickson had beaten Carl Crook in the ABA final to go to the Olympics), and I sparred Dickson twice. First time I sparred him, I was delighted with the two rounds I did, as he was a tricky, sharp hitting southpaw. I thought that I coped with him very well. The second time I sparred him, he gave me a bit of a hiding. He charged out at me at the first round bell like a maniac, he stunned me early, and he never let up. Usually the sparring is light, but maybe Dickson felt that he had something to prove or maybe he and Taylor had been talking about me or maybe Taylor had asked him, 'Get him back for me, Alex.' I also sparred with many of the other boxers who arrived every day to help the Olympians prepare. Crystal Palace was huge and they could have held the Olympics there, it was so big. It was like a village and everything was on site.

Another thing I remember, is famous ITV sports presenter Reg Gutter-idge coming along to give us a light-hearted talk on some of his boxing experiences and relationships he had with some of the great boxers he covered including Muhammad Ali, Sugar Ray Robinson and many more. Reg spoke for an hour and really entertained us with his amazing and very witty stories. At the end, Reg asked us did we have any questions. There was a long pause, but no one spoke and I was bursting to ask him did he have any stories about my great-uncle Rinty Monaghan, but I was wary and self-conscious that I was the only non-Englishman in the room. I just went for it and in a broad Northern Irish accent I asked him did he have any stories about Rinty Monaghan, as he was my great-uncle. It felt like everyone turned around to look at me. I just wanted the ground to open up and swallow me, but Reg was lovely and he told a few, as he knew him quite well. That broke the ice and then other lads also started asking questions.

Harry Holland fixed me up with a landlady called Sandra Rowlands and she was the ex-wife of one of Harry's best friends, John 'JR' Rowling. She would have been in her late twenties and she had a young boy called Jonathan. I stayed with her for about nine months before moving down to King's Cross to live with guys from Ardoyne who were working there. I had a landlord/tenant agreement with Sandra and during the nine months, I would mostly go for walks, go to the gym or be round in Harry's house, which was not far away. Harry's wife, Jan, got me a job at the Thorn-cliffe Hotel, where she also worked. I was lonely though and I got friendly with a family from Derry whose son, Liam, boxed for Hogarth and his dad would be at the club most nights. I would often walk up to their house, which was a twenty-minute walk. I craved a girlfriend and to be honest – sex. What eighteen-year-old red-blooded male didn't? I had no confidence around girls and lacked confidence in general. Liam's family were good Catholics and many a night they would be saying the rosary when I called. Liam had four sisters and I really had the hots for one of them, she was stunning. Most nights when I would be leaving, she would walk me out to the door. It was obvious she liked me also, but I hadn't the courage to ask her out, as I was terrified of rejection and making a complete fool of myself.

I worked in the Thorncliffe Hotel for around nine months (until I moved to King's Cross) and it was ok. It was a holding hotel for Pakistan nationals who travelled to Britain for a better life and stayed in the hotel until they got a flat or house somewhere. There were some hygiene issues, including people using sinks (wash-hand basins) as toilets, as children would shit in them. We had to clean the mess up and bring them into the bathroom and point to the toilets telling them that is where you do that. They had a sink in their room and there would have been toilets on every floor. Each family only had one room so there could be six, seven in a room. We tried to explain to the parents about toilet needs, but they could be awkward, ignorant and indifferent. There were also issues involving children's nappies but it was not that bad (or so I thought). When I left the job at the hotel, I lived in King's Cross for about three months, then I went home to Belfast. I was home only a short time, and I was sitting at home one night when **News at Ten** came on and the Thorncliffe Hotel was headline news. I screamed to my mum, 'Feck, that's the hotel I worked in.' The story was that thousands of illegal immigrants were flying over from Pakistan and staying in the Thorncliffe until they got a council flat or house somewhere. **News at Ten** warned of overcrowding and poor hygiene and it was headline news all over Britain and Ireland. The story was of thousands of immigrants coming over, staying in the hotel and getting housing before the Brits. It was even brought up in the House of Commons as MPs warned of an open-door policy regarding immigrants.

A lad called Sanji, who was about fourteen and a friend of Jonathan's, was in Sandra's house every day, morning, noon and night. Jonathan was only about nine or ten years old so there was quite an age gap between them, but Sandra was happy enough with this friendship. I remember we all went round to Sanji's mother's for an Indian curry one night. Sanji did not seem to have any other friends, and initially we all got on and they all went to my first fight in London as it was the regional round of the NABCs and not too far away from where we lived. We were all into the pop band **Wham!** At the time. Sandra was ok, but I got no breakfast or lunch and we didn't get our dinner until about 11 p.m. I was always starving. My rent was always on time and I never once asked her for money (unlike Sanji), as I was getting a bit of work in the Thorncliffe Hotel, which was a short walk away. I remember on one occasion, Sanji and I were walking home from somewhere one night and we called into the chippy and as we left, Sanji and this boy got into some name calling. The strange thing was, they were calling each other Paki bastards (the other boy was also Asian) but I told the other boy to hit it on the head and he stepped forward from the pack of around six lads and asked me, 'Do you fucking want some too?' Sanji said, 'Be quiet Eamon', as the lad moved into my face. But I threw a left hook at him, landing a glancing blow that staggered him and I went after him looking to land the 'coup de gras', but I didn't connect flush until he landed in a doorway and I then knocked him out.

As I stepped back, I noticed that my chips (which I set down to fight) were all squashed and I said, 'Right which one of you fuckers stood on my chips?' And a fella from the pack said that I had stepped on them myself during the fight. I then said, 'Well that's all right then', and went on my way like Gary Cooper in **High Noon**. On the way home, Sanji was hyper with excitement and was reliving the fight blow for blow. The next day, I was round in Harry Holland's and his children had heard all about the fight and told me this lad had it coming as he fancied himself as a hard nut and was nothing but a bully. I would say this crowd of lads from the previous night would have been sixteen to eighteen years (I was eighteen). This boy Sanji who initially I was a hero to, started to turn on me, and he was mixing things to Sandra and I started to find him creepy. I never had a cross word with Sandra or her son Jonathan, but I got friendly with some Ardoyne lads whom I grew up with and I eventually moved down to King's Cross to be with them. I made contact with Jonathan on Facebook a few years ago and he has turned into a fine young man with a young family. His mother has been deceased for quite some time now.

I lived in London for a year and when I met Harry Holland, I was with him nearly every night until I came home to Belfast in July/August. One night, Harry brought me to the house of a mate of his to collect ticket money for a forthcoming boxing bill he was running at Heathrow. Before we went in, Harry showed me a topless photo of a girl who was this guy's daughter. She was sixteen and carried the card with the number of whatever round it was high above her head as she walked around the ring at Harry's shows. When we went in, Harry's mate was delighted to see him and they sat down to sort the ticket money out while we had a cup of tea. The girl in the topless photo rushed out to hug Harry and she smiled and said hello to me. Her name was Maria Whittaker and she went on to become a topless model for **The Sun** (page 3 girl) and became very famous. Everyman over 45 will remember Maria Whittaker and I saw her tits before any of you.

I had great support when I boxed. When Liam O'Kane, Tony Williams and I boxed in the NABCs, Harry would hire a coach for all the supporters and it was a bit like the jolly boys outing in **Only Fools and Horses**, great characters and great craic. Harry was the one who organised everything. They were great occasions and we travelled all over the country. One time, I had to box two people in one afternoon (also they were two good 'uns). I beat Danny Cooper in a bruising fight, decking him in the last round to seal

a deserved split decision win, and about two hours later, I boxed multi-titled Paul Day and what a fight that was. I put him down with a body shot
in the first round, but he boxed his way into the fight and going into the
final round, it was too close to call. It was fought at a frantic pace and the
crowd were going crazy. Harry was right at ringside screaming his head
off In the third round, I caught Day with a great right and decked him.
He rose at eight, but the ref stopped it (Paul did not complain). My crew
went mad with excitement and Harry was by now up on the ring apron
nearly in the ring with me. He needed to be very careful, as he was a pro
coach, manager and promoter. He risked losing his licence. In the *Boxing
News* the following week it read, 'McAuley is a good prospect', as some pro
managers had already noticed.

Three lads from Hogarth got to the finals of the NABCs that year, but
I was the only winner. I beat Wales' Adrian Staples by the third round
stoppage. I gave the stereo equipment I won to my uncle Gerard, who
came down to the Grosvenor House Hotel from Manchester to watch me.
I was picked four times to box for Ireland and I was also asked to box
for England at junior and senior level and after talking it over with my
amateur coach, Harry Munger, and my dad (over many telephone calls to
Belfast), I declined. I only had a few senior international fights. I beat M.
Gowans (Scotland) rsc2, R. Smyth (Wales) rsc3, O. Sindenko (Israel) KO1 and
E. McArdle (Australia) points (though I dropped him heavily in the second).
I also beat the best lightweight in England – Carl Crook (rsc2). My only
international defeat at junior or senior level, was against Ireland's, Paul
Fitzgerald in June 1984. Ireland was hosting an ABA select and there was
no one in England, Scotland or Wales prepared to box Fitzgerald, as he
had knocked out three England internationals in a row, including my old
sparring partner from Manchester, Peter English. So, I was drafted in at
the last minute (and well paid) to fight him as he was going to the Los
Angeles Olympic Games (1984) the following month and needed a fight
badly to shed rust and to keep him sharp (Paul also went to the 1988
Olympic games in Seoul). Anyway, I gave him a good fight, but he won fair
and square on points and this was the last time I boxed at featherweight
and when I moved up to lightweight, I won nineteen senior fights in a row
before turning professional in late 1985.

Regarding the night when I boxed Fitzgerald at the Europa Hotel. There
was a boxer representing Ireland called Roy Nash, who beat a Scotsman
called Joe Kelly on a cut eye and I held the catgut for the doctor to insert
the stitches into Kelly's cut. Joe Kelly was 5ft. 1in. and he would go on to box

our own Dave 'Boy' McAuley for the British flyweight title in 1986. Dave Boy stopped him in nine rounds and Dave Boy was the same height as me (5ft. 7 and a quarter). Joe Kelly would win the British bantamweight title five-and-a-half years later and would box for a version of the world bantamweight title. I also won the Hounslow sports personality of the year in 1985 and that got me sports equipment. In the semi-finals of the NABCs, I knocked out Derek Grainger in 40 seconds (Grainger had upset Roy Rowling in his previous fight and that was a big upset). Grainger would turn pro with Terry Lawless and his only defeat was when he boxed for the British welter-weight title. He retired with only one loss and a draw in 24 fights (he is a top coach now). Danny Cooper and Paul Day also went pro. Day was unbeaten in eight fights.

From March 1985 to July 1985, I lived in King's Cross where my friend, Gerry Stafford, had me fixed up at the Wardonia Hotel and I shared a room with another Ardoyne man, Gerard O'Hara. The Wardonia was facing King's Cross underground station. Gerry Stafford had previously shared a room with Gerard's brother, Andy, and he moved out to create space for me to move in. Gerry and Andy had previously lived in Bromley by Bow and when I first came down to London, I used to take the hour and a half journey to visit them and then an hour and a half journey back to Hounslow West. I remember watching the world snooker final in May 1984 in Gerry's house between Steve Davis and Jimmy White. Back at King's Cross and Gerry moved into an all-girl nurses home, where he shared a flat with his girlfriend (now his wife), Christine. Gerry kept a low profile there and the nurses didn't grass him up (if the authorities would have found out, then he would have been turfed out). Then another Ardoyne man, Paddy Gallagher, came over and Gerard moved in with his brother, Andy, and Paddy moved into my room. The Wardonia was run by husband and wife. John and Jesse (I cannot remember their surname) and John was a big boxing fan. John was from Scotland and he was also a big Benny Lynch fan. Benny Lynch was a world flyweight boxing champion in the 1930s and drank himself to death at 33 years of age. (Incidentally, I am presently helping a girl from Glasgow called Lynne Lyees get a statue of Benny in the Gorbals area of Glasgow). John was following my progress in the ABAs and would make sure I got a hearty breakfast in the mornings. I would have been in and out of King's Cross station to go to work then to the gym and back. It felt like I spent most of my day in King's Cross station. That is why it came as a big shock to me when there was a massive fire there the following year killing many people. But for the grace of God go I.

Gerry Stafford went running with me in the mornings during my ABA pursuit and he went to the Tony Graham fight when I did Graham in the first round. I remember Gerry coming into the dressing room and me asking him, 'Well what did you think about that?' Gerry said that as he entered the York Hall, I was climbing out of the ring. He had arrived late and missed my fight (one of my best wins). Gerry was at the Royal Albert Hall to see me beat Moss O'Brien and he went to Wembley to see me beat Carl Crook. Gerry also went to my fourth pro fight at the York Hall. Afterwards, he told me that he was not overly impressed by my performance, even though I had won every round, and I said, 'Gerry, in the last month I have flown from Belfast to London, London to Los Angeles, Los Angeles to Panama, Panama to Colombia, Colombia back to Panama, Panama to Florida, Florida to London, London to Belfast then Belfast to London for this fight.' I added, 'Gerry, cut me a bit of slack, please.' The last time I saw Gerry was in 2005, when I stayed with him for five days in Liverpool, as my son was boxing for Ireland in the world youth championships. Gerry's wife, Christine, is a Liverpudlian and they have two kids. During my stay, I remember Gerry bringing me to a snooker match, as Gerry was the captain and as this was a home match. Christine had spent all day doing the sandwiches for the visitors. When we got there, one of their players, Mike Kenny, didn't turn up and Gerry said, 'Eamon, do you fancy a game?' And I said, 'Yeah, okay' and Gerry replied, 'Right then, for the rest of the night your name is Mike Kenny.' Before Gerry got up to play, he whispered to me that he was a cut above the rest of them and he lost his match 2-nil. He blamed his cue, the balls, the pockets everything. He even got into a row with people in the crowd who he accused of talking when he was taking a shot. The home team were beaten 1–4. And who was their only winner 'Mike Kenny' (me). Moreover, I don't really play snooker. I would have loved nothing more than to give Gerry a good slegging, but he was in rotten form as we were returning home and I was staying in his house.

In the London semi-finals of the senior ABA Championships in 1985, I was paired against Tony Graham (St Pancras) at York Hall, Bethnal Green and this brought the crowd out as it pitted two aggressive punchers against each other, as it was the fight that everybody wanted to see (and Nigel Benn was on the bill). It turned out to be a short affair as he walked onto a short right hook that dumped him on his pants early in the first round. There was nowhere for Graham to hide after this, and after two more standing counts the ref stopped the massacre before the bell went to end the first round. In the London final, at the Royal Albert Hall, I came up against the 1978 ABA champion and Commonwealth games bronze medallist, Moss O'Brien, from Repton ABC. Moss was also the captain of the England team in 1978 and Azumah Nelson got the gold at featherweight in Edmonton (I wonder did Moss box Azumah in the semi). Anyway, Moss was attempting a comeback at 28 having been inactive for a few years. I had watched his semi-final against an old opponent, Gary Andrews. I had beaten Andrews in the NABC final in 1983. Some years later, Gary Andrews told me that he had concussion after I boxed him. He said that he was shadow boxing and was getting ready to box me, when his coaches told him that he had already boxed me and was beaten. I was quite impressed by O'Brien's performance against Andrews as he won easily on points. He was very slick and fast. He was not a banger, but was a lovely, smooth boxer, with sublime skills.

Talking about concussion, I used to spar a lad in the Holy Family club in the early 90s, Billy Boyd was his name and he was from the Shankill. His step-dad, Burt, told me a few years ago that one night he had to bring Billy to the hospital after sparring me. Burt said that they had been back home from the gym for some time when he saw Billy putting his training gear into his holdall, then putting his overcoat on. Burt said to Billy, 'What are you doing?' and Billy responded, 'I'm getting ready for the gym' and Burt replied, 'We are just back from the gym. Sure, you were sparring Eamon McAuley.' But Billy could not remember, so Burt rang Gerry Storey, who was the head coach at the Holy Family, and Gerry advised Burt to bring Billy to the Mater Hospital as a precautionary measure. Billy denied to me that this happened but Burt did tell me this and I'm 100% sure of that.

The London finals were televised each year and highlights were shown on Thames TV. I really wanted to impress and get myself shown on TV. The thing was, after Moss beat Andrews he sat down and watched me demolish Graham. I am sure it was not easy viewing for him. So in the final, he ran like a bandit and held a lot which didn't make for a great fight. He got two public warnings for holding in the last round and just about made it over the line. I was an easy winner, but they did not show highlights of my fight on TV later that night. I was not surprised. In fact, Moss was the only boxer to take me to the distance in the ABAs. I was too strong, powerful and youthful for Moss who went back to his previous job of developing the young boxers at Repton. I was in the form of my life, and I was confident because of the sparring I was getting, and I could really see a big improvement in me.

In the English semis, I was in the draw with Neil Haddock, Lee Amass and Carl Crook. I knew Amass was a southpaw and he was a banger. He had knocked out, in the first round, the well fancied Ivan Kemp and that made me sit up and take notice. Haddock was a southpaw (though from Wales, he was then in the combined services) and would go on to win the British pro-title and Crook was the favourite to win the ABA title. The one I wanted to avoid was Amass, but that is who I got. I was surprised that as he was a southpaw, it did not become an issue in the fight, but I think that was because he came to fight and was not a mover or counter-puncher (the ones who would give me trouble). He was trying to bomb me out, but I was too strong and determined for Amass, stopping him in the third round. In the British ABA semis (where Wales and Scotland come into it), I came up against an old opponent from Wales whom I got robbed against in the NABC class C semis the previous year, and his name was Robert Smyth. I was very confident of beating him, as I knew that I won our previous fight and I had now improved so much with the fantastic sparring I was getting. Well, I stopped Smyth in the third in a one sided fight. I remember him introducing me to his dad after the fight and he said to me that the first fight he had with me was the toughest in his boxing career. So, on to the final at Wembley. My club, Hogarth, had produced every champion, at every level, except an ABA senior champion. Moreover, the club would unexpect-edly close the following year. Could I be the first and the last?

The Night I Knocked Out the Para

Friday 3 May 1985 was one of the biggest days of my life. I was living in London then and I had got to the ABA boxing championship finals of Great Britain at the Wembley Arena. And the irony was, that I had to fight a paratrooper in the final. Carl Crook had been a member of the first battalion parachute regiment for around three or four years, but in 1985 he was no longer in the army. The British Army, and in particular the paras, had caused so much pain and hurt to the people of Ardoyne, and this put added pressure on me that I didn't need. I realised that if I lost, then I would have it brought up to me all my life. People in Ardoyne would have reminded me, 'Sure you let that para beat you', and with my dad being known for fighting and beating the paras on the street, then if I would have lost, I might not have been welcome back into my own family, never mind back into the district. I must admit, it did put me under an awful lot of pressure. I had a lot to live up to.

I knew that it was on BBC1 and people back home would be watching and on top of that, I was a heavy underdog. I had just turned nineteen on 4 January and it was my first real season as a senior boxer. My opponent, Carl Crook, was 21. Crook was three times combined services champion, an ABA semi-finalist in 1982, losing to Jim McDonnell (who later ended my hero Barry McGuigan's career) and an ABA finalist in 1984 (Olympic year, the big one), losing to Scotland's Alex Dickson.

The night before I boxed in the ABA final, I stayed in my coach, Harry Monger's, house as the weigh in was about 11 a.m. (or so) in Wembley Arena the following day (Friday). Harry's house was much closer to Wembley, as King's Cross was over an hour away on a train from Harry's. I remember I slept in a sleeping bag in the kitchen and before Harry and his wife went to bed, he gave me a boxing book to have a look at before I fell asleep. I remember the book well, *Give Him to the Angels: The Story of Harry Greb* (Fair, 1946) by James Fair, about the legendary middleweight boxing champion from the 1920s, Harry Greb. I remember I had a glance through it before falling asleep. I slept like a log, as I wasn't a bit nervous and saw this all as a big adventure, as it was my first season as a senior boxer and I already had a brilliant season. To be honest, I didn't really expect to win, but I knew that I was going to give it my best shot. I must be honest and admit that I didn't feel the pressure. When you're young, you're fearless, and I was. It is when you get older that you get scared and the doubts creep in.

The **Boxing News** had picked Crook to beat me. The odds were stacked against me. Getting to the ABA final at nineteen, and in my first year as a senior boxer, was a great achievement, but I knew back home in Belfast, that it wouldn't cut much ice if I lost. Ten thousand people crammed into Wembley Arena that night and ten million watched it on BBC. My brother, Paul, had come over, my dad had sent him, as my dad could not come as that court case with the boxer (I mentioned earlier in the book) fell on that date. I had seven fights to get to the final and from the quarter-finals, Crook and I had started nodding to each other in recognition (mutual respect). We both knew that we were on a collision course and were destined to meet in the final. The first round was a very quiet one with very little action, a real feeling out round. TV commentator, Harry Carpenter, thought that Crook had just nicked it, but my brother Paul thought that I won it, but then he would, wouldn't he! There was no indication that all hell was about to break loose in the second round, in one of the most violent rounds ever seen in an amateur contest.

Twenty seconds into the round, I caught Crook with a clean right hook, which staggered him back and knocked his gumshield out. He got a standing count, but was brought back to his corner to have his gumshield washed and put back into his mouth, giving him an extra twenty seconds to recover. When the ref said, 'Box on,' I was on him like a harbour shark and was well on top. In fact, Crook was close to receiving a second standing count such was my dominance when suddenly, he caught me a left hook that landed flush on my chin and nearly took my head off. There was no physical effect, my legs did not go, but I must admit I was stunned. I defiantly walked towards him staring at Crook as I received an eight count. I thought to myself, 'I have lost the initiative, he's got it now, I must get it back, I must.' My inexperience started to show as I charged recklessly towards him, leaving myself exposed to a sharpshooter like Crook. Now I was making mistakes and he was making me pay for them. I lunged in and put everything into a hail Mary of a left hook (both my feet left the canvas) and Crook caught me with a sharp right and I lost my balance. The ref came in and gave me a second standing eight count thinking that I was hurt, but I protested to him that I was off balance. Crook thought that I was hurt also and I am sure he thought to himself, 'One more count and it's automatically stopped.' So, he came in to finish it, as all the momentum had swung his way.

I remember my dad always used to say to me that if you catch your opponent as he's rushing in, then it doubles the impact of your punch (you're almost punching twice as hard). And that's what was going through my mind at that moment. I thought to myself, 'He's going to rush in now to try and finish me, I am going to catch him coming in, and I am going to put everything into this punch.' And that is what happened. Crook came steaming in and loaded up on a big right, but like a sharpshooter, I beat him to the draw. My right landed just a fraction before his, catching him flush on the nose. The sound of the punch landing and Crook's nose breaking reverberated around the arena, an awful crunching noise. Crook went down in a heap as I walked to a neutral corner thinking to myself, 'He's not getting up from that,' but damn it, he started to rise and he did get up. However, such was the damage to Crook's nose that the ref had no choice but to stop it. The blood was gushing out of his nose and his nose was badly misshapen, in fact it was nearly touching his ear. He had two breaks across his nose and one down, reported the **Boxing News** magazine. Crook told me later, in 1991, that he had concussion and couldn't remember anything about the fight. I had broken his nose in three places. The crowd was going crazy with excitement. I had become only the second man from Belfast to ever win the ABAs, Jack Gartland being the first in 1928.

As I stepped from the ring I was mobbed. Two guys from the Bone, called Cheeser and Rab, introduced themselves. My brother Paul, uncle Gerard, Gerry Stafford and guys from my boxing club, Hogarth, were hugging, kissing and dancing with me. A bottle of champagne appeared and it was poured into the cup as we all drank from it. Colin Hart from the **Sun** grabbed me for an exclusive interview. The next day, the headlines in the **Sun** were, 'Eamon nose he's a champion.' Guys from Belfast who were working in London suddenly appeared from nowhere to congratulate me. It was incredible. I had previously thought that there were only a handful of supporters there for me, how wrong I was. I will never forget the roar that went up when Crook was introduced at the start of the fight. Where were his fans now? Someone shouted, 'Let him get back to the dressing room.' I was a bit embarrassed, as they all followed me back to the dressing room, which I was sharing with two boxers, John Beckels and Rod Douglas. But they both hugged me and were very happy for me. In fact, they also won their fights that night.

The last I saw of Carl Crook was when I was having a shower and the medical people went to rush him past me on his way to the hospital. We had time for a hug. A handful of us had a celebration back at Gerry Stafford's flat. Later, when I went back to my room in the Wardonia Hotel, there was a telegram from my mum and dad and also another bottle of champagne and a big card from the owners, John and Jessie. John had been at Wembley for the fight. The day after the final (Saturday 4 May), I was in attendance at a professional boxing show run by Harry Holland. Harry Carpenter was doing the commentary and the camera zoomed in on me and Harry told the viewers that I had won the ABAs the previous night with one of the best punches he had ever seen (some compliment). In addition, that day at the boxing show, I was introduced to the great Tommy Farr, who took Joe Louis the distance for the world heavyweight title in the 1940s. We had a photo taken, but unfortunately it got lost down the years.

Two days after the final, police arrived at my dad's house in Holmdene Gardens. They had come with a summons for my dad. My dad just happened to be watching a re-run of my ABA final on the video recorder as they entered the house, as the front door was opened. The cops got caught up in the fight and asked which one I was. Their excitement was obvious. They were ducking and diving and ooooohing and aaaaaing and when I won, they congratulated my dad and were asking questions about me. Then they left. About five minutes later, they arrived back looking a bit sheepish as they had forgotten to hand the summons to my dad. But my dad was long gone. He had pulled his shoes and socks on and left out the backyard door.

Carl Crook went on to win the British and Commonwealth professional titles and defended those titles five times. He also boxed twice for the European title and was No. 5 lightweight in the world. I met up again with Carl in Romford, Essex in 1991, when I joined the Barry Hearn Stable. When I entered the gym on my arrival and I was looking for Barry Hearn, Carl was there, and he rushed over to me and hugged me (that is respect in a moment). Carl stayed in Romford for a week when I was there before going back to Chorley. I also had a win over Carl's brother, Nigel, in 1983.

A few years ago, I typed Carl Crook's name into Google to see what had become of him after his boxing days. I was stunned to find out that Carl's dad, Peter, killed his wife (Carl's mother), Charlotte, 25 years after Charlotte had told Peter that she had once had an affair. Peter could never get over this and rows would flair up from time to time, with Peter wanting to know more details about the affair. He just couldn't get over it and in 1998, he strangled Charlotte and then tried to kill himself, but was discovered, rushed to hospital and survived. He was sentenced to six years in jail for killing his wife. I pray for Carl and his family. But for the grace of God.

When I boxed for Sacred Heart ABC, my coach, Eamon Maguire, used to talk about a great boxer from the Oldpark/Bone area called Barney Burns. Barney won three Irish senior titles and boxed many times for Ireland at senior level. He went to live in Birmingham in the early 1960s, and got beaten in an ABA middleweight semi-final by the late great Chris Finnegan, but in 1961, Barney got to the ABA final at Wembley, where he lost a tight majority decision to Peter McCann. A dozen or so fellas from the Bone Oldpark area came over for the fight and they were joined by dozens of Paddy's who lived and worked in London, and had gone along to give their fellow Belfast-man some support. Burns was looking to become the first Belfast-man to win the ABAs since Jack Gartland won in 1928 (Gartland also represented Great Britain in the London Olympics that year). My coach, Eamon Maguire, and my friend, Paddy Maguire (no relation), who became a British bantamweight boxing champion in 1977, were also in attendance to support their friend Bernard Burns. Barney just came up short that night, I made sure that I did not. Rest in peace Barney.

When we were in London in the summer of 1985, Gerry Stafford, Andy O'Hara, Paddy Gallagher and I went to see Barry McGuigan boxing for the WBA world featherweight title against Panama's Eusebio Pedroza at Loftus Road (home of Queens Park Rangers FC). We got free tickets as Paddy's dad, John, worked on security for Barney Eastwood, and John let slip that his son was sharing a bedsit with me. This was Barney's first approach to me, but it was certainly not his last. We worked all week, but on a Friday and Saturday night, we would have gone to a bar in Covent Gardens which was pretty famous then, simply called 'Blitz', and it was a place where all the new romantics hung out. In the bar one night, we were offered tickets to some big pop concert at Wembley Stadium featuring a lot of big names, the guy was looking for £50 a ticket. We thought they were a bit pricey and we casually rejected his offer. Talk about regrets. It became known as Band Aid (Live Aid) and on the bill were Elton John, David Bowie, Duran Duran, The Who, Paul McCartney and many, many more 'giant names'. As Frank Sinatra used to sing, regrets, I have had a few.

I also had the chance to go to a live *Top of the Pops* show. This was when I was living with Frankie Woods. Frankie's son had invites (or tickets). We gave it a bit of thought, then we decided just to go down to the Three Kings on the Fulham Palace Road for some real ale. When I was in King's Cross with the Ardoyne lads, we used to go to a pub (I cannot remember its name) and actor Phil Daniels used to be in it sometimes. Occasionally, Gerry would have a game of pool with him. Phil was allowed to bring his German shepherd dog into the bar, the guv'nor was okay with this. I can still remember Gerry introducing me to Phil and Gerry gave me the big build up about me being on TV and knocking out the para a few weeks earlier. I thought Phil was going to ask me for my autograph. Phil smiled and we shook hands. Don't forget, that I was a mod a few years previously (for four years) and Phil was the most famous mod in the world, as he was the star in the cult film *Quadrophenia* (Sting was also in the film playing Ace Face). Phil also played 'grandad' in the *Only Fools and Horses* prequel, *Rock n' Chips*, and he was a regular character in *EastEnders* and featured in the pop band Blur's video 'Park Life'.

I was having the time of my life in London. I was getting £25 a day in work, my digs were paid for, and then Margaret Thatcher, the British Prime Minister, brought this new rule in that to get your digs paid for, you had to be 25 or over. I was nineteen and up until this new law, I was getting my bed and breakfast accommodation (in the Wardonia Hotel) paid for by the government. This new rule affected me, and I had no other choice, but to come home to Belfast, as I could not afford to pay for my digs, which was a small bedsit that I shared with another Ardoyne lad, Paddy Gallagher. Incidentally, Paddy Gallagher's son (also called Paddy) is a boxer and won a Commonwealth gold as an amateur in 2010. During his recent professional career, he suffered a controversial loss to Chris Jenkins for the British and Commonwealth welterweight titles in August 2019, when the fight was stopped due to cuts to Jenkins' face.

When Rocky Kelly boxed Kosta Petrou for the vacant British welterweight title, Harry Holland hired a rated welterweight called Chris Blake to spar Rocky to get him in shape, but he wasn't giving Rocky the work that he needed, and Harry was disappointed. This was just before I won the ABAs and I was cutting back on the sparring after having nineteen fights (all wins), in a tough brutal season. Harry came to me and pleaded with me to spar Rocky and made the point that Rocky had helped me no end (which was true), and I wouldn't have done so well in the ABAs without Rocky and himself (which was true also). Harry had been paying Chris Blake to spar Rocky, but he was not prepared to pay me and he said that I owed Rocky and it was now time to pay him back. This was absolute bullshit. I had sparred with Rocky for many of his fights and all I got was a free ticket. Shows I can remember going to that Rocky boxed, on the under-card featured Mark Kaylor v. Tony Sibson at Wembley, Barry McGuigan v. Esteban Equia at the Royal Albert Hall and Clinton McKenzie v. Terry Marsh at Shoreditch (and there were more). The sparring was of mutual benefit for Rocky and me and it worked both ways. I was working in London at that time, and had just moved to King's Cross where myself and my housemates were having the time of our lives. Harry expected me to take an hour-long tube (and an hour back) to Chiswick (after a day's work), to spar Rocky and I wasn't being paid. Rocky boxed Petrou two weeks before my ABA final and would get stopped in nine rounds (after hurting Petrou early). Harry and I fell out after this and didn't talk for a couple of years.

Home Is Where the Heart Is

When I came back from London in 1985, I remember saying hello to the first recognisable face I saw and he blanked me. The next day, I called up to an old school pal (and former neighbour) in Estoril Park and he told me in no uncertain terms that he was dating a girl and he wanted to spend all his time with her. I sat in the house for weeks waiting for someone to call; nobody did.

The first person to befriend me was a guy called Mickey Wasson, who was two years older than me. I bumped into him in Etna Drive and after a long chat, he told me where he lived and invited me up for dinner the next day. I went up and his girlfriend (who was very pretty) cooked us a lovely meal and I looked around his house and thought to myself, 'This guy has it made'. He had everything you could ever want: a beautiful house, a stunning-looking girlfriend, a good job in the post office and he was also a very fit athlete. On top of all that, he was an amazing dancer, the best I ever saw live or on TV, and that includes Michael Jackson and my hero, Prince. And I really mean that with all my heart. Mickey and I started knocking about together and we would go running in the mornings at 10 a.m. and when we would run together, I could not keep up with him for a long time, as he just seemed to glide. We had three different runs to choose from, the large run was very steep and included running around the horse shoe bend and up the Ligoniel mountain, the medium run would have been about four miles and the short run, which I still do over thirty years later, was just under three miles. When we did the short run, we would time ourselves and try to beat the previous time every run.

North Belfast has some amazing runs as there are loads of hills. We would do the short run in twelve minutes, as I remember, and this really improved my fitness and I enjoyed running with Mickey. As I moved up the ranks as a pro boxer, I started to beat Mickey in those early morning runs and he stopped running with me. Mickey had a big ego and didn't want to be overshadowed. We never fell out or anything, but I missed not running with him and it was lonely out there in those early morning runs and as I had no one to compete against, it affected my fitness as I got lazy and slowed down my pace.

We were always telling Mickey to enter the dancing competitions in the GAA club in Ardoyne on a Saturday night. There were some great prizes and we knew Mickey would walk it, but he wouldn't enter and I think he was terrified of losing or embarrassing himself, as Mickey was competitive and had that big ego (as I stated earlier). On a Saturday night, no one would be on the dance floor until Mickey arrived and when he did, he would just walk in and throw his coat to his sister. Una. and walk on the dance floor as everyone followed him. The dancefloor would then be full in seconds. The Magic Fly roadshow DJ, Gerard McGreevy, would also give Mickey the big build up. He was like John Travolta in the 1970s classic **Saturday Night Fever**. One time, as we all entered the disco, McGreevy shouted, 'Here comes Mickey and the diet coke kids' (we all drank diet coke) and Mickey loved that one as his name stood out over mine. Mickey was very confident and very witty and a riot to be around (a great craic). I went to Spain for two weeks with Mickey and three other postmen around this time.

Then, out of the blue, Mickey started to smoke grass and his life started to unravel. He broke up with his girlfriend, stopped training, lost his job, hit a neighbour, and got into trouble with the IRA over it. His beautiful house turned into a drop-in for people to come and smoke weed. I remember calling one day and there were people in the house and he had a giant Jamaican flag on the living room wall and he had moved his settees from the living room up into the front bedroom. It was a mess. Then just like that, Mickey was gone. We eventually found out he was living in the Isle of Wight and through time, he got his act together and by all accounts is a hard grafter on the building sites. He has a partner, Tina, and a wee daughter, so good luck to him and I wish him well. In the last 25 years, he has been back to Belfast four or five times and has never once come looking for me. I went to his mother's funeral a number of years ago, and

I called to the wake to offer Mickey my condolences and we chatted for a while. You just try your best and move on – that is my outlook in life. Another friend of mine and Mickey's called Tony McNulty, once said that if Mickey had been born and lived in America, then he would have been a big star and a millionaire, as he had talent to burn. And Tony was right. I wouldn't deny Mickey that compliment.

I was only home a week when my dad had me picked to box against Australia. He had also fixed me up with Gerry Storey's Holy Family boxing club (I had wanted to go back to my old club Sacred Heart). I won on points against the Aussie, dropping him in the second. Then Gerry Storey, in his infinite wisdom, had me go into the Mater Hospital to have an operation on my nose. The reason for this was, I was complaining of my nose being sore and it bled a few times down at the Holy Family gym, but what I really needed was a rest. I had had nineteen hard fights in one season (all wins) and some brutal sparring with Billy Hardy and Rocky Kelly. All my nose needed was a few months with no one punching it. So Gerry had me go in to get my nose cauterised (congeal the blood) just to impress me, as I think he had a good contact there, Dr Darcy. After a week or so, I was back in sparring again as I was getting picked for internationals like the TSC multi-nations in Berlin. As soon as I got a punch on the nose, the pain was unbearable. Therefore, Gerry booked me in for another operation. This time I think I gave it longer, but when I went in to spar, bang – the pain! So, unbelievably, I was booked in for a third op. Listen, when all is said and done, I ended up out of boxing for a year and I was in the form of my life at that time. I missed international after international. It was the worse time of my life. The abuse in the house with my dad was at its height also. Looking back, my dad and Gerry should have had me rest for a few months, but I am also to blame, as I would have done anything to box. I wanted to box for my country and I wanted to box in major competitions and travel the world.

My dad got involved in my boxing career when I came back to Belfast from London in the summer of 1985. He had me lined up to fight for Ulster against Australia and after my early morning runs around the Waterworks, which has two ponds, one big and one small, he would take me up to the Crumlin Star social club for a game of snooker. Sometimes, it felt like I was out running again, as I would be running around the snooker table taking the balls out of the pockets as my dad would be potting balls left, right and centre. My dad was an excellent snooker and billiards player and he had won many titles. I remember growing up and there would be silver cups on display in the living room with a list of names engraved on them that are tattooed on my mind. Names like, Paddy Morgan, Jimmy Miller, Eddie Sharkey and Sammy Pavis (who was also a great footballer who played for Linfield). I am not sure what titles my dad won, but he won quite a few individual titles and he used to have a scrapbook that I always used to look at. It was full of newspaper cuttings and photos of his snooker, billiards, boxing and darts achievements. My dad really excelled in sports. Perhaps that is how I inherited my own athleticism and sporting abilities. What I would give now to have that scrapbook, which has been lost for many years.

I remember being picked to go to the House of Sport in Belfast along with ex-boxers Hugh Russell, Ken Beattie and Gerry Hamill to represent the boxers in a pre-Commonwealth games event with representatives from all the sports there. Past and present athletes were there to meet, among others, Mary Peters and the Duchess of Kent. Russell, Beattie and Hamill had won medals at previous Commonwealth games, and I was seen as Northern Ireland's brightest medal hope for the current boxers. What they did not know was that I had already signed to go professional with Barney Eastwood, but it was not announced to the public yet. No one knew except Barney Eastwood, my family and me. A press conference would be held a month later. The Duchess of Kent, assisted by Mary Peters, went around a large hall talking to all the athletes. There were four representatives from each sport. The athletes who were going to represent Northern Ireland in Edinburgh in 1986 were at the front, with the other athletes from their sport in a line behind them. Gerry Hamill was known for being a terrible wind-up merchant, but I didn't know that then. I was a very naive nineteen-year-old and if someone had have told me that the world was flat, then I would have believed them. Well, Gerry told me that when the Duchess comes to me, I was to curtsy and say, 'Hello Ma'am.' When the Duchess finally came over along with Mary Peters, I did just what Hamill told me to do, I curtsied and said, 'Hello Ma'am.' I heard the chuckling behind me and I knew then that I was set up. The bastards! I went bright red with embarrassment, but I remember the Duchess talked to me for ages. She must have felt sorry for me. Men bow, women curtsy, and I will always remember that.

I first met Barry McGuigan in 1985 in Mr Barney (BJ) Eastwood's gym in Castle Street, Belfast city centre, just shortly after Barry's first defence against Bernard Taylor. I wasn't at the Taylor fight at the King's Hall and although the fight was shown live in England, Scotland and Wales, it was not shown live on local TV. So some smart arse worked out that, if you turn your TV aerial towards Napoleon's nose up on the Cave Hill (where Rinty Monaghan trained and got his goat's milk), then you could pick up Scottish TV which was showing the fight. I remember it so well. Belfast was in the middle of 'Barry mania' at the time and workmen were charging money to go up on your roof and turn the aerial to get the fight. I sparred Barry one day in Eastwood's and I learned a valuable lesson that would stand me in good stead for the future. I was still an amateur then, and my coach, Bobby McAllister, who was familiar with the gym, failed to tell me something significant that nearly got me knocked out. This was a professional gym and was different in many ways to amateur gyms. Bobby should have explained to me that when the buzzer sounded, it meant that there were ten seconds left in the round and when the round was over, the buzzer stopped. I didn't know this. Well, Barry always sparred hard and I sparred hard and we were going at it hammer and tongs, then the buzzer buzzed and I dropped my hands thinking that it was the end of the round and Barry clocked me with a big right. I did not go down, but I was stunned. I fell back on the ropes and Barry put his hands on my shoulders and said, 'You alright, Eamon?' and I remember thinking, what does he want me to say, 'Not so bad Barry. And, how's yourself?' Bobby should have warned me about the buzzer. He should have told me that when the buzzer goes off, then keep fighting until it stops. When I joined the gym and trained there, I used to warn Barry's sparring partners about the buzzer. No one warned me, I learned the hard way. Barry and I only sparred a few times and I would not lie and say that we were great friends at that time, but we certainly knew and respected each other. As I mentioned earlier, I had signed to go professional with Barney Eastwood and the next chapter details my early days as a pro.

Top: My mother and father on their wedding day, with my two grannies

Middle: Me and Tanya in the Bone park

Bottom: Tanya, Paul and me with Santa

Fairfield Street 1972

Top: The funeral of next door neighbour David McAuley. The British Army attacked the funeral; that's our house far right

Middle: Posing at my dad's car in Fairfield Street in the 1970s

Bottom left: The McAuley clan

Bottom right: Our next-door neighbour, Margaret McCorry (right, white top). Shot dead in 1971

Holy Cross Football team 1976

Lucky to be alive –
Patsy 'Coco' McAuley

Me and Paul in Holy Cross

Top: Hard to believe my dad came out of this car alive

Middle: The aftermath of the 1977 bomb in Etna Drive

Bottom left: McAuley kids with Granny O'Kane

Bottom right: Me and Danny Trainor at Solitude after winning the Northern Ireland cup

Teenage kicks in Ardoyne

Normal everyday life in Ardoyne in the 1970s

We used to jump from the school onto the mobile hut; miss and you are dead

With sparring partner Rocky Kelly, and Harry Holland

Promo Photo

Me, slightly drunk, with
Karen on her 18th birthday

Knocking out Derek Grainger with this punch in 40 seconds

Decapitating Les Remickie, Ulster Hall, 1986

Catching Robert Smyth with a right. ABA semi-finals 1985

Top left: Getting introduced at the King's Hall, Belfast, 1987

Top right: Me and Barry McGuigan outside his house in Kent, 1991

Bottom: Me and Paul Hodkinson with Michael Nunn

Top: Sacred Heart ABC Ulster and Irish Champions

Middle: My brother Paul on the right, with Anthony 'Monkey' McBride, the man who started me boxing

Below: Me, my dad and my brother, Paul

Top: My brother, Paul, and his girlfriend, Lillian

Middle: With the keys of my first car, 1988

Bottom: The soldier I went to war with in the 1985 ABA final

On the door at the Bellevue Arms with Robert McCartney, second left

The night I nearly got killed with a pipe bomb

Top: With George Chuvalo

Middle: With Smokin' Joe Frazier

Bottom: With old opponent Ben McGarrigle

Two Eamon McAuleys

Just completed the Belfast Marathon; Karen by my side as always

My son Shea with Carl Frampton

With Liam Neeson

Top left: Me at the statue for my great-uncle, Rinty Monaghan
Top right: Me with hitman Ricky Hatton, Europa Hotel, Belfast
Bottom: Sammy Vernon, Neil Sinclair, Paddy Maguire and Me. Four ex-pros; Sinclair and Maguire were Lonsdale belt holders (British champions)

Mural of Sacred Heart Boxers

Me with new Ulster senior champion Paul McCullough and an old opponent, Dermot McDermott, who I beat in December 1982

With Hands of Stone
Roberto Duran

11

Turning Pro

I hadn't wanted to go pro. I had wanted to represent my country going to the Europeans, the world's, and the Olympics. Now I could not do that. Turning pro had robbed me of my dream. However, Barney Eastwood is a very persuasive man and when he sets his sights on something then he goes for it 100 per cent. He said that he had seen me knockout the para in the ABA final, he said that he loved big punchers and was looking for someone to come along after Barry McGuigan to carry the baton. He said that I was the man. I had already turned Mr Eastwood down a few times. He had sent Brighton millionaire, promoter and matchmaker, Paddy Byrne, to my house in Ardoyne and he had my amateur coach, Bobby McAllister, bring me down to the Castle Street Gym to talk to him a few times. One time, Barry McGuigan even had a good long talk with me and he told me how much BJ had done for him and if I'm thinking of turning pro, then Eastwood was the best man to go with (and in the light of what happened with those two), I told Barry that I had no wish to go pro at that time.

Mr Eastwood's first offer to me was a £2,000 signing-on fee; I said, 'No.' Then he offered me £5,000 and I knocked him back again and I asked him for £10,000, thinking that would chase him away, but after a while, he sent for me to go up to his house to talk. Anytime he wanted to talk, he would send a driver (Ray Boyd) to pick me up in one of BJ's blue Mercedes and bring me to his house on the Hollywood Road, facing the Cultra Inn and the Culloden Hotel. BJ had four or five blue Mercs and a Rolls Royce outside his house. I eventually turned pro with Mr Eastwood and the deal was done that day. I got a fantastic deal. I ended up getting a £6,000 signing-on fee and a promise of £1,000 for each of my first eight fights. I was promised a day job (working for one of Eastwood's guys, Ray Boyd, who had his own car-cleaning business), I was also promised driving lessons and I got a few hundred pounds worth of sports equipment. In addition, my dad got a few quid that day from Barney also (Judas). I brought my dad with me this time. My mum had begged me to bring him. My dad and I hadn't been talking in a while. In the past, when I talked to BJ, I was on my own and I felt like a salmon in a sea of sharks. I thought it was time to give my dad another chance and it would get him off my mum's back for a while. I had mixed feelings about going pro. I remember shortly after this, another one of BJ's men (Al Dillon), bringing me round to the Bank of Ireland and that's where I put my money, in an Isle of Man account (tax free). The manager, Davy Wells, even came out to greet me. Everyone treated me well as they all thought that I was the next big thing.

When you think that Barry McGuigan got no signing-on fee from Eastwood (only promises) when he turned pro, Dave 'Boy' McAuley got nothing when he signed for Eastwood and Paul Hodkinson didn't get a signing-on fee (and they won world titles), then you will understand how highly Eastwood thought of me.

When I had my press conference a few weeks later, the media went large with their coverage. 'The New McGuigan', said one headline; 'Better than McGuigan' said another, which quoted Mr Eastwood who commented, 'This boy hits harder than Barry.' I felt the pressure and expectation, I really did, instead of boosting my confidence, this was having an adverse effect on me. I now had to live up to all this hype and money Eastwood had given me. I hadn't boxed in a year with this damm nose injury. The only spar I had, was that one with Barry McGuigan in Eastwood's gym when Bobby McAllister brought me down.

When Barry McGuigan defended his world title against Stevie Cruz in Las Vegas in June 1986, I had this tantalising option put to me. Mr Eastwood said to me, 'Do you want to make your debut on the big London bill at Wembley Arena featuring Lloyd Honeygan in a world title eliminator? Or would you like to make your debut in Madison Square Garden on the Edwin Rosario v. Hector Camacho undercard on 13 June, then come with us to Las Vegas to help Barry prepare for his world title defence?' This bill in Las Vegas also featured Tommy Hearns and Roberto Duran and was called 'the triple Hitter.' Sounds like a no brainier choice, doesn't it? Well I picked the London show (regrets again) and the reason I picked London, was that

I was really feeling the pressure of having to deliver the goods. I hadn't even sparred in a year with this nose injury and that was why I didn't want to go to Vegas, as it would have put extra pressure on top of the pressure that I was already trying to cope with. Paul Hodkinson took my place.

My professional debut was to be on the undercard of gym mates, Roy Webb and Dave 'Boy' McAuley, who were boxing British title eliminators in April 1986 and I was up to the high doe with nerves. My confidence wasn't good and my form wasn't good. I remember sparring Gary 'Peppy' Muir in Eastwood's gym and he gave me a bit of a hiding, as I was struggling to find the form that I knew I was capable of. I hadn't boxed in a year and I was really feeling the pressure and expectation of having to deliver the goods. **Belfast Telegraph** journalist Jack Magowan wrote that the 'Drums have been beating long and loud for McAuley and he now must show us what he's got.' Peppy was just an average boxer, but my confidence was at rock bottom. I really thought that I should just give the signing-on fee back to Eastwood and go back to the amateurs, but I had signed contracts and he could stop me from ever boxing again. These were just some of the thoughts going around in my head in the build-up to my professional debut. I had no self-belief, only self-doubt. The night before the show, which was at the Ulster Hall, my opponent Craig Windsor pulled out. To be honest I was relieved, as I just didn't feel right mentally or physically.

In May, I made my debut at the Wembley Arena where, exactly a year previously, I had knocked out Carl Crook for the ABA title. I boxed a journeyman that night at Wembley, called Dean Bramald, and although I was still not 100 per cent, I won every round and finally I was off and running. This would give me some confidence and I had shedded a lot of ring rust after having been out for a year. I was on my way. I said my goodbyes to Eastwood, Eddie Shaw etc. at Heathrow Airport as Bobby and I were going home to Belfast, and Eastwood and Eddie Shaw were heading to Vegas to meet up with Barry McGuigan and their team for Barry's ill-fated world title defence against Steve Cruz.

My second pro bout was in the Ulster Hall in Belfast, and this was my Belfast debut with the Belfast crowd getting their first look at me. My confidence was growing and my form was improving, but the Belfast crowd are a hard lot to please; they do know their boxing and now was the time for me to live up to all this hype, but boy was I nervous. It didn't help that as I was making my way to the ring (trying to be focused), they were carrying Scotsman Danny Quigg past me on a stretcher. He had been knocked unconscious in the previous fight by the Shankill's Rocky McGran. This was the last thing that I needed to see. I tried to remain positive and focused, but I remember I kept looking back behind me and thinking, welcome to the world of professional boxing. Thank God, I clashed heads with my opponent Les Remickie and he came out of it the worst, causing the ref to stop the contest in the second round, with me being declared the winner, because my nerves were wrecked. I remember going to the BBC a few days later, to collect a video of my fight and, as I'm talking to the late Joy Williams, I saw this guy with a guitar on his back struggling to get through the revolving doors and I rushed over to help him (which I did) and the ignorant git didn't even acknowledge me and he just pushed on past me. I was close to pulling him, but I just decided to let it slide. I enquired as to who he was and the receptionist told me his name was Owen Paul and that he was late for his performance. He was there to perform his number three (in the pop charts) song 'You're My Favourite Waste of Time' which was his one hit wonder, but it stayed in the top ten for sixteen weeks and made him a very rich man. He was lucky he didn't get a dig in the gob that day.

When BJ signed Liverpool featherweight Paul Hodkinson in 1986, it really took a lot of pressure off me. Paul became BJ's new focus and new toy and I was no longer the new kid on the block. My confidence returned, and I started producing amazing form in the gym. I had been sparring with Paul, but in legendary journalist Jack Magowan's own words in the *Belfast Telegraph*, 'McAuley looks too heavy and rough for the tearaway Hodkinson who, some think, is a better prospect than McGuigan was at the same formative stage of his career.' Well they stopped me from sparring Paul and moved me up to spar the heavier Andy Holligan and Eamonn Loughran. There was less than half a stone between Paul and I as I would have been about 9st. 7lb. and Paul was around 9st. 3lb. I was a light lightweight. Of course, Paul would go on to win the British, European and WBC world titles. When I settled, my form was outstanding and I remember Bobby McAllister saying to me that I was the best of them all, and I was thinking to myself, 'Tell me something I don't already know.' This was after Barry had left the gym though. Barry was the 'greatest'; I was just the 'latest'.

One of my dad's best friends, Pat McAllister, suggested one day that he would take me out on a cycle ride. Pat would have been around twenty years older than me but was a very fit man for his age. I thought we would be cycling and talking as we took in the sights. I remember we went along the Antrim Road, past the zoo, then on to Chimney Corner at a ferocious pace, with Pat quite a bit in front of me, and somehow we ended up at the Black Mountain as I was gritting my teeth trying so hard to keep close to

Pat. We stopped for a break on the Black Mountain, as Pat had stopped as he had lost sight of me and he waited for me to catch up. I cursed Pat at least a hundred times, as I had never expected this to be so hard, murderously hard. When I got off my bike, my legs turned to jelly and I fell to the ground. I got up, then I fell to the ground again. I felt like the boxer Trevor Berbick after he got knocked down by Mike Tyson around that same time.

My third pro fight was in the King's Hall, and was a rematch against my previous opponent, Les Remickie; the date was 19 January 1987. It was on a card headlined by Barney's new signing, Herol Graham, who was the No. 1 middleweight contender for Marvin Hagler's world title. Graham was boxing the American Charlie 'Cho Cho' Boston. This was my first appearance at this famous venue, where my great-uncle Rinty Monaghan had won the undisputed world flyweight boxing championship in 1948. My confidence was growing and I hammered Remickie, who quit in his corner at the end of the second round. It was a good win even though Remickie was a journeyman, but he was tough and durable and not many stopped Remickie. (Journeyman is a term used for a boxer who, even though he might have many losses on his record, he will still try his best to win and give you a good test).

After the boxing was over, Barney Eastwood threw a big party at the La Mon Hotel (scene of an IRA bomb in 1978, in which twelve people were burnt to death). My crew arrived in two cars. I had never seen a party like this in my life, as no expense was spared. All sorts of the finest food and drink were available and there were lots of local celebrities and famous boxers (past and present). Liverpool's Paul Hodkinson had a brilliant win that night in only his fifth pro outing, where he outclassed former British champion Steve 'Sammy' Simms from Wales. Legendary sports commentator Harry Carpenter stepped on stage with microphone in hand and spoke for ten minutes about Paul Hodkinson, saying that he was blown away with his talent, and that he had a very high regard for Paul's opponent, Steve Simms. He added that he was shocked that a young kid in just his fifth pro fight was able to take him apart. He said 'Hoko' (pronounced Hok-o) was the best prospect that he had ever seen and he was convinced this kid was going to be a future superstar (some praise, eh). Everybody clapped and Harry sat down.

Then well-known boxing manager and promoter Mickey Duff went on stage, took the microphone and talked for ten minutes about how good I was. He said that I had the potential to be a future world champion and boxing legend. He went on, and said that he had been keeping his eye on me ever since I knocked out Carl Crook in the ABA final. Well, I never signed as many autographs in my life and Barney Eastwood was introducing Paul and I to all his millionaire friends (society's finest). In my company that night were Jimmy McNulty, Tony McNulty, Gerard McVeigh, Terry Short, Mickey Wasson and Tommy McKeogh. Terry Short was in his element that night and was drunk and mingling with society's finest and he was acting like a big shot ordering them drinks (the drinks were free anyway). He would click his fingers and shout to the waiters, 'Garcon '[French for boy], some drinks for my friends.' It was some night. A couple of days later, I received a phone call from Mr Eastwood. He said, 'Pack your bags. You and Hoko and I are going to Los Angeles tomorrow.' Things were really happening in my life then, my confidence was sky high, and better still, I had just met the girl of my dreams.

Karen

I still remember the first time I set eyes on Karen. It was in the Larry Kennedy lounge of the Shamrock Bar in Ardoyne in the summer of 1986. Larry Kennedy was an independent Belfast city councillor who was murdered by Loyalists at the Shamrock club in 1981. I was in the lounge that night with Paddy Gallagher, who I shared a bedsit with in London, and when I went to the bar to get a drink – that's when it happened. Karen was behind the bar on her own and she served me my drinks. I was instantly besotted with her beauty. I was well and truly blown away. It was the first time in my life that I ever felt like this and I know it sounds corny, but what can I say, I was struck by Cupid's arrow. When I went back to Paddy, I was on a different planet. Paddy was talking away but I wasn't listening. I just said to Paddy, 'Do you know who that girl is?' He replied, 'No.' I was not intending to go into the disco part of the Shamrock that night, but Karen was switched from the lounge to the disco (cabaret room) and Paddy and I followed. Karen was just sixteen at the time (I was twenty). I am sure Paddy Gallagher was wondering what was wrong with me. I am not a big drinker, but I was banging pint after pint into me, as I was distracted from everything and everyone around me, except her. I decided that I was going to ask her out, but the thing was, that I was very drunk. She casually rejected my advances with a polite, 'On yer bike!' Later, I staggered home (on my own), but the next day, I just couldn't get her out of my head. I just couldn't stop thinking about her. 'Who is this girl and where does she live?' I started to go to the Shamrock three times a week!

I kept my distance and worshipped Karen from afar. I was in Eskdale Gardens one day with my friends Noel Magee and John O'Halloran, when Karen walked by. I rushed to the window and said, 'Quick lads, come here, do you know who that girl is walking down the other side of the street?' I think it was Noel who said, 'I think her granny lives up the street.' Another day, I was on the Ardoyne Road when the bus pulled up and all the workers from McWilliams sewing factory in Ligoniel got off, and there she was. Better still, my sister Tanya got off the bus, as she also worked at McWilliams. When I spoke to Tanya, she said she didn't know Karen and had never spoke to her before, but I was still making progress. I used to be up on the road everyday watching Karen get off the bus. She must have noticed me: 'the stalker.'

I was very shy around girls, very shy and the fact that she had already knocked me back, made me extra reticent. Then I got devastating news from John O'Halloran who told me, 'Eamon, see that girl you're stalking, you want to be careful as she is going out with Gary McKillopp.' It was like a thunderbolt. Well, that was that as far as I was concerned. I was heart-broken. But as time went by, I heard from someone that Karen and Gary had broken it off. Was Karen opening the door for me? Did she know that I was interested in her? Did someone tell her? These were all the things that were going around in my head. I was doing well then, as a boxer and was well-known in the area. She must have known me. I made up my mind that I was going to pluck up the courage to ask her out before someone else did. At the same time, I was terrified of rejection. Every time I went to the Shamrock, I dragged Tony McNulty along (well, I couldn't be sitting there on my own). I am sure I put Tony's head away with, 'Karen this' and 'Karen that.' Many a night, Karen would be there even if she wasn't working and this one night, she was there (off duty) with her friends and the slow section came on (or 'erection section' we called it) and 'Lady in Red' by Chris De Burgh blasted out. Tony said, 'Why don't you go over and ask her up for a dance?' He had said this many times before, but I hadn't the courage previously. This time, however, I just went for it and I went over and said, 'Would you like to dance with me?' and, she said, 'yes!'

I knocked out Jim Docherty (not the same Jim Docherty that I competed against on sports day which I mentioned earlier in the book) clean out in the GAA a couple of months before that, as he shook hands with me and wouldn't let go of my hand for well over five minutes. I pleaded with him to give me my hand back, but he just kept saying that he could take five of my punches and I said, 'That's very good, but could you release your grip on my hand?' I should have just asked someone to go and get the doormen, but in the end, I just banged him. As he was sitting down at the time, he just took off up into the air and brought two tables of alcohol with him and the doormen carried him out, but didn't say anything to me, as I just sat down to drink my diet coke. About an hour later, as I was at the bar buying drinks, I look over and saw him walking through the front door and he spotted me and made a bee line for me and I was thinking, 'Fuck me, this is all I need, as he was a big heavy lad.' And as he gets to within five feet of me, he throws his hands up as a sign of peace and says to me (as God is my witness), 'Eamon, some cunt banged me earlier and I'm looking for him. Would you back me up?' I replied, 'Yeah, that's no problem Jim.' And I went and got the doormen and told them to put him out, and they did. Next morning, he called to my mum and dad's house, but I wasn't there as I must have touched for a girl and had not come home from the night before (I hadn't met Karen yet). He had brought his toddler son with him and he wanted to apologise. I didn't really start drinking until I was 28. I had a wee go at it from sixteen to nineteen, but I didn't really like the taste, the hangover or the humiliation I felt from the night before. I didn't like embarrassing myself and had low self-esteem as it was.

A big regret of mine, was that I couldn't really relax and enjoy those great years from 1985 to 1988. So much was going on in my life, and I was seldom off the TV or in the newspapers and I was a bit of a local celebrity and had loads of friends, but I was also deeply self-conscious. Why was that? Was it pressure and expectation from the boxing? I just wish I had the confidence then that I do today. When I look at some of the current local boxers, like Michael Conlan and Carl Frampton, I marvel at their confidence and self-belief and how they are living in the moment and enjoying their boxing and their lives. I look back and think it is really sad that I did not have that self-belief. When I was in the ring I did, but outside the ring I struggled to express myself. This put pressure on me regarding chatting to anyone, and I just couldn't relax and be myself. Perhaps the environment in which I lived didn't help. Sometimes trouble came my way when I didn't want it to.

One night, just before I dated Karen in 1986, I was in the Shamrock club in Ardoyne with my friend Tony McNulty and we were bopping it out on the dance floor (men used to dance together then, as we would be putting the vibe out during the mating season). Suddenly, this drunk guy banged into me and it was me that said, 'Sorry,' and he went right into my face and said, 'What the fuck are you slabbering about?' But a few local Republicans quickly intervened and said, 'It's okay Eamon we will sort this out.' And the next thing I saw, is the doorman, 'Haystacks', who was a man mountain of a guy, dragging this guy out while firing uppercuts into his face. I felt sorry for the guy. One of the local Republicans then came over to my table and said, 'Don't worry Eamon we will look after you as you bring a lot of pride to Ardoyne.' The Ardoyne black taxi drivers wouldn't charge me when I got a taxi from Ardoyne to Castle Street (and back) to go to the gym and it was five or six days a week. that I went to the gym. This was right through 1986–1987 and it was their way of supporting me and getting behind me. When I boxed in the Ulster Hall and King's Hall in 1986–1987, half of Ardoyne would have been down supporting me.

On another occasion in the GAA club in Ardoyne (1986), shortly after I had started going out with Karen, I was dancing with Karen on the dance floor and two mates, Mickey Wasson and Tony McNulty, were bopping it out beside us, when two guys came over and started to dance next to us. This was fine, but then the guy banged into me and didn't apologise. I let it go. Then it happened again, and I knew instantly that these guys had picked me out quite deliberately. I should have walked away, but I was with Karen (I was only just going out with her) and my manhood (ego) was being challenged. So, I bumped the guy back and that's what they wanted and he turned to me and aggressively went right in my face, but before I had time to think both guys were lying on the floor knocked out. My fists were quicker than my brain. The bouncers carried them out, but never said a word to me, and I went and sat down. My mates were awestruck, and couldn't understand how I had seen the other guy approach me on my right side and I couldn't give them an answer, as I didn't know myself. I threw a right and then a left hook. It was instinct that came through that night. As a professional boxer, I preferred to do my fighting inside the ring, but when challenged, I would not back down when others were starting the confrontation.

For me, concentrating on the professional boxing and trying to avoid altercations was my priority at this time. In the next chapter, I discuss an exciting and important period in my professional career.

Living the Dream

One of the highlights of my boxing career happened in early 1987, when Paul Hodkinson, manager BJ Eastwood and myself visited Los Angeles, Panama and Colombia. Mr Eastwood took Paul and I into some of the roughest, toughest gyms in the world, and what an education that was. In Los Angeles, we trained with Joe Goossen and his boxers. That is where I sparred Hector Lopez, former world champion, Jamie Garza, and future world champion, Gabriel Ruelas. Then we went to east Los Angeles where I sparred Marcos Villisana and Antonio Esparragoza (two future world champions) and Hector Lopez also came along with us that day. Believe it or not (I have a write up to prove it), I was down to spar *Julio César Chávez* that day and I was very excited and honoured. Mr Eastwood was forking out a lot of money by taking us on this trip, but if Barney saw talent or, in Hodkinson's case 'a dead cert', then he would back it to the hilt. Chavez never came that day and I don't know why. I was disappointed, but didn't like to ask Mr Eastwood any questions. I sparred Villisana and Esparragoza and held my own, but it was just light sparring.

In addition, training in the gym that day, was a young prospect that had a handful of fights just like Paul and I had, but he seemed light years ahead of us. His name was Genaro Hernandez and he died tragically young. Paul and I looked on as he hit the pads, which were being held by his uncle, and then did a bit of sparring with his uncle. The reason I asked someone what his name was and the reason I remembered his name, was because he looked awesome. I thought, 'Wow, I must remember his name.'

He also looked massive for a super featherweight (he was 6ft.). Hernandez looked much more advanced than Paul and I. Indeed, he would go on to become world super featherweight boxing champion and made many title defences, including beating the great Azumah Nelson.

We also went out for a run one morning with one of Joe Goossen's boxers, Michael Nunn (Nunn would go on to win world titles in two weights, then his life spiralled out of control as he got caught dealing drugs and got sentenced to 24 years in prison). We found Michael a very friendly guy. He brought Hoko and I up to his hotel room, showed us his newspaper cuttings, and was asking all about the No. 1 middleweight contender and our stablemate, Herol Graham.

Also in the gym one day, was the (late) legendary former world heavyweight boxing champion, Floyd Patterson. He was with his adopted son, Tracey Harris Patterson, who would also go on to win a world title. Paul and I had a chat with Floyd, who was lovely, and he told us about the great time he had in Dublin quite a few years previously. What I noticed about Floyd, was that he found it hard to make eye contact. Floyd had a deep-rooted inferiority complex (which is a cause very close to my heart). However, he was happy to chat with Paul and I and we got a photo with him, which was taken by his son.

My good friend, John McNally, won a silver medal at the 1952 Helsinki Olympic games in Finland. John said that when he was in the dressing room after winning a tough contest in the semi-final against 'Kang Joon Hoo' of South Korea, he was in agony with rope burns as he had spent much of the fight on the ropes, as he tried to fend off the aggressive Korean. In the dressing room, John lay on the rubbing table as two American boxers, Virgil Akins and Floyd Patterson, each held one of John's hands as the Irish coach poured pure alcohol over his back. John squealed in agony, but he said the pain was temporary as Floyd Patterson spoke words of compassion into John's ear. John never forgot Floyd's kindness. Floyd went on to win the gold at middleweight later that day, and Akins would go on to win the world welterweight title. I never knew John McNally in 1987, otherwise I would have brought his name up to Floyd.

One day, we went to see Eddie Shaw's sister and her family, and that night Paul and I went to a party in Hollywood with Eddie's nephew and his girlfriend. It was a big swanky party. Anyway, we were staying in the hotel (beside the Inglewood Forum) with Roberto Duran's manager, Luis Spada, as one of Spada's boxers, Bernardo Pinango, was defending his super bantamweight world title against local guy, Frankie Duarte. Pinango won on points and we all headed to Panama to train with Panama's legendary world boxing champion, Hilario Zapata, who was getting ready to defend his world flyweight title against Colombian, Fidel Bassa, in Barrenquillia, Colombia in a weeks' time.

The only highlight I can remember from Panama, is BJ, Paul and I having dinner in Luis Spada's mansion. During the dinner, Roberto Duran rang from Florida, where he was living at that time. Duran and Spada had a conversation and I was tempted to say, 'Let me talk to Roberto, let me say hello.' I eventually got to meet my hero Duran, but I had to wait another 30 years when he came to Belfast's Europa Hotel for 'An evening with...'

I showed Duran the t-shirt Spada had given me that time, claiming that Roberto had worn it and Duran signed it for me. One other thing I remember from Panama was, one day Mr Eastwood asked Paul and I if we would like to go out for dinner with him one evening rather than having dinner in the hotel, as per usual. We didn't fancy having to wait until later as we were starving, and we asked would he mind if we just had our dinner in the hotel, as we could not wait until evening (the hotels we stayed in were truly out of this world). The next day, Mr Eastwood told us that he had a wonderful evening and an excellent meal with boxing legend Eusebio Pedroza. Why did he not tell us that Pedroza was coming along? I would have jumped through hoops to meet Eusebio Pedroza. And so, on to Colombia, where I would bump into another boxing legend, but this legend was practically a down and out, unlike Pedroza, who was a very smart man and was involved in politics in Panama after his boxing career ended.

Panama was okay, it was like America caught in a time zone. It was more like America in 1947 instead of 1987, with old fashioned clothes and old cars. Colombia was much poorer. I witnessed immense poverty. People were living in mud huts. It was a real eye opener for me. I remember being introduced to Colombia's most famous boxer – Antonio 'Kid Pambele' Cervantes. It was at one of the many Zapata-Bassa press conferences and I think this one was at the hotel we were staying in. The media circus was in full flow and Paul and I even got interviewed by reporters. The press were everywhere. I remember three men approached us and one said to us, would you like to meet Kid Pambele, one of Colombia's legendary boxing champions. I looked at the guy in the middle, to whom this guy was referring to, and he looked meek, downtrodden and humble. I asked, 'What is your name?' But the guy who spoke earlier answered for him, 'Kid Pambele Cervantes.' Then the penny dropped. Paul Hoko didn't really know a lot about former boxers (he thought 'Sugar Diabetes' was an American welterweight), but I considered myself to be a boxing historian then, and I still do. I said to Cervantes, 'Peppermint Fraser' and the joy in them was obvious. Alphonso 'Peppermint' Fraser (from Panama) was Cervantes' great rival. They knew then that I knew who this old looking guy was. The other two guys then gave me a hard luck story about Cervantes and I gave him a small amount of money. I still remember that and it makes me sad.

There was a fierce rivalry between Colombia and Panama and this fight was massive. Having said that, I can still remember the Colombians telling me that they did not think that Bassa had much of a chance, as Zapata had already defeated better Colombians than Bassa. Zapata had made twenty defences of his light flyweight and flyweight titles.

We ran with Zapata some mornings. He was a superstar and he had all the trappings of a superstar. He was dripping with gold jewellery and had a stunning blonde wife (or partner). He even had gold teeth. There was this welterweight in Spada's camp and he was due to box world rated Colombian, Thomas Molinares, on the Zapata/Bassa card. Molinares stopped this guy in four rounds and would go on to win the WBA world welterweight title against Marlon Starling. Anyway, the Spada camp used me for light sparring on the week of the fight to keep their boy sharp. The gym where we sparred was open to the public, and hundreds of Colombians crowded in to watch Zapata train and spar. There was seated around the ring (not chairs, but benches) just like in an arena. When I was sparring this guy, Alberto Lindo (I had to check Molinares record on the internet to get this guy's name), the crowd were going crazy rooting for me. Every time I landed, the crowd would be on their feet cheering and this light spar had all the energy of a title fight. The truth was that, the guy was just sparring light with me, and fair play to him, whereas I was going at full throttle (the more the crowd roared, the more I steamed in). I am lucky this guy didn't just knock me out, I am sure he could have. To be honest, the crowd was cheering for me, not because they liked me, but rather because they did not like him, or his country.

Mr Eastwood had to pay someone to mind our clothes in another gym in Colombia, as they would have been stolen. Even the boxers were begging Paul and I for t-shirts etc. And he also paid guys to spar us and there was even heavyweight boxers trying to say they were lightweights, so as they could spar us and get some money. I shouted to Mr Eastwood that I am not sparring anyone until they get their weight checked on the scales. I remember I sparred brilliantly in Colombia and more than held my own with them all. I recall after one spar, Paul Hodkinson saying to me that

I was brilliant. They were lining up to spar us. I also remember there was one gym that had no roof. Such was the level of extreme poverty, they were desperate for money and living with inadequate resources.

On fight night, Zapata lost his title in controversial circumstances. For eight rounds, Zapata was coping okay until some lunatic jumped onto the ring apron and punched Zapata, knocking him out. After a break of maybe, ten or fifteen minutes, the fight resumed and Bassa came on strong to win the decision and the title. After the decision was announced, there was a free for all in the ring and, as Zapata was led from the ring under a police escort, he was bombarded with all sorts of missiles as he made his way back to his dressing room. I had never seen anything like it (and if you do not believe me then go on YouTube and watch it). A few months later, they had a rematch in Panama and it ended in a draw. There were riots, which lasted for days, and it was headline news around the world. I remember thinking to myself at the time, 'Please God, bring me back to beautiful Belfast.' A couple of years later, Zapata came over to Belfast to help Dave 'Boy' McAuley get ready for a world title defence. I had left Eastwood then, but both John Breen and Paul McCullough (who coached Dave Boy after Eddie Shaw had died), told me that Zapata was incredible and they also told me that Dave Boy couldn't lay a glove on him.

The roughest and toughest guy that I was ever in the ring with, was a guy by the name of Hector Lopez. I have sparred over a dozen world boxing champions, some sparred hard like Barry McGuigan, Gabriel Ruelas (still an amateur then), Paul Hodkinson and others sparred light, like Antonio Esparragoza and Marcos Villisana. Hector Lopez sparred like I had mugged his mother! Lopez beat some good fighters including, Bernard Taylor, Juan La Porte and had lost a close decision in Australia against Kostya Tszyu (Tszyu said that Lopez gave him his toughest fight). When I went to Los Angeles, my first spar was against Olympic silver medallist and world rated featherweight, Hector Lopez. To be honest, I was a bit jet lagged and he got the better of the two rounds that we sparred. The next morning, Paul and I were having breakfast in the hotel, when coach Joe Goossen came by and he asked could he join us for breakfast. He then paid me the greatest compliment of my boxing career. He turned to me and said, 'Hector told me that you caught him a good shot yesterday.' Wow! I must have stunned him for Hector to say that to Joe. When you look at Lopez's career and the guys he boxed and would go on to box, he was never put down until his last fight against massive puncher Randell Bailey, then I was never paid a greater compliment. And with 16oz. gloves also.

One more thing about Los Angeles, was that Paul and I met Sylvester Stallone at the Inglewood Forum, on the night of the Pinango/Duarte fight. I still remember he had a brown v-neck jumper on and his face was shiny. I wondered, 'Did he ever get plastic surgery?' One morning, Paul and I also ran at the same spot where Rocky and Apollo Creed did their sprints in *Rocky 3*.

My fourth pro fight was in London (York Hall), a week after coming back from America/Panama/Colombia and I won every round against Telford's, George Jones, but hadn't the snap on my punches that I normally did. This could have been because I was still suffering from jet lag or it could have been because I was the lightest I had been in a few years, 9st. 5lb. I had aspirations of getting down to super featherweight as I was a light, light-weight. My fifth fight was on the undercard of Larne's, Dave 'Boy' McAuley's, challenge for the world flyweight title against Colombian, Fidel Bassa, at the King's Hall in April. I knocked out Tony Borg from Wales in four rounds.

The next month, I was off to Bellamadina in Spain for two weeks in the sun with my mates. Then Karen and I got a nice wee flat off the Clifton-ville Road and things couldn't have been better. I was 21 and everywhere I went in Belfast, I was getting asked for autographs and photos. Then, very unexpectedly, I lost to Hammersmith's, Andy Furlong, and I sank into a depression that lasted over ten years.

First Loss

I had been on a long winning streak, having previously won my last nineteen amateur contests. Things were going well for me, both inside and outside the ring. My sixth straight win as a professional came on 29 October 1987, when I hammered Swindon's Nicky Lucas, in three rounds. It was at the Ulster Hall and I had him down twice and the fight was shown on TV that night. It was an awesome performance. The next day, Karen and I went into town. As I walked around, the town people were pointing at me and shouting, 'Well done!' In addition, I signed quite a few autographs. Boxing was huge in Belfast then. It still is, hosting sell-out shows in the SSE Arena, Windsor Park and the Falls Park. Barry McGuigan had lost his world title the previous year, and was in a semi-retirement after an acrimonious fall out with Mr Eastwood. Nevertheless, there were still huge crowds that went to the Ulster Hall and the King's Hall when I boxed. That day in Belfast city centre, I spotted this boxing glove beanbag in Bannon's shop window and if my memory serves me right, it was £30. I thought that it would be lovely for the flat so Karen and I went in to buy it (and I still have it). Frank Bannon himself was in the shop that day and Frank loved his boxing and was best pals with Ardoyne's boxing hero, Freddie Gilroy, in fact, Freddie worked there, but I don't recall him being there that day. Anyway, Frank would not let me leave the shop and I was there for well over an hour drinking tea, signing autographs and chatting to the staff. Work came to a standstill (everybody loves a winner don't they). Everywhere I went, I was the centre of attention. Later, the Crumlin Star club officials asked me if

I would be available to present prizes to club members who had excelled in snooker, darts, etc. I also remember being in the Dockers club in Pilot Street (scene of where my dad was once shot) at a boxing show, and I was mobbed. My confidence was really growing and at long last, I was really starting to believe in myself.

My next fight was lined up for 3 December at the Ulster Hall with Dave 'Boy' McAuley boxing Panama's Roy Thompson. Dave Boy was having his first fight back after the titanic struggle for the world title against Fidel Bassa. Dave Boy had been in front on the scorecards after twelve rounds, but Bassa came on strong to stop Dave Boy in the fourteenth round. This fight was one of the last ever fifteen round fights and was voted fight of the year by *Boxing News* readers. Bassa was making the first defence of his title against McAuley and don't forget, I had seen Bassa win the title against Zapata in Colombia. This next opponent, Roy Thompson, had been one of Dave Boy's sparring partners, helping him to prepare for Bassa. My original opponent, Dougie Munro, pulled out two days before fight night and I think it was the day before the big show, that I remember Barney Eastwood pulling me aside at the final press conference to tell me that he had got me a guy at short notice. However, there were a few things he needed to run by me before he gave it the green light. Well, so he said.

He told me that they had been shopping around and it was not easy to get me an opponent and this was the only guy to take it. He said Andrew Furlong had only two losses in eighteen fights, but one of those losses was a second round stoppage defeat to Peppy Muir, who was one of Eastwood's boxers before going over to live in England. He was from East Belfast and was an undercard boxer and no more (so said Eastwood). Eastwood said to me that Peppy wouldn't go four rounds with me. I said, 'What are the other things you want to run by me?' He said, 'Oh, Furlong's a southpaw and a light welterweight.' I remember saying something like, 'Well if you're happy, then I'm happy', and added, 'Furlong's getting knocked out.' I had gone from having no confidence to being over-confident, as I now thought that I was unbeatable, untouchable even. Andy Furlong didn't weigh in on the day of the fight, as I and all the other boxers did; why was that? The *Boxing News* said the following week that he weighed in at 9st. 11lb., but I'm not so sure.

To be honest, looking back, I had a big problem with southpaws and I had not even been sparring southpaws whilst getting ready for this fight.

The previous week, I had been up to Belfast Zoo with Karen. On our way to the zoo, I had gone over on my ankle whilst showing off, doing a balancing act on the cribby, as we walked down the Westland Road. It was swollen and painful. Anyone with any sense would have gone straight home to get ice on it to get the swelling down, especially if they were a professional athlete with a big fight the following week. Sadly, I had no sense then and I walked on to the zoo, hobbled around it and got a taxi home and then I put ice on it, but it was too late, much too late. The damage had been done. I was head over heels in love with Karen and I didn't want to let her down by not going to the zoo, but I know Karen would have been telling me to turn back, forget the zoo, another time Eamon. I don't even think I wore an ankle support for the fight. The ankle went in the first round and in the video, which is on YouTube, you can see me stumbling and pointing to the canvas (that was my way of saying I have hurt my ankle). I knew right away that I could not put weight on it for punching power after that, as it was badly swollen. I know what you are thinking, 'Excuses, excuses,' but let me tell you this, Furlong might even have beaten me if my ankle was 100 per cent. He was a tall southpaw who, worse still, was a counter-puncher, the worst kind off southpaw. All I am saying, is my corner retired me at the end of the third round with a twisted ankle, as I could hardly stand. I had Furlong down and nearly out in the second round. I didn't quit.

The crowd booed, as there had been a few early retirements that night. It was ignominious and humiliating for me. My own people booing me. Two months previously, they had been stomping, cheering and singing, 'There's only one Eamon McAuley' when I knocked out Nicky Lucas. How fickle people are. It reminded me of when Jesus arrived at Jerusalem on a donkey and they threw palms at his feet singing, 'Blessed is he who comes in the name of the Lord, 'Hosanna in the highest'. A week later, they had him crucified. Barney Eastwood said to me, 'We live to fight another day.' But I was heartbroken.

In the dressing room afterwards, I remember being on my own. There were normally lots of well-wishers around after a good win. Dave Boy was on straight after me. My dad entered the dressing room. It was just him and me. We hadn't spoken in two years. I had to get away from that hell-hole in Holmdene Gardens to concentrate on my boxing. It was all down to his drinking. He sat down beside me and we talked. Then I broke down and he held me in his arms. As a dad myself now, and looking back, I can see how hard it must have been for him that night. Probably the hardest thing that he has ever had to do, to be there for me. And he was.

Andy Furlong would go on to take WBC super-middleweight boxing champion, Robin Reid, the distance.

My first professional defeat could not have come at a worst time. I was set to top the bill at the Ulster Hall in my next fight, but the defeat scuppered that and Andy Holligan took my place in topping the bill in a small hall show. Topping the bill would have been a dream come true for me and this was a very bitter pill for me to swallow. In fact, I was devastated, a broken man.

15

Some Tales from Barney Eastwood's Gym

When I was training and boxing in Barney Eastwood's gym in Belfast, from late 1985 until early 1988, I watched many world-class boxers and also some amazing characters come through the doors. One of them was a lad from Liverpool (now deceased), by the name of Keith Wallace. I remember watching him spar Roy Webb and Dave 'Boy' McAuley as they prepared for British title eliminators in February/March 1986. Keith had been having his way with them both, but as I watched, I noticed that Webb and McAuley had much smaller gloves on them and Keith's gloves were huge (I would say 16oz., maybe even 18oz.). I thought that this was unfair, as they were all about the same weight. So the next day, I mentioned to Keith that he can borrow my 12oz. gloves (I had 12oz., 14oz. and 16oz. gloves, as Mr Eastwood had given me a few hundred pounds with the training gear when I turned pro). Well. Keith looked at me with a real deadpan expression, and said softly, 'Do you want me to kill them?' and then walked on by. Moreover, Keith was way past his best then. Unfortunately, Keith, like a lot of us, never fulfilled his potential. He should have been a boxing legend. Sadly, alcohol got a grip on Keith and he died a young man, but this is one wee personal memory that I will remember. Rest in peace Keith – former ABA champion and Commonwealth professional champion.

One time, as I was waiting to go into the ring to spar in Eastwood's gym, John 'Rocky' McGranaghan came over and started to talk to me. I am sure it was Barry McGuigan I was about to spar. As I am trying to get focused and work out a game plan to tackle Barry, John turns to me and says, 'Eamon you know I touch for women in the town some weekends and I bring them back here to the gym.' A few of us, including me, had three keys to open the shutter at the bottom of the stairs, the door at the top of the stairs and one for the dressing room, where the showers etc. were. As I am stepping into the ring to spar Barry, John shouted, 'Eamon, it isn't just sparring that goes on in that ring.' John was implying that he was bringing girls back to the gym and having sex with them in the ring. I lost my focus thinking about what he said, and nearly got knocked out by Barry. What a character!

John McGranaghan threw himself over the Westlink Bridge on the Crumlin Road one time, in an apparent suicide attempt and went through the windscreen of a passing car, which just happened to be passing by. The car broke John's fall, but left John very badly injured. As luck would have it, this car was being driven by a top surgeon who was on his way in to work in the City Hospital. The surgeon escaped any damage when John came through his window and when John was taken to hospital, it was this same surgeon who performed life-saving wonders to save John. What are the odds? John started to follow God after this and would regularly be seen in the Mustard Seed Faith Hall singing and praising the Lord.

John was from the Shankill Road and was a big handsome guy, and either his mum or dad was Scottish, which gave him this lovely softly spoken accent. And, boy he could get the women. Sadly (once again), alcohol got a grip on John and his life took a downturn and he died a sad and ignominious death. I was at his funeral on the Shankill Road. I watched a big crowd come along Lanark Way from the Catholic Springfield Road to be at the funeral service. I remember feeling emotional at that moment when sport, especially boxing, had the power to unite both communities. I thought it was a beautiful moment when people of both faiths came together for John. Everybody loved John, and in life they tried to help him (and many did), but with alcoholics, they have to help themselves. Only they can change their destiny. And I know more than most, as alcohol killed my dad, and my brother.

I had been training in Eastwood's gym from just after Barry's first defence against Bernard Taylor. I was there for his second defence against Danilo Cabrera. I went down to Dublin for the Cabrera fight with the rest of Eastwood's fighters who were boxing in the big show. I wasn't boxing on the bill, but Mr Eastwood thought it would be a good experience to go anyway. We travelled to the venue in a van with 'Barry McGuigan's Official Van' printed on both sides and we were mobbed the whole way to the venue, with people banging the van and cheering and screaming, 'Here we go, here we go, here we gooooo.' They thought Barry was in the van but it was a decoy. Barry travelled behind us in an unmarked car with tinted windows. While everyone was hammering on our windows, Barry's car slipped into the venue unnoticed. In our van, everybody was quiet and nervous (especially Dave Boy as he got very nervous before a fight). Later that night, after Barry's harder-than-expected win against Cabrera, Mike Tyson's former coach, Teddy Atlas, sat at our table and was the centre of attention as he rattled on about Mighty Mike. Later, Mr Eastwood introduced me to some very important men in world boxing and told them I was the next Barry McGuigan. They were Roberto Duran's manager, Luis Spada, and top WBA official James Binns.

In April/May 1986, the world's media was in the gym to take photos of Barry, as Barry was preparing for his world title fight in Las Vegas against Fernando Sosa (who would later be replaced by Stevie Cruz). I was in the ring shadow-boxing but I was aware that all was not well, as Barry wouldn't come out of the changing room. Mr Eastwood was acting as a go-between with Barry and the media and he eventually came out of the changing room to tell the media (on Barry's behalf) that there will be no photos taken of Barry, but he then went on to say, 'But feel free to take photos of Eamon McAuley, who is in the ring shadow-boxing and who could well be the next Barry McGuigan.' I think the sticking point between Barry and the media was money, but the press all left straight after, which didn't do a whole lot for my confidence.

When Barry McGuigan and Mr Eastwood had an acrimonious breakup after Barry lost his WBA world featherweight title in June 1986, I took the opportunity to claim ownership of Barry's dressing room locker in the Castle Street Gym. I stripped off the white tape that had Barry McGuigan on it, and replaced it with white tape with my name on it. I didn't do his out of disrespect for Barry, I did it out of respect. Barry was my hero and I knew that he was not coming back. That really bothered me, as Barry was one of the main reasons I turned professional with Eastwood.

Barry used to come to the gym in Castle Street in Belfast with disguises on, such was his fame (Carl Frampton hasn't yet come close to Barry-mania). Barry would walk into the gym with a hat, sunglasses and a fake beard on. Honest to God. I witnessed this many times. I remember being in Eastwood's gym one time, and there was a kickboxer who had come up from Dublin for sparring. He was European kickboxing champion and that sounded huge to me, plus he had a team up with him and they all had this guy's name printed on the back of their sports tops. It looked very impressive. I was picked to spar this guy and I was a bit keyed up as he was the same weight as me, and I didn't want this kickboxer getting the better of me. I was representing my sport. I need not have worried a jot. This guy was no Conor McGregor that's for sure and I lay on him a vicious beating. He just about got through two rounds, but Eddie Shaw wouldn't let him come out for a third round. To be fair, the guy wanted to go on, but his face was covered with blood and I clearly remember Eddie Shaw saying, 'We don't let that go on in this gym.' I take it he meant one-sided sparring. To be honest, I should just have gone easy on him. It was wrong of me to unload on him and I am sorry I did. I was just like a bully (and I would claim to hate bullies). The guy was not great with his hands, but I am sure if we would have been using our feet, I would have been the one covered in blood. Eddie Shaw thought the whole episode was hilarious and he was trying his best not to burst out laughing (wicked sense of humour that Eddie Shaw had).

In late 1986, I was to fight in Sheffield and close to fight night, I was sparring Paul Hodkinson, when I got cut inside my mouth (my gums) and ended up getting six dissolvable stitches. That in itself was bad but then I got an abscess in my gums and tongue (little yellow pimples) and I couldn't eat anything solid, as the pain was too great. I remember Mr Eastwood ringing me up to see how I was and if I was fit for fighting and I couldn't even talk, all I could do was mumble. He couldn't even make me out and pulled me off the bill right away. A very similar thing happened when I was on the undercard of the big world title bill featuring Dave 'Boy' McAuley against Colombia's Fidel Bassa (about six months later) and again, I got cut inside my mouth and again, it was while sparring Paul Hodkinson (and I used to handle Paul easy enough). This happened about three weeks out from the big show and I wanted to pull out as I couldn't spar.

Sparring is so important, as it sharpens the reflexes and it's also good to build your stamina up, as it's the closest thing you can get to actual boxing. That's why I was so concerned, concerned enough to want to pull out. This time I was put under pressure to box, and I received a surprise visit (in the gym) from Mr Eastwood's son, Brian, who insisted I boxed on the undercard and started telling me how good his dad had been to me and how much his dad had done for me. I eventually relented under the pressure and boxed Tony Borg (without sparring for over three weeks) and after a slow start, I knocked him out in the fourth round. I remember bumping into Mr Eastwood later that evening, and he gave me a big hug and he seemed very happy (or relieved!).

I absolutely loved the sparring and the fighting, but I was not so keen on getting up at 7 a.m. to go for my morning runs (running four miles) or all that gym work. I did it though. I would run three days in a row then take the fourth day off (three days on, one day off). It was the Sheffield boxer, Herol Graham, who told me that this was his routine, so I copied him. I actually sparred the very skilful Herol Graham a few times. He was the number one contender for Marvin Hagler's undisputed middleweight title and I was a novice pro. He just used me for speed and I don't think he threw a punch in anger at me. He was impossible to hit to the head and I cut the ring off and chased after him, but it was like trying to catch a fly on a wall, so I just concentrated on whacking him to the body.

I am still friends with former world featherweight boxing champion Paul Hodkinson to this day. He was over in Belfast a few years ago and I brought him to a Cliftonville football club match. Then we had a lovely meal and a drink at the Europa hotel at the invitation of promoter Mark Dunlop, who was running a professional dinner/boxing show. I left early, as I know my limit with alcohol, but Paul and John Lowey (who was another world class boxer) headed round to Thompson's Garage nightclub, but Hoko had left his phone on and his partner heard him talking to women in Thompson's. The next day, I was to bring him to the airport but I slept in. He rang me from Liverpool that day and told me the story of what happened with the phone in Thompson's. He said that when he went home to Liverpool she was gone and had taken all her stuff. He then said that she went into his wardrobe and cut all his suits and shirts with a pair of scissors! Having said that, they are back together now, as I was over in Liverpool last year and I had a lovely meal and drink with them both.

I loved watching the boxers from Panama in the gym, boy could they do some tricks. They would hit the speedball (in rhythm) with their head and elbows and they could even lift their feet to hit it. Have you ever seen anyone skipping backwards? Well, some of them did, amazing. There was this guy called Jose Marmolejo, who would hit the heavy bag and he would almost limbo under it as the bag would be about two foot from the ground, and he did it effortlessly and with such grace. He was the No. 1 rated featherweight for Barry McGuigan's WBA title at that time. Mr Eastwood had a great connection with Panama and its boxers and coaches through Luis

Spada (who managed Roberto Duran). When Puerto Rico's, Wilfredo Gomez, turned professional after winning the world senior amateur title at seventeen, he based himself in Panama and in his TV documentary **Bazooka**, he said the reason for doing so, was because Panama had the world's best coaches. Gomez went on to be a three weight world boxing champion and made seventeen defences of his world super bantamweight title, winning them all by knockout. Barnardo Checka had been the No. 1 rated featherweight in the world in his boxing days but in 1985–1988 (before he got fat and lazy), he was an amazing coach in Eastwood's gym. Fabrice Benichou was the IBF world super bantamweight king and he was in the Castle Street Gym a couple of times and later, would fight Paul Hodkinson for the world featherweight title. So I take it Mr Eastwood had a connection or had options with Fabrice. I also remember Harry Robinson, an amateur coach from the Shankill, would bring two brothers down, Alan and Wayne McCullough. Alan would spar with Hoko and I and would turn pro only having three fights, but Harry would get in the ring with Wayne, who was only sixteen, and do the pads with him. Harry wore this big oversized foul protector and Wayne would be hitting the pads and hitting the protector, which covered Harry's whole body. We used to laugh at the site of this oversized jockstrap and some of the Liverpool lads took photos of each other while wearing it, but fast forward 30 years, and you will see that all the pro coaches are wearing them now while holding the pads for their boxers, while they switch from head to body. Harry was away ahead of his time. Harry's protector looked a bit different and I don't know if it was original to him but that's the first time we ever saw anything like that. And Wayne McCullough? Well, he went to two Olympic Games (1988 and 1992) and he won a silver in the 1992 Olympics before turning professional, winning the WBC bantamweight title in Japan in 1995.

I remember one Sunday around March/April 1986, and Dave 'Boy' McAuley and Roy Webb were due to top the bill at the Ulster Hall against Charlie Brown (Scotland) and Peter Harris (Wales) in the British title eliminators, and I was to make my pro debut on the undercard against Craig Windsor from Scotland. This particular Sunday, Barney Eastwood had arranged sparring, as he had brought in two sparring partners, Shane Sylvester and Rocky Lawlor, from England to spar Dave 'Boy' McAuley and Roy Webb. Webb and Dave Boy were from Larne, but Roy Webb didn't turn up and Mr Eastwood was furious and took his anger out on Roy's coach, Bobby McAllister. I had never seen Mr Eastwood so angry. Poor Bobby took a torrent of abuse, but he did fight his corner saying, 'What can I do? I can't go up to Larne and get him out of bed, he's a grown man and a professional and he should be here.' I felt sorry for Bobby, as he received the full wrath of Eastwood's anger, but he was right, it was not his fault. Mr Eastwood made the point that he was paying the sparring partners and they weren't getting used. Roy Webb was a real talent, but like me, he used to cut corners and when he boxed Peter Harris that night at the Ulster Hall, he ran out of steam (after building up a huge lead) and was stopped in the eighth round. Roy was never the same as a boxer when his brother Kenny died suddenly in 1986, as Roy and Kenny were very close and Kenny travelled everywhere with Roy. In fact, the sparring partner I mentioned earlier (Rocky Lawlor) came over in January 1987 and stopped Roy in seven rounds at the King's Hall, as Roy ran out of steam again (and Harris and Lawlor were his only defeats in eighteen fights).

Kenny Webb was a great boxer himself in his day and had gone to the Commonwealth Games in Edmonton in 1978. Kenny had a great sense of humour and was a practical joker. I remember being with him in Dublin when McGuigan beat Cabrera in a world title defence (Roy had a great knockout win that night) and later, in the hotel as a party was in full swing, Kenny pulled out his lung tester and I innocently enquired as to what it was and he gave me this spiel about having to blow into it and it would give you a reading as to what condition your lungs were in, but unbeknown to you when you blew into it, it shoots out black soot which once again unbeknown to you, covers your face. Well after washing my face, Kenny and I had a ball that night getting millionaires and VIPs to blow into the trick lung tester and Kenny would give them a fake reading, and they would walk away with black faces and we would quickly get offside and move on to the next victim. I never laughed as much in my life looking around the big room at all the black faces. It was such a tragedy and a shock when Kenny was taken from us in 1986. Rest in peace Kenny, my friend.

When Barney Eastwood signed Herol 'Bomber' Graham, Herol was the No. 1 contender for Marvin Hagler's undisputed world middleweight title. He was unbeaten in 38 pro fights and was the British and European middleweight boxing champion, having previously held the British, Commonwealth and European light middleweight titles. As an amateur, he was also an ABA champion. He was a precocious talent, no doubt about that. Herol's previous manager and coach, Brendan Ingle, had made a deal with Mr Eastwood and even though he was there in Eastwood's gym, he would have sat at the back of the gym, and it was Eddie Shaw who was in the ring with Herol showing him moves. The thing that struck me and is tattooed on my brain, was that Eddie was trying to change Herol's style. Eddie was trying to get Herol to be more aggressive and move his head more (roll underneath the punches, instead of using his fast feet or swaying out of harm's way, which was Herol's style). Barney Eastwood in his infinite wisdom thought that if he made Herol more aggressive, then Herol would be a more marketable boxer and sell out venues. Brendan Ingle must have been having palpitations at the back of the gym watching Herol turn into a Barry McGuigan clone (Ingle obviously still had some role in Graham's career). It was not just tweaks Eddie was making, it was a complete overhaul.

I had the privilege of watching some great coaches in my time but come fight night, I never listened to my coach in the corner. I didn't put a lot of importance on the coach. Maybe a good coach would be of importance in the gym or in the build-up of a fight, by way of getting you in great condition or putting you though circuits and stuff like that. I was impressed with Joe Goossen when I was in Los Angeles for a week in 1987, and I also watched Teddy Atlas and Brendan Ingle in the Castle Street Gym then later, I watched Eddie Futch while I was training with Wayne McCullough in the Holy Trinity gym in Turf Lodge in 1993. Goossen, Checka and Atlas were good motivators, while Eddie Futch had all that experience and knowledge (he was once on a Detroit boxing team with Joe Louis).

Larry Holmes, who I am a big fan of, says in his book, **Larry Holmes: Against the Odds** (Holmes, 1999), that all the trainers he knew well, and that includes Angelo Dundee, always liked to take far too much credit for the successes fighters had and none of the blame for their failures. Larry never once heard a trainer say 'it was my fault, I gave my fighter bad advice'. Every time Larry had a good round, his coach would say it was because he had followed his instructions and every time Larry had a bad round, it was because he hadn't followed his instructions. Larry swears there were plenty of times he knocked out an opponent doing what he had figured out by himself, and damn near got knocked out listening to a coach's advice. 'For most trainers it's heads I win and tails you lose' (Larry Holmes). I remember that Irish final in 1982 against Bill Nicholson, when my corner told me to go out there in the final round and up the tempo and take the fight to him, well this played into Billy's hands, as I was a counter-puncher then and was not used to being the aggressor, and lo and behold, I walked on to a haymaker from Bill. That was the only time my coach, Eamon Maguire was, not in my corner and that was the last time I ever listened to a trainer/coach. I trained myself for my last five professional fights and didn't have a coach.

Two more things I remember about Eastwood's Gym was that legendary SDLP politician Paddy Devlin loved his boxing and would call in to the gym regularly, and he and his son would often give me a lift home to Ardoyne. He was a lovely man. Also Barney Eastwood sometimes carried a gun with him and I witnessed this a few times. He would have a holster underneath his coat and the gun would be in the holster.

Difficult Times

Between 1988 and 1998, my confidence disappeared. I was to be on the undercard of Dave 'Boy' McAuley's rematch with Fidel Bassa at the King's Hall, in February 1988. I trained really hard for this, as I was coming off my first loss as a pro. I ran up the Cave Hill mountains with Sam Storey (three days on, one day off) and we did sprints in the Waterworks. Sam was a very fit guy, but I kept up with him. I was super fit and determined to get my career back on track. I had also moved down to super featherweight (9st. 4lb.) as for most of my fights I was 9st. 7lbs. or 9st. 8lbs., below the lightweight limit. But a week before the big world title rematch, Barney Eastwood pulled me off the show. He told me he was going to give me a rest since I had been going at it hammer and tongs since 1986. But why did he wait until a week before the show? I had put so much work in. I was devastated. What was he doing? What was he saying? I needed to come back with a vengeance after the loss. This was a new weight, a new beginning. On the walk home, coach, Bobby McAllister, and I were discussing the situation, when Bobby suddenly out of nowhere said, 'Why don't you retire?' I was a month short of my 22nd birthday. Why did he say this to me? Mr Eastwood had been getting Eddie Shaw more involved and Eddie was having a greater input in coaching me since my loss. Bobby was being phased out and Eddie was coming more to the fore as my coach. Bobby was being undermined. Was that why he asked me to retire? At 21!

It was Bobby who planted the seed by telling me to retire and mixed in with the anger of being dropped from the big show and my immaturity,

I started to give it serious consideration. But I had no other skill or trade. Then sometime later, Mr Eastwood rang me to ask if I would be interested in boxing Peppy Muir for the Irish lightweight title, as he was convinced that I would be too much for Peppy and thought it would be a good ticket seller. I explained to Mr Eastwood that my future now lay at super featherweight and with regret (looking back), I didn't take the fight. But I have a lot of regrets in my boxing career. I also thought that I was also getting my own back on BJ for pulling me out of the big show in February.

That was the last time I spoke to Barney Eastwood, until he came to the Rinty Monaghan statue unveiling, 28 years later, in 2015. But once again, I was only punishing myself. Shortly after this Peppy would take his own life and I drifted away from boxing. Karen had our first child, Ciarán, in October 1988. The day he was born, I went into town to get Karen flowers and as I was passing Eastwood's gym with a giant bouquet of blue flowers trying to look inconspicuous (anything but), I heard the window of the gym upstairs rapping and I looked up to see Eddie Shaw smiling and giving me the thumbs up. Eddie had fallen out with me and ignored me a few times, as I had stayed away from the gym for about six months (a place I had practically lived in for over two years). Eddie really believed in me and thought I had unfulfilled potential. Anyway I smiled back at him and gave him the thumbs up and went on my way up to the Royal Victoria Hospital on the Falls Road. That was the last time I ever saw Eddie Shaw.

Karen and I lived in our wee flat throughout 1988, which was another very bad year of the Troubles. I remember an incident that happened around the time, of a spate of ghastly murders starting with the murders of three IRA members in Gibraltar. At the funeral of one of these IRA members, Michael Stone killed three mourners. Then at the funeral of one of the mourners, two off duty soldiers drove into the funeral and they were shot and killed. Also an innocent Catholic was shot dead around the corner from my flat (Cliftonville Road) as Loyalists walked into his house and shot him dead, then sped off in a waiting car. All these incidents happened in less than a week and fear and hysteria were in the air.

It was to the backdrop of this that, Karen and I (who was pregnant with our baby, Ciarán) were asleep one night when my bell rang at 3 a.m. I jumped out of bed and opened my flat door but I was very concerned. The doorbell then rang again and I shouted, 'Who's there?' But no one answered. I started to get very worried, then the bell rang again, and I again shouted, 'Who's there?' and once again, there was no reply. So I walked along the hallway to the front door of the flats and the bell went again.

This time, I poked my head out quickly as curiosity got the better of me and the first thing I saw was the British Army across the street and I felt relief, but also anger. I thought to myself, 'Did these pricks ring my bell to wind me up?' Then the bell rang again and I looked to my left, and there was a man standing two feet away from me and I came out from behind the door and I said to him, 'What the fuck are you ringing my bell at 3 a.m. in the morning for, you fucking prick.' Obviously I was fuming.

As he walked towards me, I could tell that he was very drunk and he looked at me and said, 'What the fuck are you slabbering about?'

'Slabbering about', I said. 'Here' – wallop, 'have some of this', and I chinned him.

The army (whom I had forgotten about) then came over and I got the good cop, bad cop from them as one wanted to ring the police and let them handle it, and another one had compassion for my predicament. In no time at all, Karen was by my side and a neighbour, whose identity I will protect for her own reputation, came forward to say that she knew the man and he was looking for her flat (no mobile phones then). The soldiers helped the guy up and tended to his needs. It ended up that the guy had a car and he eventually got into the car and drove off (drunk as a skunk) in full view of the army foot patrol as Karen, myself and the neighbour went back into our flats.

On 8 August 1988, Karen and I were on our way back home after a visit into town, as we had been getting some baby stuff for heavily pregnant Karen. As I was driving down Alliance Avenue, a car came racing out of the Berwick Road and was being pursued by a hostile crowd, who were throwing bricks and bottles at the fleeing car as it came right towards me at high speed. I had to swerve left and mount the footpath to avoid the car crashing right into us. I could see the people in the car as it came towards me and one of them had a Glasgow Celtic football top on. The car had missed me by inches as it continued to speed up Alliance Avenue, as the baying crowd couldn't keep up. When I pulled over and spoke to people in the crowd, they told me that so-called Loyalists had shot two men dead in Etna Drive and were making their escape. I immediately went to talk to an RUC officer and told him what I had seen and I was able to give a clear description of the men in the fleeing car, but he dismissed my story and told me that the car the killers had used had been found burnt out in a Loyalist area, and the car I had nearly crashed into was of no concern to him. As you can understand, there was a lot of confusion and fear in the area at that time. What happened was a young lad called

Seamus Morris (eighteen) had been sitting on a wall on the Brompton Park/Etna Drive corner with some friends including his brother, Conor, when a car pulled up and young Seamus was shot dead. I knew Seamus to see and he was inseparable from his girlfriend and his brother. As the killers made their getaway, a lorry reversed out from the Highfield entry nearly blocking their path and a gunman got out of the car and shot the lorry driver, Peter Dolan, dead. Peter Dolan was not from the district and had just been making a beer delivery in the Highfield Club, just off Etna Drive. Loyalist gunmen, as usual, were looking for easy Catholic targets to murder, and these young men were just that (easy targets). Regarding the car that nearly crashed into myself and Karen, I was later told that there were two cars with Loyalist gunmen roaming the streets of Ardoyne that day. I was told that the car involving me had fired shots in and around the Farringdon Gardens area and there was reports that a fella had been shot, but the bullet had only grazed him and he was not badly injured. I had given the RUC my name and address that day, but I never heard anything from them regarding that incident, even though I could describe the Loyalists in detail. I am good friends with Conor Morris today and he has never recovered from witnessing the horrific murder of his teenage brother that day over 30 years ago.

Looking back, 1988–1989 were not great years for me. I had self-doubt and low self-esteem and I had got myself into a terrible rut. I didn't train. I didn't really do anything. I would go to bed around 4 a.m. and get up about 1–2 p.m. I had thrown my dream away of becoming a legendary boxer, like my great-uncle Rinty Monaghan, and spent two years wallowing in my own self-pity. God bless Karen, as she had to cope with my mood swings and a baby. I just spent those two years spending my money. I even got Karen to pack her job in at the Shamrock, because of my jealousy and insecurity. She still had a day job working in the town. I didn't spend my money on myself, I spent it on Karen buying her mostly stupid things. I did buy my first car in 1988 though.

After my one and only defeat, I sank into a depression. It didn't matter that the guy was heavier than me or that my defeat was by an unfortunate injury. I remember being in Eastwood's gym at a press conference just after my loss, and I smiled and said hello to a guy who would normally break his neck to get talking to me, but he snubbed me and was all over Paul Hodkinson and Andy Holligan. It nearly killed me. I felt hurt, shattered, betrayed and humiliated. It destroyed me! Looking back now, I am kicking myself, why did I let this sycophant get to me so much?

I was starting to lose my confidence and this was heightened when I joined a year's training course in my own area, to get close and reach out to lads around my own age, that I had gone to school with. I had a very hard time doing that. I was struggling so much that I felt inferior to these guys. From 1988 to 1995, I really struggled and looking back, I can clearly see it. I found it very hard to express myself and I couldn't even tell a joke in public, as I had very low self-esteem. Things came to a head when I worked in a youth club in Ardoyne called the Pop Bar which was a youth drop-in centre for fifteen to 25-year-olds. I was there two or three years and I was at my lowest ebb, when the boss, Michael Stevenson, asked me if I would be interested in doing a cursillo. It was God working through Michael Stevenson and the cursillo and all the amazing Christian people I have met over the years, that has given me my confidence back and praise the Lord for that.

I eventually came back to the boxing in 1989, when I signed for London promoter and my old coach and mucker, Harry Holland. I didn't have many options, as I had no trade or no skills. I was working on an ace scheme in Ardoyne at the time and Karen, Ciarán and I had moved back into the district, as we got our own wee house in Highbury Gardens. I went with Harry, as Harry used to be a great motivator and I felt at this time that my heart had gone out of boxing and maybe Harry could work his old magic on me, as he had in 1985, when I never lost a fight for Harry (nineteen wins), and won an NABC title and an ABA senior title with him and Hogarth. I had two pro wins while with Harry, Greg Egbuniwie (won on points) and Ricky Bushell (won RSC4) and I got cut for the only time ever against Bushell and received four or five stitches but the cut didn't bleed. A few times I flew over to box on Harry's shows and my opponents pulled out the day before the fight or the day of the fight. It's a nightmare when this happens, as all the training and effort has been for nothing and I was also out of pocket because I had to fly over and back (Harry did cover the cost a couple of times).

I remember one fight that fell by the wayside, was when I was scheduled to be on the undercard of Nigel Benn's fight with Marvin Hagler's half-brother, Robbie Simms. I was to box a guy called Peter Gabbitus. The fight was to be at an agreed weight and for the first time as a professional, I was unprofessional. I came in 3lbs. overweight. As I remember, this fight fell over a holiday period (could have been on St Patrick's) and the gym, where I trained in Belfast, was closed so I couldn't train. I did some running though instead and trained in Harry's gym the night before the fight (light training) and got my weight checked and was something like 2lb. over-weight. It was a wee bit of a concern but I thought, 'I will dry out and I will be fine.' The weigh-ins in those days were on the day of the fight and not the day before, like they are now. I made a big mistake the night before, at Harry's house, when I had a wee sip of juice just to take the bad breath away, but I was shocked when I stepped on the scales and I was 3lb over the weight. My opponent was just under the weight. An argument ensued with my coach suggesting to Gabbitus's coach that I would try to skip some weight off. I said, 'There's no way I could skip three pounds off.' Harry then said to them that he would pay them extra money if they still took the fight. They refused. Harry didn't need this bullshit, as he was co-promoting the whole show, which was being televised by ITV. This was Mickey Mouse stuff for him and this was my fault as I had come in 3lb over the agreed weight. Gabbitus's coach said it was unprofessional of me to come in over the weight and that their boxer had made the effort to make the agreed weight. He was right. Harry once again offered them more money, but they said no and that was that.

The fight was off. It had cost me money to fly over and back and two months hard training had been for nothing, as I wouldn't be getting paid, but I had no one to blame but myself. To be fair, Harry gave me money to cover the cost of my flights. I had been looking to put on an awesome display, to get myself on TV. The weigh-in was at the famous Thomas 'A' Beckett gym (I had trained there before) and as I am sitting in the gym (feeling sorry for myself), who is standing right beside me but 'Marvel-lous' Marvin Hagler. I instantly forgot all my troubles and rushed into the toilets to get my camera ready for a photo with Marvin and me and as I am fiddling about with the camera, it slips though my hands and falls and smashes all over the ceramic floor. The thing was, it was not even my camera, it belonged to my brother Paul's girlfriend Lillian. I had to buy her a new camera. Things were not going my way but I ran back out to the weigh-in and plucked up the courage to approach Marvin, but I hadn't picked a very good time, as his brother was just stepping onto the scales. I can clearly remember what I said. I rattled on about being a pro boxer and I told him I was boxing on the undercard (which I was not now). I told him that I rated him the third greatest middleweight of all time, behind Harry Greb and Sugar Ray Robinson (I'm sure Hagler saw himself as the greatest middleweight). Marvin turned round to look at me full on the face and he gave me the same stare that he gave Alan Minter and Tommy Hearns and then he spoke to me, he said, 'I am busy man.' That was it, that's all he said. It just was not my day. Harry Holland asked me did I want to stay and go to the show that night, but I said, 'Harry, I just want to go home.' I felt like saying, 'Never mind the weigh-in, where's the weigh out?' (way in, way out). When I got home, I ended up having a row with Karen and we went to bed not speaking. No romance after a week of abstaining from sex. What a day. Harry Holland rang me the next day and said, 'Eamon, you should have stayed because after the boxing finished Hagler, Simms and I and their team went out for a lovely meal and a drink and Marvin was in great form!' If I had have stayed, I would have been with them as I was staying with Harry. Another big regret!

Two of my mates loved that story about Hagler. Even now, 27 years after it happened, my friends, Neil Sinclair and Seán McNulty (a former Irish junior champion), would reply if I texted them asking to meet up, 'I am busy man.' I broke Neil's nose in sparring one time at the Holy Family club. It was in 1994, the year he went to the Commonwealth Games (I am not sure if it was before or after the Games). I do remember catching him with a powerful right that landed flush. I knew right away that I had done damage. I stepped back, as Neil was on the ropes and the blood was just gushing from his nose. Neil and I sparred many times, but I think that was the last time we sparred. Neil was only about eighteen or nineteen at the time, but he was heavier than me and even then, he could really bang. I had to be on my toes and on my game with Neil. I would never rush in with Neil (which I loved to do, trying to knock everyone out). I moved, I boxed, I feinted, trying to get him to lead so as I could counter. You had to be smart with Neil and I could be a smart counter-puncher when I wanted to be. I was not just a one-trick pony. But to be honest, I would rather be aggressive and throw bombs. I didn't want to be a boring counter-puncher. Neil Sinclair would win a Commonwealth gold as an amateur and a British title as a pro, as well as winning the Lonsdale belt outright by making three successful title defences. Neil also boxed for the WBO welterweight title.

Around 1989–1992, I had lost a lot of weight as I was now a full-blown veggie and I weighed about 9st, 2lb (before I became veggie, I weighed around about 10st 2lb). I didn't eat red meat, white meat (chicken and fish) and eggs (veggies can eat free-range eggs, I didn't). I was not in the gym that much around that time (only one or two fights). When I did train, it was in the Holy Family ABC where Gerry Storey would let me spar with his amateur boxers Neil Sinclair, Billy Boyd, Seamus McCann and Johnston Todd. I must give credit where credit is due, and say that I had trained in the Holy Family (on and off) for eight years and Gerry Storey never asked me for one pence in dues (and I appreciate that), but regarding the sparring, it was just as beneficial for Gerry's boxers to spar me and that worked both ways. I handled Neil Sinclair and Billy Boyd handy enough, but Seamus was a southpaw and I would never shine against southpaws, but regarding orthodox boxers, then I dominated them all. I can't think of any orthodox boxers who got the better of me from featherweight to welterweight. I dominated, or at the very least held my own with, boxers from all over Britain and Ireland.

I remember I used to spar Johnston Todd who was an Ulster and Irish senior champion and he had joined the Holy Family club from Ballyclare ABC. Gerry Storey used to make me do two rounds with a lighter fighter, then two rounds with a heavier lad. Johnston was only a bantamweight, but he was a tough kid who had power in both hands. Johnston was also a southpaw, but an aggressive one, and not the kind of southpaw who made me look silly - the counter-punching type. I found Johnston to be an easy spar and I should have just gone easy on him, as he was a nice quiet fella who put me in mind of Sonny Liston (he hardly talked and hardly smiled). The coaches in the club and the men who used to come to the club to chat and gossip, would be drooling over Johnston as he was the talk of the town as he had knocked out Jim Conlon, Roy Nash, Joe Lawlor and many others and this was just before Johnston lost in the Ulster and all Irelands to Wayne McCullough (who many Holy Family men fancied Johnston to beat).

To be brutally honest, I was a bit resentful of some Holy Family coaches and supporters, as these were the same people who used to drool over me and now, I would just get a nod or a hello and that was all. I would take my frustration and resentment out on Johnston and instead of sparring light with him, I would hammer him and lay into him and I knew that I was hurting him, but I wouldn't let up (shame on me). He would only do two rounds with me, then I would do another two rounds with someone heavier, like Boyd or Sinclair, but whenever Gerry Storey used to say, 'Right Johnston jump in and do two rounds with Eamon.' I would look at Johnston and would see his face drop and I knew deep down, that he didn't want to spar with me. I first got to know Johnston when the Sacred Heart ABC used to go up to Ballyclare and I remember Johnston used to have three or four brothers who boxed and their mum and sisters would be there squealing and shouting when they boxed. The last time I saw Johnston was in Ardoyne, and he was working on a building site and was driving one of those dumper trucks and we chatted for a short period, as Johnston was uncomfortable talking. Johnston was a heavy drinker, who drank himself to death in his late twenties/early thirties. I liked Johnston; he was a nice fella and would have made a great professional boxer. Boy could he punch. Rest in peace my friend and sparring partner.

I remember I had flown over to London to box, and my opponent pulled out the night before the fight and Harry was scrambling around trying to get someone to fight me. If my memory serves me right, it was my first comeback fight with Harry after being out of the ring for nearly three years. Harry said to me that a kid from Manchester was prepared to fight me and he told me his pro record, which was a bit patchy, and he also told me that he had lost his last fight, but lucky for me, I knew my boxing and I said to Harry that the guy who was prepared to box me (Paul Burke) lost a British title eliminator in his previous fight to Tony Richards and he only lost it by one round (Burke would go on to win the British title). I said, 'Harry I am not ready for a fight like that yet.' The next week Burke's coach, Phil Martin, contacted the **Boxing News** to tell them that they were up for the fight and I wouldn't take it. The story said, 'We offered Eamon McAuley a 6x3 round fight, but McAuley's camp were not keen on it.' Then Harry Holland contacted Sheffield's Brendan Ingle, to see if he had anyone for me. Brendan knew me from Barney Eastwood's gym and knew that I was a good fighter and Brendan told Harry that he had this guy, but he has only had a few fights and he's a bit of a novice and would I take him the full six rounds without hurting him (I was in the same room as Harry and was listening to this conversation). Harry turned round to me and explained that there was a kid and he was only a novice and would I carry him for six rounds and I said, 'Tell Brendan to fuck off.' I wasn't falling for that bullshit and I was surprised that Harry was. It was probably Prince Naseem Hamed or Junior Whitter. I knew Brendan Ingle was an Irish hustler with the gift of the gab. Maybe he remembered that my grandad, Harry McAuley, knocked his brother John out in two rounds and was seeking revenge. I ended up boxing a guy from Hackney called Greg Egbuniwie and I beat him over six rounds, knocking him down twice in the second round, but I couldn't finish him. I was exhausted as I wasn't fit. I think this was my worst performance ever, but at least I shed nearly three years of ring rust. In the crowd that night cheering his head off for Egbuniwie was Kirkland Liang, who once beat Roberto Duran.

Barry Hearn

I never heard a thing from Barry McGuigan until 1991, when he rang me (he got my number off someone). He said that when he was at boxing shows in London or wherever, people would bring my name up from time to time. He said to me, 'Why are you not boxing?' He asked me what was I doing with my life and I replied, 'Not much.' I was still on the yearly ace scheme, which taught you skills and trades. Barry sounded excited and passionate and he said, 'You could be a fucking world champion.' He told me he could fix me up with Barry Hearn, and asked would I be prepared to give the boxing another go. He said that I would have to be prepared to come over to England, to be based the way Ballymena's Eamonn Loughran was, but I told him I had a partner and a two-year-old son and that was not possible. He then asked would I be prepared to come over a few weeks before my fights to get the best coaching and sparring. He said it's all there in Romford and there was a big house where the boxers stayed, Barry Hearn's office was next door to it and the gym was just across the road.

I agreed, after talking to Karen, and started to get myself fit. I went to Paddy Fitzsimmons' Dockers gym in Belfast and was very well looked after. Paddy had been to the 1964 Tokyo Olympics and had beaten Ken Buchannan as an amateur (and what a win that was). I sparred against amateurs, but light-welters and welters. I sparred Steven McCloskey and Eddie Fisher, among others. I also sparred great stylists like, Joe Lowe and Mark Winters, which brought out the best in me and I handled them handy enough (I once sparred Joe Lowe in Eastwood's gym on Christmas day

1986). I trained at Paddy's gym for two months and got into great condition, as I thought this was my last chance with the boxing and I didn't want to let myself or Barry McGuigan down. I went over to Romford a whole month before my fight. I thought it was too long. I missed Karen and my son, Ciarán, and I also missed Ciarán's third birthday, but these are just some of the sacrifices that you have to make if you want to be successful. I understood that.

Eamonn Loughran looked after me in Romford. He said to me that if I had 75 per cent left of what I had in Eastwood's gym, then I would still be head and shoulders better than the motley crew that was available in Barry Hearn's gym. He said there was one or two guys that he rated, Carl Crook was one, Michael Ayers and Herbie Hide, were two others. When I arrived in Romford, I left my stuff in the house where the boxer's stayed (it was two houses knocked into one big house). The place stank, with training gear hanging everywhere to be aired and boxers at the house tended to go to the laundrette every three days to get them washed and freshened. Someone in the big house told me that Barry Hearn was over in the gym across the road, so I headed over there. As I entered the gym, Carl Crook was there. We hadn't seen each other in six years when I won the ABAs and broke his nose. Carl was a British and Commonwealth champion now and was down preparing for a European title challenge in Italy. He was big-time now, but that didn't stop him from rushing straight over to me and giving me a big hug. Barry Hearn said that he would have a one-to-one meeting with me in his office later that day (after I get myself sorted and settled). But there was no sign of my mate Eamonn Loughran. I enquired about Eamonn to the lads in the gym, asking did they know where he was.

They looked at each other. Then they told me that Eamonn and heavyweight Herbie Hide had an altercation earlier and that's why Barry Hearn was there (and I thought he was there to greet me). What happened was, words were exchanged between the two of them and Herbie decked Eamonn. Well Eamonn's much smaller than Herbie and he knew that it would be silly to get involved in a punch up, so Eamonn left and returned two minutes later with a hurling stick which he had bought prior to this incident. Eamonn made his way to the gym (hurling stick in hand), but they could see him coming and they locked the doors to prevent Eamonn from entering. After much mediation, Herbie and Eamonn calmed down and eventually shook hands. An hour later I arrived. Later that day, I had my meeting with Barry Hearn in his office, which was next door to our accommodation. Barry McGuigan had been telling Hearn how good a boxer

I was, and Hearn had sorted Harry Holland out with a few quid to free me from my contract to Harry, which meant I could now sign a new three-year contract with Barry Hearn, which I did. As soon as I had signed and before the ink had dried, Hearn told me how much he would be paying me for a 6x3-minute round contest up in Cardiff in four weeks' time. It was not huge money. I then said that I am fit enough to box 8x3 minute rounds and asked how much he would pay me for that. His reply caught me off guard, he said, 'You will box for what I fucking tell you to box for McAuley.' I was really scundered and went bright red. What a cheeky, ignorant so and so, I thought.

Later, I told Eamonn Loughran what Hearn had said and Eamonn said that was just the way Hearn was, but he was okay when you get to know him. Eamonn then said that Hearn was just testing me, as he had done with him. Eamonn had been living in Romford for over a year and Hearn paid him a weekly wage that he could live on and his boxing money was separate. I ran with Eamonn in the mornings and Eamonn was amazed that I could keep up with him (the first time we ran, he tried to run me into the ground). He said that Steve Collins and Neil Sinclair were also good runners and that they were the only two that could keep up with him (now make that three). This boosted my confidence. We were allowed to go to the exclusive Romford snooker club (if my memory serves me right it was beside the gym or above the gym) where I was introduced to the former six-time world champion snooker player Steve Davis. Steve said that he was a big boxing fan and Eamonn Loughran told me that Steve was a fan of Carl Crook. It was Eamonn who introduced me to Steve Davis and Eamonn said to Steve, 'Steve, this is Eamon McAuley. He knocked Carl Crook out in two rounds and broke his nose in three places.' I said to Steve, 'And I'm barred from those three places' (joking). I also went over to the gym to watch Nigel Benn train. He trained at 9 a.m. which was strange. I would pop over after my run, then go back to bed for a few hours before training, then dinner, which we had to buy and cook and then over to the snooker club again. Graham Moughton introduced me to Nigel, who was really friendly (nothing like the angry guy I always saw on TV). I told Nigel that I had won the ABAs in 1985, the year he had lost in the London semi-final (at York Hall) to Rod Douglas. Benn avenged that loss in 1986, going on to win the ABAs that year.

A week later, I went to Nigel's fight against Lenzie Morgan and Nigel had to have a big last round to win a split decision. I remember I sat with Michael Ayers that night, and he told me that he was going out with an Irish girl. Both Eamonn Loughran and Herbie Hide boxed in Germany during my stay in October 1991 and both won. Herbie was a bit of a bully, but just like a typical bully, he backed off when Eamonn Loughran put it up to him. However, they came back from Germany with respect for each other and Eamonn went back home to Ballymena for a short break, leaving me with a crowd of strangers. Before Eamonn left, I had sparred him and he was full of praise for me. 'You still got it kid. You still got it,' he said. I also sparred with Paul Harvey, Ojay Abrahams, Tim Driscoll and Michael Ayers (Jim McDonnell who ended Barry McGuigan's career, gave us a standing ovation at the end of the spar). I did really well in sparring and the coach, Graham Moughton, was very impressed. McGuigan had told Graham to keep me and Floyd Havard apart in sparring. When I was in Romford, Barry McGuigan came down one weekend to bring me up to his place and I stayed over. It was in Faversham, Kent. I remember it so well. That night Barry, his wife, Sandra, and I sat in front of a big open fire and Barry said that he was going to show me the greatest movie ever made – **Pretty Woman**. He loved it and we sat there and watched it.

Another memory I have, is of Frank Bruno ringing Barry to ask him for a lift up to Wales. Barry's landline phone was in the hall and I was in the living room, but I could hear Barry talking to Frank. We were going up to Cardiff the following week and Barry and Frank were going in a working capacity (Eurosport I think). Herbie Hide and Floyd Havard were joint top of the bill. Anyway Barry was all subservient, 'Yes Frank, that's no problem Frank, anything for you Frank. It would be a pleasure Frank.' Then he said his goodbyes to Frank and walked into the living room. He looked at me and said, 'Do you know who that was?' Acting daft, I said, 'No who was it?' And he said, 'That was Frank Bruno,' I replied, 'Never.' Barry then said 'I can't believe that guy, he wants me to go and pick him up next Saturday and drive him up to Wales, can you fucking believe that? He is one fucking lousy fucker.' I remember thinking at the time, 'Barry you're one two faced so and so,' (joking). Listen, anybody who says they haven't done the same thing some time in their life is a liar. Some people do it every day. Bruno did have a reputation for being very lousy and mean with money. I remember former manager, Harry Holland, telling me how tight Frank Bruno was with money. In fact, I remember when I stopped Ricky Bushell in four rounds at Battersea, seeing with my own eyes Frank running after Harry shouting, 'Arry, Arry I had to pay in at the door just now, sort it out 'Arry.' Frank had met his match in Harry though, as Harry was running away from Frank shouting, 'I am busy Frank, I am busy. I will sort it out later.' I asked Harry later when I was back in his house, 'Did you sort Frank out?' And he laughed and said, 'No I fucking didn't.'

As Barry was taking me back to Romford, he was driving at high speed and I was a bit concerned as he was doing over a hundred miles per. hour. I knew that Barry used to drive rally cars, but suddenly, right out of the blue a 'road closed' sign came up, and this was the road that we were going to take and Barry had to slam on the brakes, as metal fences were situated across the road to prevent anyone from driving down that road. I remember we swerved and skidded around and ended up with the car facing the opposite way we were going. It had been a close call. We were both shaken up and Barry tried to joke it off. Thinking back to that incident over 26 years ago, it's hard to remember all the facts, but I remember Barry kept going back and doing handbrakes trying to tell me he was always in control, maybe he was, but he was in a cold sweat. And I remember thinking, 'But why do you have to drive so fast giving yourself less time to react?' But I said nothing to him. I might have ended up in a pub quiz question, 'What was the name of the other guy in the car who died with world boxing champion Barry McGuigan in a car crash in 1991?' Thank God that we didn't crash and die.

That night when I was back in Romford, I rang Karen and she gave me devastating news. She told me that Hugh Magee had been shot dead. Hugh was a good friend of mine. Hugh was a taxi driver and as he slowed his taxi down to go into Rosapenna Street, Loyalist gunmen walked up and shot him dead at point blank range. He had passengers in the taxi and it was an awful ordeal for them. Hugh would never charge me when I was in his taxi, so what I used to do, was give him boxing videos of all the top boxers past and present (Hugh and his brother Jim were very good boxers for St Gabriel's as juveniles) and he would talk about them with glee when I next seen him. Hugh had one child, a boy, and the young lad went badly off the rails with the loss of his dad. I know everybody says nice things when someone dies but Hugh really was a gentle, gentleman. Rest easy Hugh, my friend.

On the way up to Cardiff to box Kelton McKenzie, I shared one of Barry Hearn's stretched limos with Herbie Hide (who was top of the bill), coach, Freddie King and in the front, Barry Hearn and driver Robbo. There was a built-in TV in the back for us to watch but Herbie and I hardly said a word as we were keyed up for our fights (which were being televised live). We stayed in the Holiday Inn and we were on the same floor as the All Blacks rugby team. The Rugby World Cup was being held in Cardiff at the time (1991). I remember they were approachable, accessible and very friendly.

During our stay, stars from TV's **Neighbours** visited the All Blacks and they were hugging and kissing and I was there in the middle of them. Mrs Mangle, who was my favourite character from the Australian soap, was not there, but two or three of the top actors, who I instantly recognised, were. I regret not going out and buying a rugby ball for the All Blacks to sign their names on it. The All Blacks were the favourites that year, but Australia won it (only beating Ireland by a point in an earlier match). I weighed in and on the night, after the show had got underway, I got the news that I didn't want to hear – my opponent had pulled out.

A crowd had come down from Manchester to cheer me, on including my brother Paul who had been working there. I know why the guy pulled out, but I can't be 100 per cent sure. Kelton McKenzie's brother, Tony, who was a former British champion, was training with me in Romford and he knew how good I was. He watched me sparring and was there with Carl Crook the day I arrived. He had heard all about me. Well I think Tony has rang his brother Kelton and told him how good I was. But, I wondered, 'Why leave it so late to pull out?' Although the fight didn't happen, I was glad to see my brother and I remember Barry McGuigan telling me that South African boxing legend, Brian Mitchell, was in the house and he pointed to where he was. Mitchell was over for the Rugby World Cup and saw a poster about the boxing show and on a whim, decided to come along. He was one of my boxing heroes and hadn't long retired (in fact he came back for another couple of fights after this). Mitchell had only one loss (twice avenged) in 49 fights and made thirteen defences of his WBA world super featherweight title. The amazing thing was, he made all thirteen defences in his opponent's backyard (country). Because of apartheid, Mitchell, a white guy, couldn't defend in his own country. Before I rushed over to speak to Mitchell, I remember Barry saying to me that he found him a bit cocky, he was not - he was drunk! I remember telling him that my opponent had pulled out and would he fill the void, as we were both super featherweights, he laughed and he was happy to pose for a photo with me. He was in a fun mood and when I jokingly asked him if he would box me, he started to shadow box. Only the hard core boxing fans would have picked him out, and I think that he was pleased that I recognised him and we chatted for a while.

After the show (Herbie won by stoppage), we had a meal at the invitation of co-promoters (two Welshmen - Kevin Hayde and Dai Gardner) with Barry Hearn being the main promoter. It was a fascinating experience to be in Hearn's company as he was some character, as well as a self-assured, self-absorbed, cocky and arrogant so and so. Hearn told me that I would be boxing the following week on a televised show, but I told him that I needed to go home to see my loved ones. I told them that I would come back the day before my proposed bout, but the truth was I knew that I was not coming back. I had my fill of boxing. I had been terribly homesick for four or five weeks. A very dear friend had been murdered while I was away and I couldn't even attend his funeral and all this to no avail, as my opponent pulled out and I only got a third of the money. I was fuming about that, as I had done everything asked of me including being under the weight. That, and Barry Hearns' cheeky attitude, were the final straw for me.

A week or two after that, I went over to Rusholme in Manchester and stayed with my brother, Paul. I worked with Paul, for a guy called Paul Doherty, formerly from Ardoyne, from late October until a couple of days before Christmas. We worked nightshifts seven days a week and I came home with a good few quid for Karen. Eamonn Loughran would go on to become a world champion and after he retired from boxing, he became quite a successful businessman. Eamonn is a Christian and a lovely guy who I still keep in touch with and a few years ago, him and I carried a banner around Belfast city centre at a pro-life rally attended by over a thousand people.

I tried another comeback in 1993, with Belfast promoter Owen McMahon, and boxed at the Ulster Hall against Salford's Russell Davidson. This was five-and-a-half years after I last boxed in Belfast, against Andy Furlong at the same venue. I had become a full-blown veggie a few years earlier and was losing out on a lot of vitamins, but hadn't the intelligence to subsidise by getting these vitamins from other products. I was not even taking vitamin tablets. I hadn't the sense to realise that as an athlete, I was losing vital vitamins. Where was I getting protein, calcium, iron etc. from? I lost my strength, I lost my power and as I was not knocking them out any more, I lost my friends. I can look back on old videos of me boxing then and I am shocked how skinny, how weak and how unhealthy I looked and I think to myself, 'How did it take me so long to realise what I was doing to my body?' However, I did beat Russell Davidson over six rounds in a half decent fight.

The following night, I was at 7 p.m. Sunday Mass in the Holy Cross Church in Ardoyne and right out of the blue, Fr Kenneth Brady said, 'There is a young lad sitting here tonight who has won his tenth professional boxing contest in the Ulster Hall last night. His name is Eamon McAuley and I think he deserves a round of applause.'

And everyone started to clap. This never happens in Mass. I didn't know where to look or what to do. Everybody was looking at me and clapping.

This was 1993, when there would be a good crowd at Mass, unlike nowadays, where numbers have declined. I never expected Fr Kenneth to do this, but I have a good idea why he did it, and why he wanted to give me a heads up. The previous night, I had stood in the rain with my holdall (containing my boxing gear) on my own, waiting for a public black taxi to take me down to the venue (or as close to the venue as the taxi went). As I was waiting in the rain in Balholm Drive waiting on a taxi, my aunt Kathleen came over to talk to me. Kathleen was not my real aunt, but her husband, Owen O'Kane, was my mum's cousin and we grew up calling her Auntie Kathleen. She was great pals with Fr Kenneth. She knew that I was boxing that night and she wished me good luck. I joked with her that a few years previously, I had someone to carry my bag for me and I had a team around me with friends busting to drive me to the venue. Maybe she felt sorry for me? Maybe she thought that it was ignominious or humiliating that I was standing in the rain waiting on a public taxi, on my own? I really think that she mentioned this to Fr Kenneth, but I am not sure if she told him to give me the heads up, maybe that was Fr Kenneth's idea?

I had two more pro fights after the Davidson fight. In June 1993, I beat Peter Buckley on a card topped by Wayne McCullough and that was held in the Maysfield Leisure Centre. Legendary coach, Dean Powell, bandaged and taped my hands that night and was in my corner. Dean tragically took his own life a few years later. Then I boxed Colin 'Kid' McAuley at the King's Hall on the same bill that my great friend, Eamonn Loughran, topped, successfully defending his WBO world welterweight title. I won both those contests on points, but once again, I was very light and very weak. I was then lined up to box again on the undercard to one of Eamonn Loughran's WBO world title defences. This time I was lined up to box 10x3 minute rounds for the Irish lightweight title against a guy that I had already beaten in my previous fight - Kid McAuley. I trained very hard, as the most I had ever boxed was 6x3 minute rounds. This was my first title fight as a professional and as I had beaten this guy clearly in my previous fight, I thought that it was a handy one for me. I wanted to put on a better display this time though, as I hadn't impressed in my previous three fights. About a week before the big show the whole thing was cancelled, and I am sorry I can't remember why. And that was that for me. I packed it in. This sort of thing had happened to me too often. It was a sickener.

With my dreams of boxing success and my professional boxing career now over, I had to find other ways of making a living.

Security Consultant (Bouncer)

I started to do the door aged 26. I started in the Manhattan Bar in Bradbury Place in Belfast, under Terry Johnson, and the Eglantine Inn (nicknamed the Eg) on the Malone Road, under Jim McDonnell. Ciarán McGuigan was the manager in the Manhattan, and Gerard Deery was the manager of the Eglantine. They were both fighting for my services and they were both pals with each other. Ciarán McGuigan was a big boxing fan. I usually worked two nights a week in each. But sometimes I got more nights in the Manhattan, as I couldn't say no to my boss, Tony Agnew. Sometimes I was working seven nights a week. Down the years, I have done the door in many places. I have come through knife fights, bottle fights, death threats, court cases etc. I have been called a Fenian bastard. I have even been called an Orange bastard. Two guys got shot dead in places I had just left, doorman, Seamus Dillon (Glengannon) and Edmund Treanor (Clifton Tavern). Bill Gilmore (doorman) got shot in the stomach the night Edmund Treanor got killed, but he survived. Bill died shortly after this, and his family believe the shooting accelerated his death. It was me that got Bill started in the Clifton Tavern, as I told the manager Peter McGrath that I needed another doorman.

When I first started doing the door in the Manhattan, we would wear blue jackets with white shirts, black trousers and blue dickie bows. In the Eg, we would wear cream coats, white shirts, black trousers and red dickie bows. We were like ice cream salesmen. Loyalists from the Donegal Road tried to muscle in at the Manhattan (when I started there it had just opened and it was the place to be). Many a night, we had to pull the shutters down as they tried to muscle in and they threatened to come back and shoot us. The same crowd would later murder a Protestant girl called Margaret Wright, thinking that she was a Catholic girl. They cut her throat in a late night shebeen (illegal drinking den, bar/club). Two of the Loyalists, Elliott and Hamilton, were murdered by other Loyalists shortly after this (one the next day) for killing the girl. I doubt if they would have been killed, if the girl was a Catholic. Indeed, a Catholic girl from County Armagh had her throat cut (and killed) in the same area around that time, as she too had been in a late night Loyalist shebeen, but no action was taken against those men.

One night, Mickey Mooney (a well-known drug dealer) turned up at the Manhattan and issued a threat. I was working in the Manhattan that night, but I was upstairs and not on the front door (I am too small for the front door). The boys on the front door told us later that Mooney said to them, 'You all know what I do lads, you do your job and let me do mine.' And he opened his coat to show them a UZI sub machine gun. None of the doormen spoke to him and he then left. What he was saying was, that he was going to have guys inside and maybe outside, selling drugs so just ignore it. When he said, 'You do your job,' well, our job is watching out for anything like that going on (especially in the toilets) and throwing the scumbags out. A few months later, he was the first drug dealer to be shot dead by the DAAD (Direct Action Against Drugs – which was a cover name of the IRA). He was taking a bogus phone call at the top of the stairs at the 18 Steps bar in Ann Street in Belfast, when the DAAD ran up the stairs and riddled him. Another guy that I did the door with, Paul Daly, was also shot dead by the DAAD. In fact, we moved into his house when his family moved (1981/1982) from Holmdene Gardens in Ardoyne. The very first night that I did the door, I hit someone. It was in the Eg and the manager, Gerard Deery, said to my boss, Jim McDonald, 'I hope that fella (me) isn't too quick in lifting his hands.' He knew that I was a professional boxer. Jim assured him that he would take me under his wing and calm me down, and he did.

I was blessed with working under Jim. Jim was a talker and not a fighter (a good doorman). He would say hello to everyone as they entered and goodnight to everyone as they left. He would banter with customers and build up a friendship with them. As he used to say to me, 'One day you might need them to back you up.' Jim thought of everything, but deep down Jim (or JR as we called him as he bore an uncanny resemblance to JR from the TV show *Dallas*) was all for self-preservation. He reminded me of the character Norman Stanley Fletcher who Ronnie Barker used to play in the

TV comedy sitcom *Porridge*. I only ever saw him angry once. He got into a row with some young lad on the front door and the kid punched him (I think the fella was just walking by and wasn't coming into the Eg). I ran down the stairs (I worked on the top floor) as I heard the commotion in the street. Everybody was holding JR back and he was livid (I had never seen him so angry), but this young guy was still provoking him, so I went over to the lad and I said, 'Clear off,' and he got cheeky with me and I hit him a big slap in the face and he hit the deck. Seán Murphy (the other front doorman) released his grip on JR and JR said to me, 'Eamon, that's the hardest punch I ever saw,' and I said, 'It wasn't a punch, it was a slap.' But they didn't believe me. I went over to the lad to help him up and he was okay with me. To be honest, I hit him a slap as I didn't want to punch him and hurt him (the slap probably hurt more). The speed of me and the sound of a big slap, plus the young guy falling, made it seem worse than what it was. I helped him up and got talking to him for about ten minutes and him and JR shook hands and he went on his way. At the end of the night as we had our usual 'one pint' before we left for home, Seán Murphy turned to me and asked, 'Eamon, was that really a slap?'

I remember Jim telling me that my dad filled him in when they were living and working in London when they were eighteen. He told me that some Belfast guys accused him of bullying them and they threatened him that they would get Coco down to sort him out. Jim said, 'Get Coco down then,' (thinking it was just talk from them). The next thing is, Coco turns up at his door. Jim said that they had a fair fight, but my dad was too much for him and at the end, they shook hands and stayed friends. Jim held my dad in very high esteem.

You have to have great instinct on the door, mixed in with a lot of bluff. It's about spotting a row and acting quickly before it comes to blows. Even going over and standing beside them without saying anything, sometimes makes them back off. Making them aware of my presence. I try to joke my way through everything and if someone called me a bouncer, I would reply, 'Security consultant, please.' But when the first punch is thrown, then it's time to earn your money and you have to be brutal, but I try to avoid this at all costs. Sometimes, you have to show them that you mean business and this can make them back off. I normally say my wee poem to people as I am clearing them out, 'Lift your glasses and shift your asses, do your talking as you're walking.'

I have been very fortunate that I have only had one or two punches thrown at me in over 25 years (and, thankfully, they both missed). I have good instincts and discernment and these are good qualities for a doorman. I was trying to count how many punches I have thrown in all those years and it's under a dozen (that's not bad). Usually one punch is all that's needed. That's why I am extra careful not to take one. As I remember from the death of my friend, Seamus McCloskey, one punch can lead to a fatality. One punch attack, especially after too much alcohol, can lead to a death. Think first before throwing a punch.

I have also dragged people out, thrown them out or just held them down. I was running this guy out of the Hercules bar in Castle Street and his head cracked against the glass part of the door (very thick glass with a design/logo on it). He must have been struggling with me, and to be honest, I am not sure if I did it on purpose (self-preservation kicks in), as I worked there on my own.

When I worked as a doorman in the Eg and the Manhattan nightclubs, my boss was Tony Agnew, and he was quite a character. Tony was only about 5ft. 4in., but his ego was much bigger. He had all these big, burly doormen working for him and he could be a cheeky chappie at times, but deep down, he was a decent enough fella. One time I got done for assault and I got a £250 fine and Tony tried to wriggle out of paying it, as by the time it went to court, I had left Tony and worked elsewhere, but I got hold of him on the phone and persuaded him to pay the fine (which he did).

One night in the Eg, a guy was giving me a bit of hassle, as he wanted to bring his pint glass down the stairs as we were trying to move them out at the end of the night. I tried to explain to him that this was not allowed. He started slabbering to me and he had two mates with him to back him up (the other doorman, heavyweight boxer Paul Douglas, must have been downstairs at the time) and he just said, 'Fuck you!' And continued to walk down the stairs with his pint glass. He had crossed the line and I went after him and as we got to the landing on the middle floor, I tapped him on the shoulder and said, 'Hey you', and as he turned around he lifted his hand with the pint glass in it and as the other doorman, JR, was about to move in, I smacked the guy. I saw the guy's nose go from left to right and the blood just started to spurt out spraying JR's cream jacket and shooting right up the wall and onto the ceiling. It was just like the ABA final when I broke that para's nose. It was like reliving it all over again. It really was a bloodbath. His two friends helped him down the stairs which brought him out onto the street. I had to be held back. I was convinced that he was going to stick the pint glass into my face.

I want to state quite categorically, that I don't see myself as a hard man. I am only a small guy (under 5ft. 8ins.) and at that time I weighed about ten stone (I am about eleven and a half stone now). I have worked with big strong men who would snap my spine like a twig. I have seen doormen in action and thought to myself, 'Wow, I wouldn't fancy messing with him.' I would be half-decent for my age, height and weight, but I do know my limitations (always did). That's important. It's also important not to let the ego get out of control with the 'I am the man bullshit.' I am not the man. Never was, never will be and wouldn't want to be.

My dad, Coco, was a hard man. Harder and tougher than I could ever be. But he had a miserable and unhappy life. The shootings and bombings he came through made him drink, and when he went into pubs and clubs to drink, people would start on him, challenge him or just generally torture him and he brought this all back into the house. He also worried about Republicans shooting him again when he had run-ins with certain individuals, maybe shoot him dead this time. He hated the fact that these were cowardly bastards picking on him, while hiding behind that organisation. That did his head in, plus we would get threatening phone calls and death threats through the post. They wouldn't leave him alone.

During a period of tit-for-tat killings by Loyalists and Republicans, a tragic incident I will always remember was the Shankill Bomb on Saturday 23 October 1993. I was in Belfast city centre and had gone for an interview at Debenhams in Castle Court, for a Christmas temp position. I had previously worked there. You could enter Debenhams's office through Gresham Street then, and I remember a radio blasting out that a bomb had gone off in the Shankill and there were many deaths. That was the first time I heard about it. Ten people died that day, including one of the bombers, Thomas Begley. Thomas Begley was from Ardoyne, as was the other bomber, Seán Kelly. It was Johnny Adair and C Company of the UDA that the IRA were after. Johnny Adair was like the bogeyman to Catholics and Johnny likes to say he brought the war to the IRA, but of the forty or so murders under Adair's command, not one was an IRA man, they were all innocent Catholics. Incidentally, Johnny Adair is a big boxing fan and I have been told by a source from the Shankill (Glen Kane), that Johnny has watched all my fights on YouTube, and is a big fan of mine. Apparently, he wants me to send him a signed photo. You just couldn't make this up. Glen Kane was jailed for nine years in 1993, for kicking a Catholic lad called Kieran Abram to death. Kieran was kicked to death by Kane and other Loyalist thugs in 1992.

Anyway, I knew both the Begley and Kelly families very well. I had grown up with their brothers and played football with them regularly as kids. That night, I worked on the front door of the Eg on the Malone Road and I must admit, that I was very worried. There was going to be retaliation for the Shankill bomb, no doubt about that. It was a very dangerous night to be on the front door (two doormen didn't come in to work and we had to scramble round to get men). I normally worked in the top bar, but as we were short of experienced men, I got moved to the front door. Paul Douglas from the Shankill and Dave Ballantine didn't come into work that night (the door staff in the Eg were mixed, but none of the Protestants came in). The Eg was mostly made up of Catholic students and I had witnessed this a few months later, when Ireland played Italy in the World Cup and the three floors were packed to the rafters with Republic of Ireland supporters. That night, 18 June 1994, Loyalist gunmen attacked a small bar in Loughinisland killing six Catholics as they sat and watched the match. The fear and tension in Ardoyne at the time of the Shankill bomb was palpable as the bombers were from there. As I am working on the front door of the Eg that night, a car was stopped on the nearby Lisburn Road and four Loyalists (with guns) were arrested.

This was a story that reached us and I am not sure if it was true or just a rumour, but there was no doubt that fear and hysteria was in the air that night. Furthermore, I have to be brutally honest, and say that when Loyalists attacked Greysteel the following week and killed eight innocent people, two of whom were actually Protestants, it was a relief. It took the pressure off, for a while. Somebody was going to pay a heavy price for the Shankill Bomb. That's just the way it is here (tit for tat). I was just glad that it wasn't me or anyone in my family.

In mid-1990s Dublin, ex-pro boxer Joe Egan worked on the door with me in the Eg for a few months and he was a good craic. Joe took Lennox Lewis the distance as an amateur and had a good win against another former world heavyweight champion (WBA), Bruce Seldon. Big Joe was also a sparring partner to Mike Tyson, when they trained up in the Catskill Mountains, when Cus D'Amato was alive. Joe said that Tyson never knocked him off his feet and Joe said that Tyson called Joe the toughest white man on the planet. Joe also has a book out **Big Joe Egan: The Toughest White Man on the Planet** (Egan, 2006). I was in Manchester in 2006 with some mates, to go to the Joe Calzaghe—Jeff Lacy world title fight. After the fight, we hit the town and we had a great night. The next day, I'm walking the streets with the worst hangover ever. As I'm walking randomly feeling sorry for myself, I spot Joe Egan heading into a hotel and I shout, 'Joe, Joe', and I walked towards him. I said, 'Joe, it's Eamon McAuley; we used to do the door together.' Joe was doing really well at this time and could have walked on or just said, 'Hello Eamon,' but Joe gave me a big hug (it was twelve years since I had last seen him). Then Joe said, 'Hold on until I get you something' and he went to the boot of his car and handed me his book, which had just came out. Then he said, 'Come on into the hotel, I want my friends to meet you.' When I went in, there were a few famous boxers, including Richie Woodhall and Glen McCrory, and they were signing autographs for a line of people. Big Joe shouted, 'Lads, come on over so I can introduce you to a very special friend of mine.' Richie and Glen came over and Joe said, 'See this guy here, he was a great, great fighter, but see his dad, Coco, well, he was the hardest man in Ireland.' And as God is my witness, the fans who wanted Woodhall and McCrory's autographs, now wanted my autograph as they had heard Joe giving me the heads up. Joe smiled and winked at me as he left me with a line of strangers who were looking for me to sign whatever. That was the last time I saw Joe, but I did enjoy his book. I remember thinking at the time that the guys back at the hotel are never going to believe this story that I'm going to tell them.

Even though I work in bars and clubs, they are not places I would frequent outside of work. I also remember a night when I was on the door at the Manhattan, and if my memory serves me right, it was the night of the Ulster senior boxing finals (1993) and two local boxers I knew, Paul Ireland and Wayne McCullough, were in the downstairs bar. I heard that they were downstairs, but I just let them be. I remember speaking to Wayne in the town one day, and this would have been right after he got the silver in the Olympics (1992), and I was glowing in praise of him. Well I had never really spoken to him before, but when I did, I was furious and I wish I hadn't have bothered. After ten minutes of talking about him, I mentioned that I had signed with Barry Hearn and he said, 'Yeah they could do with six round fighters.' Calling a boxer a six round fighter, is basically saying the boxer has found his level at six rounds and isn't good enough to progress to eight, ten and twelve round fights. What a prick and because of my low self-esteem, I didn't challenge him regarding what he said, but I feel myself getting angry now as I write this. Then I said to him that I was sparring some top boxers over in Romford and he said, 'Yeah, they will only use you as a sparring partner.' Nobody ever used me as a sparring partner. I never took any beatings off anyone. Ever. What an arrogant, cocky person Wayne McCullough was. Maybe he was upset that

I beat his brother Alan (who's a lovely lad) in the Shamrock Club in 1981, giving him two counts.

Back to that night in the Manhattan, and Wayne and Paul were quite drunk. I don't think that Wayne drank much, but Paul did, and he was barred out of a lot of places for fighting and causing trouble. As I am standing in the middle bit of the Manhattan, I looked out the glass windows and the next thing I saw, is Paul Daly dragging Paul Ireland out of the front entrance. I ran down quickly, grabbed Paul and said, 'Paul it's okay, I know this guy please let me sort it out.' Paul Daly was one of the strongest men in Ireland and believe me, Daly would have tied Ireland and McCullough in knots. Fair play to Paul Daly, he released his grip on Ireland and the next thing is Wayne McCullough came out of the front entrance shadow boxing (throwing punches in the air). It was pathetic and laughable. I grabbed the two of them and told them both to catch themselves on as McCullough was shouting at Daly, 'Come on ya wee fat fucker, me and you now.' I quietly told McCullough, 'See if you go toe to toe with this guy then believe me, you will never box again.' Anytime I released my grip on McCullough or when him and Ireland broke away, I noticed that they kept their distance from the doormen. It was all bullshit bravado (Ireland had already felt Daly's strength). The manager, Ciarán McGuigan, told me just to leave them be and they eventually drifted off. Having said that, they knew me and didn't once get nasty with me. I must admit, that I was tempted to throw McCullough at Daly to let Daly maul him after the way McCullough treated me that day in the town. They must have gone to the newspapers, as it was in the Sunday papers the following week. They said in the report that they were minding their own business, while out celebrating with a glass or two of orange juice. McCullough said that they were picked on because of who they were. Bullshit. They were warned a few times about their behaviour and given a bye-ball because of who they were. The third time Daly went to warn them, Ireland threw a punch which missed and Daly dragged him out. I also remember one night in the Eg, turning Paul Ireland and his brother away (their reputation proceeded them) and as they walked over to the other side of the road where the Botanic Inn is, Paul's brother punched this poor innocent young lad for nothing. The lad just happened to be walking past at that time.

I had a chance to spar Wayne in 1993, when he came back from America to top the bill at the Maysfield leisure centre and I was to box on the undercard. This was up in the Holy Trinity gym and with Wayne this particular day, was the legendary coach, Eddie Futch. I declined the opportunity to spar

Wayne as I felt very weak, and I knew that I wouldn't be able to do myself justice and I would end up full of regrets. This would have been three days before my fight with Peter Buckley, which was a poor performance due to me losing too much weight and being very weak. I would normally have jumped at the chance to spar Wayne (who would go on to become world bantamweight boxing champion) and if I was at myself, I had no doubt that he would have been easy enough for me to handle. The Eamon McAuley from 1986–1987 (the lightweight) would have hurt Wayne McCullough, but then Wayne was only a bantamweight and I was a lightweight.

Before I boxed Peter Buckley (on a card topped by Wayne McCullough who was making his Belfast professional debut after turning pro in America), Barry McGuigan had arranged for Karen and I, Eamonn Loughran and his wife, Angela and Wayne McCullough and his wife, Cheryl, to meet up at the Wellington Park Hotel for a get together. Eamonn and I have always been good mates, even to this day. However, I didn't really know Wayne and in the back of my head, were those two incidents where he was very disrespectful to me in Belfast city centre in 1992, and the behaviour of him and Paul Ireland some months later at the Manhattan nightclub. Since then, Wayne had turned pro (and got himself a broad American accent), but he was in great form that night in the Welly Boot (as it's locally known), as he was the centre of attention, talking about, well, mostly himself. On the other table Cheryl held court as she told Karen and Angela all about her recent big Las Vegas wedding to Wayne. Wayne didn't mention that crazy night in the Manhattan and neither did I. The drinks were flowing that night, diet coke all round.

Paul Daly, Saul Devine and Tommy McKeogh would come to the Eg sometimes. At this time, they were mixed up in drugs and I knew what they were at. I had seen McKeogh operating at a big rave called hellraiser (or firecracker) in the Ulster Hall. I was doing security, but everybody was at it (dealing drugs) and the rest of the doormen were turning a blind eye. Initially, I was stopping it, but then I got a death threat from Loyalists and I said to myself, '£40–50 isn't worth getting shot dead over', and I never worked another one. I had spoken to Tommy that night at the Eg and he assured me that there was no drugs being sold or taken this night. Tommy seemed hurt when I said to him and he said, 'Eamon, I have people who do that for me', he sounded like a real Godfather. I knew that Tommy liked and respected me. Shortly after this, all three were named in the *Sunday World* newspaper as drug dealers and Daly and Devine were shot dead by the DAAD and McGeough fled to England, where he still lives to this day. I also remember one night in the Eg, when they were drinking (about four or five of them) and there was a crowd of rugby players around them. I recall it was the night Ireland beat Italy in the 1994 World Cup, and we all watched it on the big screen as Ireland won 1–0. Ended up with a bit of bumping and barging with Tommy's crew and the big rugby players. I thought to myself, 'Fuck, this is all I need, this to kick off.' Even Douglas backed off. I came up with an idea. I went over to Daly's table and made a big deal of going around and shaking all their hands in front of all the big burly rugby players. I got the other doormen to do the same and make a big point of doing so. I was letting the rugby players know that these were our friends (ex-friends) and if a row does break out, then we will be on our friends' side.

It worked like a charm. The rugby players backed off and left. Thank God it worked and I breathed a sigh of relief. All the doormen did. Paul Daly was very drunk and I don't even think he realised what was going on. Sometime later, I bumped into Paul after parking my car in Little Donegal Street. As I came out of the car park, he was right there sitting in a car. I was a bit agitated to see him, as he was regularly pictured in the *Sunday World* with stories claiming that he was a top drug dealer. 'King Coke' they called him. I remember saying to him (as God as my witness), 'Paul, why don't you move away from here? You're gonna end up getting shot dead.' But to be honest, he protested his innocence and said that he was not a drug dealer and that if he is, then he's a skint drug dealer (if there is such a thing). He also wanted to brag about the run-in he had with another doorman friend of mine, Seán Glackin, but I said, 'Ack here's the wife Paul. Have to run, speak to you another time.' He was shot dead just round the corner from where we spoke a week later. He was sitting in a car outside his sister's house in Stephen Street, when he was shot ten times.

In 2002, I was doing the door in the Bellevue Arms up in Glengormley with Pablo Hamilton. It was a Sunday night and among the last to leave the premises was a young lad called Gerard Lawlor. I didn't really know him, but I knew that he was involved in a fight in the Bellevue car park the previous week. The build-up to the fight happened in the upstairs bar and I had been trying to calm things down. I witnessed an eejit provoking Gerard and offering Gerard to a fight outside. Gerard was up for it and we had to stand between them. Our head doorman then, Seán Murphy, liked Gerard, but warned him that if he fights on the premises (which includes the car park), then he would be barred from the club. Gerard was okay with us, but this drunken eejit kept shouting that if Gerard had any balls, then he would go outside and they would sort it out. Gerard's manhood was being called into question and he probably thought that a man had to do what a man had to do. We understood this, and Gerard went outside and filled the guy in. It was not even close and I was impressed with Gerard's strength. He played GAA for St Enda's. We decided not to bar him as he was provoked and we let him off with a stern warning. So just over a week later, Sunday 21 July 2002, he was one of the last to leave the Bellevue and as he was leaving, he turned to Pablo and said, 'Do you think that I will get into the Chester with these jeans on?' The Bellevue closed early on a Sunday, but a way on down the road there was a disco in the Chester that stayed open until 2 a.m. Gerard must have changed his mind about going to the Chester because he was walking down Floral Road with Chinese food in his hands (while wearing a Celtic top), when Loyalist gunmen pulled up beside him and shot him dead.

The strange thing was that the day before (Saturday night), I was standing at the front door of the Bellevue when John Docherty (Glenard/Ardoyne taxis) called me over. John was just dropping a fare off. He said to me, 'Eamon, do you know who that is that just walked into your club just now?' John said that this guy was a prominent Loyalist from around the turn of the road area in Ligoniel. Also that night, as I am walking past his table, he stops me and asks me to take a photo of him and his friends and handed me a camera. The Bellevue was then and is now a bar which is predominantly frequented by Catholics (although I knew one or two Protestants who drank there). Was it a strange coincidence that a prominent Loyalist just happened to be there the night before the shooting or was he stalking it out or were the gunmen on their way to the Bellevue that night, where they knew two Catholics would be standing at the front door, and then just happened to see this young lad with a Celtic top on and said, 'He will do?' The Bellevue is just around the corner from Floral Road. I rang the police confidential line and reported everything to the police, but I never heard another thing. We went to the young lad's funeral, even though I hardly knew him, and there was a huge turnout of people to mourn his untimely passing. He was only nineteen and to this day, no one has been arrested or charged with Gerard's murder.

I was doing the door in the Gort na Móna GAA club off the Springfield Road/Monagh Road in West Belfast around 2007/2009, and there was a row at a fancy dress night, I think it could possibly have been Halloween. It all started when two girls started fighting on the dance floor and they grabbed each other by the hair and wouldn't let go. It's mostly girls that start fights now as they seem to be drinking more than men. I remember it was me who spotted it, and I moved in to try to break it up, but it's very hard to separate two girls who have hold of each other's hair. And when you do, there's chunks of hair everywhere. If this happens outside then I would normally shout, 'Here's the police!' and they usually let go of each other's hair. But as I went in to try and break it up, more people got involved and there was pushing and shoving as more doormen rushed in and, as we separated the girls, we moved them out to the foyer as recriminations began with both parties blaming each other.

As I previously said, most people were dressed up and the boyfriend of one of the girls had a Batman outfit on and he was furious, as he tried to attack the other party involved in the row. As we tried to restrain him and calm him, he attacked one of the doormen. He punched the doorman, 'Kapow,' and as they were wrestling on the floor, I felt that it was my duty to come to the aid of the other doorman. I punched 'Batman' as he wrestled on the floor and it had a lot of leverage on it and it landed flush and I followed up with a very cowardly stomp on his head, and his head hit the marble floor with force, knocking him spark out. It all went quiet and his mates brought him out for air and I got my comrade up off the ground. We then locked the door to keep the two factions apart and the next thing that happened was a hammering on the front door and someone's leg then came through the door. I recognised the leg, it was Batman. They were beating the door in.

We had to open the door and we ran out and came face to face with them. It was very, very tense and it was like a Mexican stand off for what seemed like an eternity. I was now standing face to face with Batman and he looked fresh as a daisy! I am not sure what these boys were taking, but they were on something. One of their crowd was an ex-boxer, who had boxed my son and his name is Conor Tohill, but he wasn't about now when I needed him (I had spoken to him earlier). If I could see him, then I could reason with him and maybe he could calm his side down, but he was not about. I was the one on my side to do the talking and I appealed to them. I told them that I was a friend of Conor Tohill. I explained that one of their men was attacking a doorman and I had to respond and that this is what they pay me for, it was nothing personal, and I didn't want to see anyone getting hurt (a bit rich coming from me). I pleaded with them to go home. I can't remember everything that I said, but I do remember the doorman who had been punched bursting for revenge. It was incredibly tense, but then, just like that, they turned and walked away (thank God). Maybe it was because most of the doormen were Republicans, I don't know. Nevertheless, I was glad but also disgusted at myself for my cowardly actions. There were two sides to me that night, good and evil, Jekyll and Hyde. I was confused.

I am 54 now and still doing the door. And for one reason and one reason only - money. Out of the last 30 years, I have probably worked 25 on the door. Sometimes it can get to you and you need a break, or sometimes you might not like where you are working or who you are working with. But I am in a position now where I have many contacts and many options, so I can suit myself. A few months ago, I was working in the Beechlawn Hotel and there was a wedding reception in one of the function rooms. The couple were from the New Lodge and there was a handful from Ardoyne and I knew them and chatted with them earlier in the evening. There was over a hundred people in attendance, including many children. I started work that night at 8 p.m. The manager in the Beechlawn doesn't want us standing at the front door. His approach is for us to sit down and drink tea or coffee and be inconspicuous, blend into the surroundings. I was to work with my mate, Mark Toal, that evening (if Carlsberg made doormen, then they probably would have made my mate Mark. He always had my back and I felt comfortable when I worked with him), but Mark pulled out very late in the evening and my boss, Tommy, was scrambling around trying to get someone to replace him. I was on my own from 8 p.m. until 11.30 p.m. when Tommy himself came in (I was not fussed, as it had been a handy night). At least Tommy would give me a hand clearing them out at 1.30 a.m.

Just as Tommy and I were relaxing with a cup of tea, a staff member rushed out from the function room screaming, 'You must get in there now, they are going fucking mad.' There are two function rooms in the Beechlawn Hotel and a big area for people to dine, as well as a bar and a reception area (as well as 42 rooms). I would occasionally check the wedding reception to check that all was well, but when Tommy and I rushed in, the place was like a riot scene. They were going crazy. There were fist fights breaking out all over the place and the bride was lying unconscious, plus her wheelchair bound dad (or dad-in-law) was knocked to the ground but was punching it out with another guy on the ground. There were chairs (with metal frames) being flown all over the place, people were diving for cover, children were screaming as Tommy and I were trying to break fights up. I shouted to the bar staff, 'get the doormen from McGlones over' (McGlones is right beside the Beechlawn Hotel and the doormen work for Tommy). I also shouted to the staff to ring the police and the manager, Tim, said they are on their way.

When the police came, they quickly realised that they had underestimated the situation and back-up arrived in riot gear. One of our doormen, Big Dougie, was hit on the head with a flying chair, which brought out a large bump. It was madness. It was shameful. In 30 years doing the door, I don't remember seeing anything as bad. We eventually got the room cleared and it was a miracle that no one was badly hurt or even killed. We were later told that it all started after the two bridesmaids previously decided to ruin the bride's big day by attacking her. It was premeditated and their tactics worked a treat (so we were told). I don't like staying in the one venue for too long, six months to a year is enough for me, then I move on. Familiarity breeds contempt. I will tell you another thing, I would rather work in a stadium with 100,000 fellas than in a room with ten drunken women.

In July 2017, I was doing the door in Voodoo in the city centre, and I was on my own 6 p.m.-1 a.m. and it was a bad night. Voodoo is normally a joy to work in and it was one of the hottest days in the year. I pulled up a seat outside, facing Voodoo and sent Karen a text which said, 'Sitting outside Voodoo basking in the sun with a cool drink, and getting paid for it.' Karen texted back, 'Lucky you.' Well from then, it started to get crazy as alcohol mixed with the blazing sun, seemed to send people crazy. All of a sudden, people started to fight and argue (and there's never trouble in Voodoo). There was a fight in the club, there was a fight outside the club. I had to break up people who were about to fight and I put out seven people in the bar in separate incidents. I ended up rolling about on the ground with someone and I ended up with cuts and scrapes on my face, plus I threw a left hook (which missed) as I was being put under a lot of pressure. I am more of a talker now and throwing a punch is an absolute last resort. To be honest I am sitting here today thinking, 'I am getting too old for rolling on the ground!'

I refute violence in every shape and form. I am very anti-violence these days. Please do not think that I am gloating or revelling in the violence, when I tell stories of hitting someone. Violence is the lowest form of humanity. What stopped me walking away from a fight then? Ego. Why did I punch people first? Fear. Why did I kick people on the ground? Cowardice and fear of humiliation. These are only a few stories of the fights I was in.

I have to see Jesus in everyone, because he is in everyone. When I punch someone, I am punching Jesus, when I kick someone I am kicking Jesus. How do I know that? Well because he tells me in Matthew, chapter 25, verse 40–41. 'Truly I say to you, whenever you did this to these little ones who are my brothers and sisters, you did it to me.'

Jasmine the Cat

In 1996 Karen and I both worked in the pop bar/drop-in centre off Flax Street in Ardoyne. I had passed a RSA youth foundation course (as a youth leader), which I believe is the equivalent to two A levels and would have got me into Queen's University. We had a cross-community programme with the stadium in the Shankill area and it was called 'the Higher Force Challenge'. The programme was a big success, with many friendships formed. On the very first day, two lads swapped football tops with each other. The kid from the Shankill swapped his Rangers FC jersey with the kid from Ardoyne, who swapped his Celtic FC top. It was their own decision to do this and they wore them for the remainder of the programme. It was an encouraging start and wonderful symbolism. We went swimming together; we went on the banana boat, we did the ropes course that they had in the stadium, 30ft up in the air. We even did a parachute jump on, believe it or not, Friday 13th (to hell with superstition). I was on the first plane (second out after Annmarie Gibney). Cowardly Karen would not go through with the parachute jump and pulled out (some leader she was). During this time, I was asked to be on many local TV programmes (political programmes), because of the cross community work I was doing. I remember one in particular, and it was on 11 July (either 1995 or 1996).

The BBC had to send a car up to Ardoyne to pick me up and also a woman (Kate Larkin), who was also to be on the BBC2's live *Newsnight* programme at 11.45 p.m. The reason they sent a car was because I had rung them to say that there had been widespread shooting on the Crumlin Road.

I explained that it was too dangerous for Kate and I to make our own way down. The interview was held on the roof of the BBC's broadcasting house in Belfast. As we were talking, we could see the bonfires in flames across the city. This was at the height of the Drumcree dispute and it was a day of tension and fear. The **Newsnight** male host interviewed Kate and I and also two Unionist politicians, both educated men, but Kate and I spoke very well and more than held are own.

While I was on the Higher Force Challenge, I met the two guys who killed Danny Carville. This one time, when I was down at the Shankill stadium with a crowd of youths from Ardoyne, a guy called Kenny McClinton came over to my squad and started to talk to them about peer pressure and staying away from paramilitaries. This talk was not on the programme, but McClinton and the other guy, Samuel McGaw, took it upon themselves to give this impromptu talk and they called themselves 'born-again Christians.' I was with the youth when they gave this talk, but I was fully aware of who they were and what they did.

At the end of the eight-week programme, we went to Norway for two weeks. Karen's mother minded our son Ciarán, and it was my mum's responsibility to come up to our house at night to feed our beloved cat, Jasmine, and let him out and then in the morning, let him back in. Simple enough, even for my mum. We had a good trip to Norway and when we returned my mum said that Jasmine never came back after the first night. This was devastating news and I regularly went around the district looking for him and calling his name. We had named him Jasmine after the princess in **Aladdin**, as we thought she was a girl. However, it turned out Jasmine was a tom cat! Karen and I were heartbroken. We printed photos of him on A4 pages and put them in shop windows with a reward if found, but with no joy. Weeks went by and just as we were giving up hope on seeing him again, this young lad came forward and tells me a story, which if true could mean that Jasmine might still be alive.

This lad claimed that he was with this fella who snatched Jasmine off the street in Cranbrook Gardens (where we lived), to bring down to the New Lodge (about two miles away) to blood the guy's Lurcher pup, to give it the taste of blood for hunting. This unpaid informant (he didn't get the reward) then said that the cat turned vicious (obviously fighting for his life) and the pup was scared of Jasmine. He said that this guy who lived in the New Lodge flats then threw our cat down the waste chute and that's the whole story, he didn't know what happened to the cat after that. Once we received this information, Karen and her sister, Mary, jumped into the car and went straight to the New Lodge flats. Karen told me that when she went to the flats she made the sound of the distinctive whistle when calling Jasmine and within five minutes of Karen calling his name and whistling, Jasmine came booting around the corner, but he was being chased by a dog and Karen said that Jasmine just jumped right up into her arms. We had finally got him back. There was so much joy in our house that night. I had done a cursillo (a three-day walk with Christ) a few weeks previously, and I praised the Lord and I promised him that I would keep my hands off this guy who had cat-napped Jasmine (his mother lived in Cranbrook Gardens so he was always up in my street).

A few months past, then Jasmine went missing again and when I saw this guy who took Jasmine previously, I followed him up an entry and shouted, 'Hey you.' and he turned around and I said, 'My cat has went missing again.' He was terrified and shouted, 'What's that got to do with me?' And I said, 'Well it was you that had taken him before', and I threw a big left hook and missed. He started screaming and I got stuck into him. This fella was a big lump of a man, but he just screamed and curled up after I landed the first blow. He was in hospital for a few days with a broken cheekbone and I saw him walk down my street a week later (through my window) and he looked bad. This isn't Christian and I did feel bad about it, but I must be honest, if I see anyone harming a defenceless animal, I don't think I could stop myself from reacting even today. By the way the cat came home the following day.

I have a big problem with people killing insects, creepy crawlies or creatures that fly (bees, wasps, etc.). Why kill them? What harm are they doing you? That's a life you're snuffing out for no reason. Is that not murder? God created that life for a purpose. They have a family. What gives you the right? They don't bother us; in fact, they try to get away from us. Some people just swat flies, wasps, etc. just for fun, or because they are being annoyed by them. This drives me mad and I get angry. What type of race are we? Humans are without doubt the most barbaric creatures on the planet. Some animals have to kill to live. We can live without killing.

Jasmine lived for another nine years and we left it a few years and then, we got another cat, Bumble Bee. We had him for two years, then he disappeared also. He has been missing about four years now. I miss him and pray for him all the time. Karen and I had three dogs and two cats and we loved them so much. They were part of our family.

Talking of cats, I remember when I was living up in Karen's house (our house) and Karen and I were watching TV when we heard this banging sound. It would have been around 11 p.m. and I asked Karen where is that coming from, and Karen said that it seemed to be coming from the back garden, so we listened and the banging seemed to be fading as I went to the back garden to check,. As I opened the door, I could see this little kitten with its head stuck in an empty tin can of our Jasmine's cat food. The kitten had stopped banging and had started to go limp, and I quickly tried to pull the kitten out of the empty tin, but it was stuck real good. I had to use all my strength to prize it away from this tin can and could hear a sucking noise as I pulled it out. As soon as the cat's head came free, it took off at a hundred miles an hour and I never saw it again. I was so happy and proud that I had saved the wee kitten's life and if it had have died then, I would have been devastated. We never left the tin cans like that again, for fear that this could happen again. When I think of this wee story (like now), it makes me smile and gives me a good feeling. The kitten had been seconds from dying that night.

I remember one sunny night on 12 July 2001, and there had been trouble at an orange parade after it passed Ardoyne shops on the Crumlin Road. There was shocking rioting and violence, as people from Ardoyne took their frustrations out on the police who had hemmed them into their own area to allow this march to proceed. After the parade had passed, cars were stolen and put across roads (and burnt) to prevent police cars and jeeps from entering into our district. This time of year really used to get me down. I was living with Karen in Estoril Court at the time, and this was a flashpoint area. Hoods would take advantage of the situation and would be making petrol bombs and they would be in their element, as they caused all sorts of chaos to their own community – recreational rioting, it is called. I used to resent these wee fuckers as they ran about like 'tin-pot Napoleons', drunk with power.

They would make paint bombs and the paint would be spilling everywhere and they would trample over gardens, lifting flower pots and throwing them at the police who would form a line across Estoril Park. If the police would just leave the area after the parade had passed, then there would have been very little (or no) trouble, but the police were on big money from the government and they were going nowhere (not when they were on double money). These people who lived in this affected area were mostly old people who took pride in their houses and gardens. We lived in the cul-de-sac and it was now filled with hundreds of people. Yes, people even came in from other areas for a game of recreational rioting. It was just a nightmare for us who lived there, decent people. I witnessed hoods smashing up pensioner's footpaths with sledge hammers to create missiles to throw at the police. The violence always turns inwards as hoods wreck, destroy and deface our own area. I swear to God, that there were some people with carry-outs (from local off-licences) enjoying the craic. I always stood at my door protecting my house and garden. I used to get very tense and angry.

This particular year (2000/2001) as I am standing at my door, suddenly there was a loud bang as something hit our metal gates (head height) on my left side as I am looking outwards and ricochets downwards and got trapped at the bottom of our gate. I heard the rat-a-tat and then it stopped. I looked down and saw a red hot (more like orange) piece of metal or lead the size of my hand. It took me a while to get my thoughts together. I looked at where this object first hit our metal railings and there was an indentation on the railings where the object struck.

When I was able to lift this object, I brought it round to the front of the road where Sinn Féin's Bobby Storey was. The police were gone by this stage. Storey confirmed what I was already thinking, that this thing that I was now holding in my hand was part of a pipe bomb and it had come within two feet of killing me. Who threw the pipe bomb? I haven't a clue, but pipe bombs at that time were the chosen weapons of Loyalist paramilitaries. However, there were no Loyalists anywhere near me. It was suggested to me later that there were hoods up in the Ardoyne shop roofs (Catholic hoods) and they were said to have pipe bombs, but very little expertise in using them. I was told that one exploded prematurely and fragments went in many different directions miraculously missing everyone. That was the rumour that reached me. I often wonder what if that piece of metal had struck and killed me (which it very nearly did) – would anybody have found the underlying cause of how I died?

Saving Lives

On the night of 1 October 2000 I was over in my mate's house playing computer games. It would have been a Friday night; games nights were always on a Friday night. We used to meet regularly, ever since I met Paul Mulvenna on 3 March 1997, as we were lined up outside Virgin Megastore in Belfast city centre to buy the latest games console, Nintendo 64 (N64). It was going on sale that day and large crowds were expected, as we were told that a limited amount of N64s were available. Paul was two places in front of me in the line. Some people had been there from the previous night with sleeping bags.

I had arrived at Virgin Megastore around 6 a.m. This young lad turned around to me and said, 'You go with Seamus Crossan's sister, don't you?' We got talking and this passed some time as Virgin Megastore didn't open until 9 a.m. I was ninth in the line and Paul was seventh and the rumour that reached us was that there would be twelve available consoles on the day. The rumours proved to be correct, but Paul and I got what we came down for (a console each) and I offered him a lift home (which he accepted). I dropped him off in the Oldpark Road and I said, 'Cheerio' and thought that was the end of that. A few days later, I got frustratingly stuck on the game Mario 64 (amazingly everybody in Britain who brought the N64 console on the day it was released also bought the game Mario 64 and there were four games to choose from) and I thought about this lad, Paul Mulvenna, and wondered could he help me get past this level in the game that was putting me round the twist. I called to see him and he did indeed help me move on in the game, and this was the start of a friendship that has lasted over twenty years. We are still both nuts about computer games. Paul went through a horrific event as a child, when one night as a babysitter was looking after him in Oldpark Avenue, Loyalist gunmen burst into the house and shot the babysitter dead in front of him. Lucky for Paul he can't remember any of it.

Well, getting back to that Friday night (1 October 2000) and we were in Paul's house with our other computer games nut, George Young, and as we were enjoying each other's company and having a drink, I suddenly-said, 'Lads, I can smell smoke.' But Paul and George couldn't smell it and sometime later, I had gone to Paul's upstairs toilet and came down and said again, 'Lads I can definitely smell smoke and something is burning.' Paul's young lad was upstairs fast asleep and this time, Paul walked around the downstairs part of the house, but still, him and George couldn't smell anything and they said to me, 'Your head's away.' Paul went upstairs to go to the toilet, but he was no sooner up the stairs when he ran down the stairs screaming, 'Next door's on fire' (the smoke had been seeping into Paul's son's bedroom). Panic came over us and Paul ran out of the house, had a quick look through the window next door, as we were trying to warn the neighbours (two sisters), but we could see the flames in the living room and Paul smashed the front window and booted the front door in. I told George to ring the fire brigade and Paul and I went in. Paul went straight upstairs and came down with one of the sisters, who had been in bed sleeping. I grabbed her halfway down the stairs and led her outside for some fresh air and I went back in. I went into the living room and I could see that the settee was on fire and there was thick black smoke everywhere. I could also see the figure of a person lying on the ground in the kitchen, and this person wasn't moving. I tried to get to this person but I couldn't get beyond the thick black smoke and Paul tried also, without success. We did all we could to get to this woman and couldn't do anymore. The fire services arrived very quickly and they were able (with the aid of breathing gear and masks) to bring the other woman out of the house and (thank God) revive her.

The fire services were glowing in their praise of our quick thinking and fast reactions and we went back into Paul's house to continue playing computer games and having a drink. Paul said to me that if I hadn't have persisted with my claim that I could smell smoke then those two women would have died and his son upstairs could have died, also from smoke inhalation (as smoke was seeping through the walls into his son's bedroom).

I felt pretty good about myself that night. Next day, the headlines on the front page of the *Belfast Telegraph* were something like, 'Next-door neighbour saves two women from certain death.' They wanted to take a photo of Paul, but he didn't want his photo in the paper. The thing was, that Paul took all the credit. He did say that a friend did help (he's too modest). Paul and his wife, who was out the night of the fire, were treated like heroes and were invited out for a five-star champagne dinner (it took him twenty years to tell me that he received a bravery certificate). Me, I had to throw out all the clothes I had on, as they stank of smoke and I couldn't get it out and they were also discoloured. I just want to say to you Paul, 'You know, I know and God knows. I am not saying that you were not a hero, you were. But I played my part also. I wanna be a hero too.' The fire services said that the two women were minutes from perishing.

The Hurricane and King Kenny

I was out with a few friends in 2000/2001, and we were in Benedict's bar on Bradbury Place, Shaftsbury Square. There were about six to eight people in my company and we were having a beer and a good time. Former world snooker champion Alex 'Hurricane' Higgins just happened to pass by outside and we could see him, as Benedict's had big glass windows. A guy in my company knew Alex, and we asked him to go and ask Alex if he would like to join us. When Alex joined us, we kept him well supplied with drinks and he didn't need to put his hands in his pockets for anything. The drinks were coming thick and fast. But I kept my distance from Alex as I knew that he could be unpredictable, as I had a few bad experiences with him before.

There was one occasion in the Crumlin Star in Ardoyne, when he was going to be a surprise guest to play Jimmy White and they had hidden Alex up in the top bar well out of Jimmy's way. My big mate Brendy Devine was doing security and he gave me the okay to go up the stairs to say hello to Alex and get a photo. When I entered the top room Alex spotted me right away and shouted to the doormen, 'Tell that cunt with the camera to fuck off.' Then he shouted to me, 'Hey you, fuck off.' I didn't know where to look and one of the doormen said, 'Eamon I don't think he's gonna let you get that photo.'

I replied, 'No problem, I'll just leave.' To be honest, he had embarrassed me. Also that night, as he's playing Jimmy White, I clearly heard him say to a child, 'Move out of the fucking way.' Such an ignorant man. So I had every right to be reticent.

When he was introduced to me in Benedict's, I was polite and told him he had once played snooker with my dad. On one occasion, they played in Hughie Hunter's house in Mountainview (beside Ardoyne). Hughie had a full size table and Alex was paid to come up and play a few fellas (one of whom was my dad). I remember my dad saying that Higgins was ignorant and obnoxious. Well, as I am talking to Alex right there in front of my friends, Alex punches me in the stomach. I couldn't believe it. I grabbed him and said, 'What the fuck do you think you're doing?' I was livid. As my friends got in to break it up and pull us apart, I shouted again, 'Don't you ever take a liberty like that again.' The doormen didn't see it and didn't bother us (thank God as there were about six or eight guys in my company, some of them big, hard, fit guys). I didn't want any trouble with the doormen. Alex lived in that area and was often seen walking around that strip of fast-food outlets and bars. I am sure he had form with the doormen who worked in that area. After we got it sorted out and Higgins left, my friend, Seán McNulty, explained to me that he had told Alex that I was an ex-professional boxer and Alex had told him that the cancer in his stomach was gone, and he was asking me to punch him in the stomach to prove it. I certainly don't remember him saying that. The last time I saw Alex was when I was doing the door in the Beaten Dockett and he came out to the front door and told me that some people were annoying him and would I have a word with them. I did just that, but I couldn't help thinking that Alex used people when it suited him. There were times I saw him fussed over, having drinks bought for him, but he didn't complain then.

Getting back to that night in the Star with Jimmy White, and as I had paid for Karen's and my tickets, we sat down and watched Jimmy White put on a masterclass of snooker against Alex and some local players. He made one-hundred-and-thirty-something in one frame. After the snooker, there was a live band and Tony and Donna McNulty joined us, but once again, I was drinking very fast and Karen had warned me to slow down, but I wasn't listening.

I ended up drunk as a skunk and a fella sitting close to me, who I didn't know, went to sit down but I pulled the chair away as he was about to sit, and he fell to the ground. I thought that it was hilarious and was killing myself laughing (I am worse than Higgins). The thing that I noticed was, no one else was laughing. Basil McAfee leaned over to me and whispered, 'That's bullying Eamon.' Well I liked and respected Basil and I was shocked and horrified with what Basil said. The fella whose chair I pulled out left shortly after with his partner. He was only a small skinny guy (a bully sure knows who to pick on). I got up and left also, leaving Karen in the club with Tony and Donna. I sat on the doorstep of Karen's and my house with my head in my hands thinking of what I had done and what Basil said. I was full of remorse. I was never a bully and hated bullies, but I also knew what Basil had said was right. I knew the next day that alcohol was responsible and I would have to stop drinking. I made it my business to find out who this guy was and where he lived. I needed to see him and apologise to him. I got the information I needed, and I bought him a present and a sorry card, and called to his house. He wasn't in, but his partner was and I told her that this was a wakeup call with me and the negative effects of alcohol. I told her that I was ashamed of myself. She was lovely and told me just to forget it (which I never have).

Basil McAfee was brutally murdered in 2011. He was spotted on CCTV going to the off-licence that day and was found dead by his mum, who had called to his flat the next day. Basil met a very violent death as he was beat viciously around the head with a blunt instrument. His murderer has yet to be caught. I remember when we lived in Estoril Park for a year (1981) and Basil happened to call for Brian Lyttle as I was in the garden talking to Brian's younger brother, Steven. As Basil opened the gate to Brian's house, Brian's dog (who was half German Shepherd) ran right at Basil snarling and growling, teeth showing while foaming at the mouth. We feared the worst. Basil was as cool as a cucumber and quick as a flash (with perfect timing) as the dog went to jump on him, Basil smacked the dog right in the mouth and the dog cowered away, whimpering. Basil never batted an eyelid and we fell about laughing at Basil's coolness. RIP Basil.

In 2002, I brought a few guys over to Spain for a white collar charity boxing event. A friend, John Rooney, had gone to London and had done well for himself, and it was John who was involved in this show. I was the coach and I had trained these lads in the Immaculata ABC (where I trained the youth boxers for over four years). All four of the guys had done a wee bit of boxing in their time, but only one of them was still an active boxer, and the rest were bodybuilders or doormen that I had worked with in the past. There was no doubt that they were a motley crew and I tried my best to coach them (honest I did), but I ended up just going to Marbella to have a nice time in the sun. We stayed in a beautiful hotel and also staying in our hotel was soccer legend Kenny Dalglish.

We approached Kenny one day as he was relaxing at the pool on his own and, as there was not many people about, he was happy to chat with us and he posed for photos (I never got to see the photos that were taken on Ciarán

Healy's camera). We didn't want to impose on him too much, but we told him that we are boxing at a big promotion at the hotel the following night and asked him would he like to go; he sounded interested and we gave him free tickets. He was lovely with us and we let him continue his sunbathing in peace and we went on our way. I found him to be a pleasant and charming man and I thought back to when he played for Celtic in the mid-1970s and he was my absolute hero. I had posters of him in my bedroom.

That same night, the boxers, Connolly O'Connor, Brian Cusack, Brendy Devine, Ciarán Healy and I went into the town and had a drink (some coach I am) and we bumped into Kenny and his wife and children. He remembered us and, as we were passing, he smiled and said, 'Hello lads.' Just then a crowd of people came out of a different bar and they spotted Kenny and started shouting at him. They were also Scots, but they were certainly no friends or fans of Kenny. I can't remember word for word what they shouted, but it was some of the most vulgar, sectarian and abusive filth I ever heard in my life (and that's rich coming from Belfast). And for Kenny's wife and kids to be subjected to it also was shocking. The strange thing was that they were calling him a Fenian bastard but Kenny is actually a Protestant, but it was the fact that he played for Celtic (a team with strong Irish Republican roots) which left him open to this vile abuse from narrow-minded bigots, and in front of his family also. The ferocity of this attack and the hate on their faces shocked me (never mind Kenny). Kenny seemed shook up and we waited there with Kenny until they walked on by. All my boxers (except me) are 6-foot and over and maybe that's why they walked on by. Maybe it was because of this gesture (on our part), that Kenny turned up at the boxing show the following night.

Connolly's opponent pulled out, then Brian Cusack got a bad decision against him (believe it or not the winner would be the guy who got the loudest clap). Steve Holdsworth from Eurosport was doing the MC. Then big Brendy Devine won on a second round stoppage even though he had drank eight or ten pints of lager that day. Devine's opponent was from Bangor, County Down, as was Ciarán Healy's opponent, Brian 'The Bull' McCue. That day in a bar, we watched Rangers beating Ciarán Healy's beloved Celtic. In the same bar that day was Healy's opponent and, worse still, he was wearing a Rangers top. Healy whispered to me, 'I'm gonna knock his bollicks in tonight', and as McCue passed us on the way to the toilets, Healy couldn't help himself and said, 'There will be no double tonight Brian.' And Devine's opponent stood up and shouted, 'You're right because there's gonna be a treble.' Brendy Devine said nothing and just smiled. It was hilarious.

That night, Brian McCue was on the receiving end of a vicious beating from Healy and Devine's opponent never landed a blow. Steve Holdsworth made me get into the ring and told the crowd that I was a world-class fighter in my day (which I was not). As for Kenny Dalglish (who supported Rangers as a boy), well, he ended up presenting the prizes to all the boxers. Incidentally, I met the great Lisbon lion, Billy McNeil, in Ayr (Scotland) in 1997. He was the captain of the great Celtic team that won the European Cup in 1967. I met him in Butlin's, where he was coaching kids, including my son, Ciarán. I had a good chat with him and I remember him saying that he had underwent a triple bypass operation. Sadly, Billy died on 22 April 2019. Rest in peace Billy.

I remember being at the opening of John Rooney's gym in Tower Bridge, London in 2004 and it was a big swanky party with a lot of famous boxers at it. I was training one of John's boxers, Ciarán Healy, in Belfast then and a lot of John's relatives and friends made the journey over for the official opening. John was born and reared in Belfast. The gym was a high-tech, state-of-the-art gym and even had a cafe built into it that served health food, tea, coffee, etc. I aligned myself with one of the guest boxers, Juan Laporte, who had flown in from New York. Fair play to John Rooney, he asked me to put clips of my fights onto a DVD (knockout clips) and they played many times that night on the big screen. I told Juan Laporte that was me he was watching and that was my introduction. I also impressed him with my knowledge of boxing and I reminded him of all the hall of famers he had boxed. Juan was once a WBC featherweight champion and had boxed (among others) Salvador Sanchez, Eusebio Pedroza, Wilfredo Gomez, Azumah Nelson, Julio César Chávez and Kostya Tszyu, giving them all very tough fights. He was never put on the mat in his career.

On the big screen that night, it also showed Juan's fight with Barry McGuigan and I stood beside him as we watched it. McGuigan boxed the fight of his career that night and beat Juan much easier than those other legends did. Juan landed flush on Barry's chin in the fifth and ninth rounds and Barry didn't even blink. Laporte hit Azumah Nelson with similar rights a few years later in Australia, and Nelson barely survived on wobbly legs to win a close decision. As Juan and I watched his fight with McGuigan, we seemed to be watching two different fights. Juan thought he was winning the fight and he told me that Mickey Duff got the time keeper to ring the bell early in the final round to save McGuigan from a knockout, as he said Barry was out on his feet, while BBC commentator Harry Carpenter thought the bell rang early to save Laporte from being stopped. Indeed, the bell did ring ten seconds early but it was not for either of these two reasons. Both Juan and Harry were delusional. Laporte had lost his world title to Wilfredo Gomez eleven months earlier and two fights after this, Barry would beat Eusebio Pedroza for the WBA featherweight title. I got on with Juan that night like a house on fire and we spent much of the night in each other's company and he revealed to me that, the only time he was ever hurt was against Kostya Tszyu and it was a body shot and not a head shot that hurt him.

When I coached Ciarán Healy as a professional (around 2004/2005), I had arranged some great sparring for him one Sunday morning with Derry's, Eamonn O'Kane, as Ciarán had a fight coming up. Ciarán turned up very late with his training bag and stank of drink. I lost it and I was shouting at him asking was he having a laugh, and as he was trying to explain, I was not listening and told him we are done, finished. Once again, he tried to explain, but I was still shouting and bawling and then he shouted, 'Eamon my mate got shot dead last night.' And there was stunned silence as everybody in the gym stopped doing what they were doing and were looking at me for a response and I remember thinking, I've heard some excuses in my time, but that one topped them all. I think I said something stupid like, 'You better not be lying,' But it was true. His mate Danny McGurk, who was a hard man according to Ciarán (which is good enough for me), had a run-in with Republican dissidents and it resulted in him getting shot dead. Ciarán won his first four or five pro fights with me as his coach, but he drank and smoked and just wanted to make a few quid from boxing (which is fair enough), but I was ambitious and had wanted to train champions. Ciarán and I parted company on good terms and he settled into a journeyman role, winning some and losing a few, but he was better than that, and I believed he had championship qualities. He did win an Irish pro-title (which was more than I ever did in my career). He is one tough guy and we have remained friends over the years. I remember Ciarán being at my brother and dad's funerals (out of respect for me) and I was at Ciarán's wedding in August 2018.

The Immaculata boxing club (which my son boxed for and for which I was a coach for four years) went to Toronto, Canada for two weeks in August 2004. This trip was all due to contacts I had, as this was the first trip the club had gone on in its history. Victor and Colin McCullough were the men who brought us over and they were my friends. I had become friends of theirs through my mate (their cousin), Anthony McCullough, who had been out in Toronto working for some time. While Anthony was in

Toronto, another mate, Seán McNulty, went over to see him and during that holiday, Seán rang me one day and during the conversation he put Victor on the phone to talk to me. It was during this conversation, that Victor first mentioned to me about bringing a boxing team to Canada. Later, his brother Colin came back to Belfast and we formed a great friendship and Colin was also keen to bring a boxing team out from Belfast. They were very proud of their Belfast roots.

Colin and Victor owned a bar in Toronto called 'the Belfast Lounge' and beside it was a nightclub they also owned called Sugar Daddies. They had moved from Belfast to Toronto as kids and had made a very successful life for themselves. Colin was the quieter of the two and he had a passion for cooking and even though he was the proprietor of the Belfast Lounge, he would be very hands on in the kitchen preparing the food. Victor was flashier and more extravagant and had flashy clothes, a few top of the range cars and a Harley Davidson motorbike. Victor did weights, had a six pack and loved the ladies. Victor handled the business side of things. Colin was married and was somewhat overweight, but I found him easier to be around.

While I was there, he showed me his million dollar dream-house, which was still being built as we were there. He wasn't being flashy or boastful as Colin was a humble, quiet and polite man. In fact, I think it was me that asked if I could see the house when we were having a causal conversation one day. There was about fifteen or twenty of us that came over from Belfast and the club's head coach, Nugget Nugent, pulled off a master-stroke when he invited Whiterock leisure centre manager, John Dunne, to come out with us. John was an ex-boxer who had once lived in Toronto for many years and he knew his way around Toronto. John came on board and was the main facilitator arranging everything. John hired us a big mini bus and drove us to the gym and back then, after the fights were over, he would take us to places like Niagara Falls, where we would get on the Maid of the Mist boat tour and be right beside Niagara and Buffalo falls, which was quite amazing. Victor and Colin would feed us everyday in the Belfast Lounge and among the Mac boxers were, Martin Rogan and Martin Lindsay, who would go on to win big professional titles. My own son, Ciarán, also made the trip and he had a scary first round knockout win which was worrying, as the badly overmatched kid lay on the canvas for what seemed like ten minutes before being helped from the ring.

One day, the legendary former world title challenger, George Chuvalo, turned up at the Belfast Lounge (arranged of course) and we got the chance to meet him, talk to him and get photos with him (Chuvalo had gone fifteen rounds with Muhammad Ali in Toronto for the world heavyweight boxing championship in 1966). It was a great honour to meet him. Moreover, I was distraught to hear him say that he had lost three sons (dead) to heroin and his wife had taken her own life. Consequently, George became a tireless worker to tackle addictions and mental health issues. He was very impressive to listen to, as he was very bright, articulate and coherent. In fact, listening to him speak so eloquently, you would never think that he boxed, never mind he took the best punches from Ali, George Foreman and Joe Frazier! In addition, never having been put on the canvas. He deeply impressed me and was an inspiration. We got photos taken with him and I must admit I was touched, if not deeply moved to listen to his story and you think you have it bad.

He was in the biggest fight of his life trying to cope with the horror of losing three sons and his wife, but there was never any self-pity in his voice, just a determination to help people with addictions and mental health issues, and I take my hat off to him. What a man. He told me a fantastic story of when he signed a contract to fight a dead man. For years, people had been trying to make a match between George Chuvalo and Charles 'Sonny' Liston, but for one reason or another, it didn't come off. Nevertheless, when Chuvalo finally signed the contract, Sonny Liston was lying dead in a motel room. Liston's body wasn't discovered for a few days and, once again, the deadly heroin was the killer. There have been all kinds of suspicions that Liston was murdered, but nothing was ever proved. The night before we came home, John Dunne's old coach came to our hotel to meet him and he brought with him a scrapbook of Johns press cuttings of his boxing career in Toronto. We were all thrilled to look at it, especially John and as the old coach was leaving, he hugged John and was crying, it truly was a beautiful moment and I think I had tears in my eyes also. I have a photo of John and Mickey Tohill and I and sadly, John and Mickey (who was some character) have passed on now and when I look at the photo it makes me sad but it also makes me smile. John Dunne was such a lovely person. Rest in peace John and Mickey.

I have lost many friends and family over the years. Some as a direct result of the conflict, some from ill health and others in more violent deaths. In the next chapter I reflect on the death of a friend of mine, whose brutal death in a bar brawl had an impact on me personally and implications for the peace process.

Bert

On Saturday 30 January 2005, I was working on the door of a place called Bar Red, which was at the back of Belfast's city hall. There would have been two men on the door on a Saturday night and that night, I was working with my big mate, Robert McCartney. During the night, we tried to get our night in by chatting about our lives, our jobs, our kids and our hopes and aspirations for the future. One thing we did talk about was our mate, Brendy Devine, who was due to go back into jail that Wednesday. Most of the conversation that night was about our friend Brendy. We were concerned for him, as he was our mate. Bert and I had a good talk and a good laugh that night. I liked to work with Bert. He had a presence on the door. He was big, strong and powerful, but I liked the fact that he wasn't a bully. He loved training and building up his body and his mates called him 'the Chest'.

One thing that sticks in my head about that night was that I told him a poor taste joke. I said to him, 'Did you hear about the wee dwarf that took his own life? He slit his ankles and took an underdose!' Bert laughed, then I suddenly realised that Bert's brother had taken his own life a few years previously (I was at his funeral). I was horrified. I remember saying, 'Bert, I am so sorry, I forgot about your brother, Gerard,' but Bert just said, 'Wise up, it's just a joke.' Suicide is nothing to joke about and is a very serious problem in our society, especially in socially disadvantaged areas of Belfast. For males, in particular, suicide is a growing cause of deaths across Ireland and the UK, tragically affecting many families, including my own. Years after this conversation with Bert, my brother took his own life in 2011 so I know what it's like to suffer the loss of a loved one to suicide and it's no joking matter. It's something I talk about in more detail in the next chapter.

Bert did mention that night that he was going for a drink with his mates the next day, but didn't say that Brendy Devine was going. The next night was a Sunday, and I went to 7 p.m. Mass in Holy Cross Church, Ardoyne and when I came back to my house in Roseleigh Gardens, my phone rang and it said on the mobile 'Bert calling.' I answered and said, 'Hello Bert', but it was not Bert, it was Brendy Devine using Bert's phone (Brendy had left his own phone in his house). Brendy asked, 'Do you wanna meet up with us for a drink?' And I said, 'No problem, where are you?' And he replied, 'Magennis's in the Markets.' I told Brendy that I would be down soon, but Brendy said, 'No, we are leaving here soon to go to the Chester and we will see you there in 30 minutes.' Then Brendy said, 'Hold on, Bert wants to speak to you.' Bert came on the phone, but he sounded blocked and he just kept saying, 'Is your dad the hardest man in Ardoyne?' He repeated this about three times and I just said, 'No, I am, see you in the Chester soon.' And I hung up.

I now had second thoughts of going, as Bert was blocked, but Brendy sounded sober. What I found out later was that Bert had been out drinking all day with his mates and got a call from Brendy, and Brendy said to Bert that he would join him for a few drinks as he was going back to prison in a few days. I got washed and changed and made my way to the Chester on the Antrim Road. I waited outside the Chester and was having a chat with the two doormen, Rory and Paul. Thirty minutes came and went and I am wondering what's keeping them. I rang Bert's mobile three times, but no reply. I then rang a fourth time and what I heard will stay with me the rest of my life.

At last Bert answered me (or so I thought) and I said, 'What's keeping you?' And Bert screamed, 'Hold on a minute.' I then said, 'Bert, it's Eamon.' And he screamed again, 'Hold on a minute.' He now sounded a lot more sober than he did an hour ago, but by the tone of his voice I knew there was something wrong. He then screamed a third time, 'Hold on a fucking minute.' I knew then he wasn't talking to me. Then I clearly heard Brendy Devine shouting, 'I never lifted my hand to anyone.' After that, I heard bottles smashing and women squealing and then the phone went dead. I said to the doormen, 'Flip, there appears to be a row going on there.' I continued waiting for a while longer, then I left. I went home and went to bed, as I had work early the next day. I wasn't overly worried about my two mates, as trouble seemed to follow Brendy and they were also two big strong, hard lads who could look after themselves in a difficult situation, or so I thought. The next morning, I switched my phone on and it went ping, ping, ping with missed calls and missed texts. My boss, Tony McNulty, left a message that simply read, 'Ring me' and when I did, Tony said, 'Have you heard?' and I asked, 'Heard what?' And he said, 'Bert got stabbed to death last night and Brendy's fighting for his life.'

Some IRA members from Belfast had called into Magennis's bar for a few drinks having just returned from a thirty-third anniversary parade commemorating the Bloody Sunday massacre which occurred in Derry in 1972, where fourteen unarmed civilians had been killed by the para-chute regiment. A row had started in Magennis's as Bert and Brendy were getting up to go and then spilled out onto the street. The row was between members of the IRA and Brendy Devine, and a certain guy in the Repub-lican side had a score to settle with Brendy. It was concerning this guy's brother who had history with Brendy. It was said in court that the top IRA man from that area, Gerard 'Jock' Davidson, had given the order for Brendy to be killed by running his finger across his own throat. It was Brendy they were after that night, and Bert tried to stop the guy from stabbing Brendy and got stabbed to death himself. 'Greater love has no man than this:, that a man lay down his life for his friends' (John, chapter 15, verse 13).

Shortly after the incident, I remember I bumped into a well-known Ardoyne Republican and friend of Jock Davidson in Eskdale Gardens and we had words and as things were getting a bit heated, the guy's phone rang and he said to me to 'Hold on a minute', but I said, 'Nah, I'm away on' (that was God working). I also bumped into Martin Meehan in the Waterworks Park and I unloaded on Martin, who had been great friends with my dad for years, but Martin was in full agreement with me and said that it was an outrage what the IRA had done. A few months later, I was at the Ardoyne Fleadh and I was drunk, when a guy called Eamon Magill called me over (Magill had worked with me and Bert in the Elephant Rooms) and he said to me, 'That's Jock Davidson over there', as he pointed to where Jock was standing with four or five people. When I am drunk, I'm a bloody eejit, a lunatic, and I went straight over to where Jock was standing and I stood right behind him as I made up my mind what to do. I thought to myself, I will wait until he turns around and then I will chin him. Well I waited, I waited and I waited as they laughed and joked and seemed to be in a world of their own. Eventually, after about ten minutes, a fella turned around and asked, 'Are you alright mate?' I responded, 'Yeah, I'm alright.' Drunk as I was, I still realised that hitting Jock would have very serious consequences, but the amount of beer I had consumed was giving me false courage, as I knew this could all led to me getting shot, maybe even shot dead, so I walked away. I must admit that when I woke up the next day, I was horrified at how stupid I was and how close I was to getting into very serious trouble, but I also praised God for watching over me and taking me away from this very dangerous situation that I had gotten myself into with ego and false bravado, but also genuine hurt for the cowardly murder of my friend. I have no doubt that God was working in my life and had plans for me.

Bert's murder was worldwide news for weeks and the peace process nearly collapsed over the alleged IRA involvement. The McCartney family were thrust into the media spotlight and were even invited over to the White House, where they had talks with President Bush.

A few years later, Gerard 'Jock' Davidson was shot dead on 5 May 2015. Another man, Kevin McGuigan, a dad of eight, was killed on 12 August 2015, as it was widely believed that he had killed Jock after a fallout. They had once been comrades in arms for the IRA. A local source said this was payback for Jock and was a warning to anybody else who may think of settling old scores with any IRA members.

I was the only one of Bert's friends to go to the trial and I went to every hearing. That was my decision, and I have no issues with any of his friends who didn't attend. I understand. That was their decision and I respect it. Three IRA men were charged with his murder and were eventually acquitted.

During the trial, the celebrated defence barrister Orlando Pownall QC held up the front page of that day's *Irish News* and on the front page there was a large photo of Brendy Devine, his wife, Ashleen, and me. We were pictured leaving the courthouse and Pownall told the judge and jury that he had noted that I was at every sitting and it is his belief that I was colluding with Brendy Devine, in making up Brendy's story and filling in the missing pieces as it went along. I was stunned, as I sat in the public gallery, listening to this nonsense. Such a load of rubbish. I couldn't believe what he was saying. He could have got me shot dead. And Pownall was thought to be one of the finest minds in Britain?

From 31 January 2005 to when I am writing this (August 2021) no one has been convicted of my friend's murder. For me, Bert's violent death was a very personal loss. It was also a tragic incident in our recent history, which would influence a change in the political situation in Northern Ireland.

My Brother Paul

My younger brother, Paul, became a dad at seventeen. His girlfriend, Lillian, was only seventeen. Obviously, it didn't go down well with both families. Lillian's dad didn't speak to Paul anyway, but now, Paul was not allowed anywhere near Lillian's parents' house. So Paul and Lillian used to come round to our house in Holmdene Gardens everyday (morning, noon and night). Things were very tense in our house at that time (1986).

My dad and I didn't speak for over two years because of his drinking and the way he was treating my mother. My dad was going through a tough time in his life, he was drinking heavily, and was abusive in the house. He was a nightmare. Sometimes he would come home and shout (mostly if I was not there) and he would take it all out on my poor mother. He would shout and bawl and sometimes throw his dinner at her. In the middle of all this, Paul and Lillian would be sitting there, with Lillian heavily pregnant. The tension in the house between my dad and I was awful. I remember there was a heavy gold poker by the fireplace and it was always in my head, that if he ever tries to attack me, then I was going to lift this gold poker and bury it in his head.

I was boxing as a professional then and I had my own pressures and these were the conditions I had to live under. I remember I was in bed sleeping early one morning, when I was woken up by his shouting and screaming. I heard him go for my mum and I jumped up, ran down the stairs and separated them as my dad had a grip on my mother.

'Get your fucking hands off her now', I shouted, and he stared at me with a deranged look. I stared back at him (I was ready), but he backed off saying, 'That's my wife', and I shouted, 'And she's my mother.' That was as close as we ever came to fighting. He blamed my mum for all his problems. Sometimes, my dad would go off the drink for periods and my mum would be running around getting him all the things he wanted (health foods, etc.) and we would be warned by my mum to stay out of his way and not to be upsetting him.

During these periods, he would be out walking in the Waterworks and lifting weights in the house and you would hear him say, 'That's me finished with drink.' Or sometimes, he would come back from a long walk in the Waterworks and my mum would have his healthy breakfast that he would require, and he would talk about how great it was to be off the demon drink and how much better he felt and how lovely the smell of the freshly cut grass was in the morning. But slowly, you could see his mood starting to turn and he would get nastier and look for faults, so as he could pass the blame onto someone else, for him hitting the drink again. This cycle repeated itself over and over and it was always my mum who was to blame (in his mind) for putting him 'back on the swall'. And for a period after that, he would come home and start his antics and blame my mum for him going back on the drink. It was a hell house I lived in. No doubt about it. To be honest, I took out a lot of my frustration on Paul. I hadn't the time of day for Paul, until I got away from that hell house. And when I did, relations improved with both Paul and my dad, but it took time.

I remember one time Paul challenging me to a sparring contest down in Ardoyne boxing club. He thought that he could hold his own with me in the ring. I remember my dad was lying on the settee in Holmdene Gardens (as usual) and he tried to warn Paul. This would have been around 1988/1989, and I hadn't boxed or trained in quite a while and had become veggie and was very thin. My dad tried to warn Paul that he was out of his depth, but Paul wasn't listening and the more Paul talked it up, the more Paul started believing in himself. I said, 'Paul, be careful what you wish for.' But Paul started getting cocky and was starting to annoy me, so I said to him, 'Okay let's do it, let's go down to the club and spar.' And we did. My dad was still lying on the settee an hour later when we returned, but he nearly fell off the settee with laughter when he saw Paul's black eye and bruises. He only did two rounds, but was exhausted. I had a wee system for novices or wild swingers (although Paul had about a dozen fights for Ardoyne ABC). I would get close to them with my hands held high and I would push them back. Paul was swinging like a good 'un in the first but as my hands were held high, nothing was getting through and I was relaxed, whereas Paul was tense and using up all his energy. I never threw a punch in the first, but in the second, I just cuffed him from pillar to post from every angle. Jabs, hooks, uppercuts the lot, and with open gloves. They were all light punches and I had him at my mercy (Paul was exhausted), but I was an ex-professional boxer and not a bully. It was only a messabout for me. Everybody outside the ring was in fits of laughter, but fair play to Paul for getting in with me and I'll tell you what, he hit hard, I could feel his blows on my arms, but luckily none got through to my chin. After the spar, Paul being Paul, said that if he had have been fitter, it would have been a different story. I said, 'Paul, I was only in first gear and I just laughed.' Paul was never fit....

Paul lived in my shadow a little bit, as I was good at all sports and won a haul of medals every sports day. I just loved sport and I still do. Paul smoked cigarettes from an early age, as did our sister, Tanya. Everyone in my house smoked except me (I was breathing in all that passive smoke). Paul was also a big-time gambler when he was younger. When he worked on a YTP programme, I used to have to go and meet him on a Friday after-noon to get my mum's keep off him, as he gambled the rest away in no time (he had been gambling the lot including my mum's keep and that's why I had to meet him to get it off him). Fruit machines were his addiction; he didn't bet on horses or play poker or anything. When he came over to London to watch me in the ABA final, he came over with money that my dad had given him. I had given him money also, but the next day after the ABA final, as we are relaxing and enjoying the craic in a pub in King's Cross, I noticed him feeding those fruit machines. Instead of joining us for some craic and banter, he was on his own for much of the day playing those damned machines.

Paul broke up with Lillian in 1989 and left Belfast to go to Manchester in 1990, and lived there for over ten years. As mentioned, I stayed in Paul's house in late 1991, while Paul and I worked for Belfast man, Paul Docherty. It was nightshift work and we were getting £50 a night. It was coming up to Christmas and we worked every night. I slept in Paul's house, but spent most of my time with former New Lodge man, Frankie Logan, who lived opposite Paul. I came back to Manchester the following year and stayed for another couple of months. I remember going to a big Prince concert which was at Maine Road, the home ground of Manchester City football club. Karen and I were massive Prince fans (he was my absolute hero and we've seen him live seven or eight times). Prince released his first album in 1978 aged just seventeen. Warner Bros gave him total artistic freedom on his first three albums and this young musical genius played all 27 musical instruments on these albums, as well as producing, arranging and composing, genius. There has never been another musician with anywhere near Prince's talent and versatility and I was fortunate to see him play live eight times.

I went to the concert with Paul and Frankie, as Paul got free tickets for all the big concerts (if he applied for them) as Maine Road was at the top of Paul's street and it was a noise pollution thing. Paul eventually met an English girl called Natalie and over ten years, had four kids with her: Patrick, Sinead, Pearse and Teirnan. For a good eight years, I didn't see Paul, but he would ring my mum from time to time. Then Paul and Natalie came home for a holiday and two of their children came with them (Pearse and Teirnan hadn't been born yet). We gave them a great time. I was happy to drive them about and I filmed their trip with my camcorder. Within a year of them coming over for a holiday, they came back again, this time to live in Belfast. They got a wee house in Estoril Park and Paul got a job.

Paul and Natalie had two more kids (Pearse and Teirnan) and for a while, things seemed to be fine. Paul liked to smoke marijuana and have a few beers and he got on fairly well with our dad and from time to time, my dad would have gone up to Paul's for a joint or two, he said it kept him off the drink. Paul was great with our dad and would never have turned my dad away if he called. Paul got on with my dad much better than me, but Paul had been away for over ten years. The drink had been taking its toll on my dad in those ten years, with constant abuse towards my poor mother. Paul was giving my mum a much welcome break when my dad called up to his house. Paul was a godsend.

If my dad behaved badly towards my mum, then Paul would bar him from his house for long periods, which would really hurt my dad, as he loved his joints and a few beers up in Paul's. Paul had the upper-hand and my dad soon got the message and his behaviour towards my mum improved considerably. Paul's relationship with Natalie was falling apart though, as Paul had lost his job and was starting to drink heavily also. Most nights, my dad would be up in Paul's smoking joints and drinking. This went on when the kids were in bed and didn't impact them. It must have been really tough for Natalie though. Eventually (over a period of time), Natalie left Paul and took the four children with her. Her and the kids stayed in a hostel until they got a lovely new house over beside the

Oldpark Road. We tried our best to help Natalie and the kids, but within a year, Natalie started to go off the rails and Paul fought for custody, as he had cleaned his act up and the children came back to live with him in Estoril Park. Paul found another girl, Jolene, and through time, she moved in with him and he had two kids with her (Shauna and Zara) and for a few years, things were fine.

Jolene McAllister had gone through a few horrific incidents as a child. She had two uncles murdered during the conflict (Martin Bradley and Francis Shannon). Jolene was in the same room as Marty Bradley, when Loyalists burst into a house on the Crumlin Road and shot Marty dead (I had spoken to Marty earlier that day). She had watched it in horror. Jolene was also holding the hand of her aunt, Isobel Nesbit, when Isobel was shot dead in Flax Street, Ardoyne in 1992. The IRA had shot her by mistake, as they were shooting at the British Army. The IRA issued a statement claiming it was a tragic accident and offered their apologies. Isobel was home on a visit from England and was due to go back to England the night that she was killed. Jolene was eleven when she had witnessed this. Two horrific events that would scar someone forever.

Paul's relationship with Jolene was turbulent, mostly down to Paul's drinking and it would be an on/off relationship. Jolene had her own wee house. I liked Jolene and she was a great wee mummy. At the heart of all this, were the kids, but I am sure that they were never affected. I tried to talk to Paul about his lifestyle and he rightly told me that it was none of my business. I remember Paul taking all his kids (except Katrina) to Salou twice and even though Paul drank, he never neglected the children. He got them out to school, he made them their dinner, he gave them money to go to the youth club, he washed and ironed their clothes and kept them clean and tidy.

From my perspective, Paul was a kind and gentle soul. The only one he ever hurt was himself. Paul always had a lot of respect for me. He was proud of me and was 100 per cent behind my son, Ciarán, when he was boxing. Paul travelled with me and loved to watch Ciarán in action. I watched Paul's temperament change and my dad no longer called, as he was bed-bound after having a minor stroke and was looked after by my mum and carers, who called regularly. Paul had moved to a lovely new house in Flax Mews and one or two people used to call to Paul's to take drugs with him, knowing that Paul had four kids sleeping upstairs (I know who these scumbags are). These parasites brought drugs to Paul's house to take along with alcohol. Paul was starting to lose control.

Karen, Shea and I were only back from Salou two days, when my front door took a hammering at 8.30 a.m., 7 September 2011. It was my sister, Tanya, and when I opened the door, Tanya screamed, 'Our brother, Paul's, hung himself.' (Tanya has a son called Paul, that's why she said 'Our brother, Paul'). Shock, horror, disbelief. I had never experienced this before, not this close. I felt numb. I feel it now. Tanya ran away, leaving me on my own as I am trying to process this awful news. I don't talk about it now and I try not to think about it. I have filed it away in my brain (compartmentalised it). I am writing this out, but then I will file it away again. I can cope better this way. It comes into my head everyday, but I chase it away, I don't dwell on it.

I strongly believe that anybody who takes their own life is getting tormented by the devil. I believe that he is in their heads, telling them they are scumbags and that no one would miss them, etc. The devil is laughing at them, while coaxing them to throw the rope up, take tablets or whatever form of suicide it takes.

A friend told me that Paul had been in a black mood a few days before this happened and was calling himself a scumbag and saying, 'Who would miss me? Sure I'm a waster.' Paul's funeral was one of the largest I saw. In part, due to the popularity of the family and in part, due to Paul's popularity. He was well liked and well respected by his children, his family and the community. He would never have left his children. Drink and drugs had ravaged him and his judgement was impaired, as his brain was not working properly. I don't think anyone who takes their own life is of sound mind. Just before he killed himself, he made a big pot of stew for the children's dinner the following day. Then he went and hung himself. Obviously, the stew was never eaten. Did he not realise that the kids would be devastated? Rest in peace my brother. I wish I could have been a better brother to you. I wish I could have been there for you. I wish you could have turned to me for help.

Paul was buried from my mother's house in Holmdene Gardens. When Paul's coffin was brought into the house, they had to turn the coffin upright to get it through the door and I watched the horror and disbelief on my dad's face as the coffin entered the living room. My dad would be lying in the bed on one side of the room and tears were streaming down his face. He couldn't talk at this time and we were not sure how compos mentis he was, but he knew, he knew, and I could tell by the intense trauma he was going through. On the day of the funeral, we had to leave my dad to go and bury his son and there was a funeral reception after in the Star social club in Ardoyne, but I didn't stay long and I went down to keep my dad company and was quickly followed by my mum and sister. At Paul's funeral, my dad's cousins and his aunt (from Portrush) came to the funeral and that was lovely of them. They were my grandad Harry's sister-in-law and nieces. It was the first time I had met them. Incidentally, my dad's aunt, who came to the funeral, was once a private secretary to the British prime minister Margaret Thatcher. We just found that out when she died in 2018.

I think I went into shock the day Paul died at the age of 42. Such was the trauma of his suicide. This was my first bereavement. I remember we called to Paul's house and as I was parking my car, a fella was coming out of Paul's house. I know the fella and he was into drugs and I am sure now that he was in Paul's house clearing evidence away that might have led to his involvement in Paul's death. What with all the shock and horror that day, I never sought to ask him why was he coming out of Paul's house and how the fuck did he get into the house? I think I went into shock that day and I started to clean Paul's house, but Paul had a lovely wee house. I think it was my nerves making me do this. I stayed on when the family left, and I think this was because this was Paul's house and I just wanted to be close to him and to try and process all what was going on, including this guy coming out of Paul's house. This guy turned up briefly at Paul's wake, but I didn't see him at the funeral. Some people then ran a fundraiser to help pay for Paul's funeral and he wasn't there. This has played on my mind for years and one day, he was coming down Duneden Park and he said hello to me and I started on him and he didn't try to fight his corner when I made accusations, he just scurried off like the cowardly bastard that he is. I have left it in God's hands now and I try not to let it bother me anymore.

Faith

Today, I live in Highbury Gardens in Ardoyne on my own. I broke up with Karen, the mother of my two sons, in 2005. It was the stupidest thing I have ever done in my life and it was all down to ego (mine). We got back together briefly a couple of times, but it didn't work out and we drifted apart. We are set in our ways now and I have been living on my own for over fifteen years. Karen is bringing up our son, Shea (I see him every day as I only live down the street). I have had twenty good years with Karen and she will always be the love of my life and my soul partner. We are in contact everyday by phone and I would text her to tell her how my day is going and to inquire about Shea. She is my crutch and my rock. I have never gone looking for anybody else in the fifteen years we have been broken up. We had been rowing constantly about me doing the door and chasing women and I left that day (January 2005). It was the worst thing I ever did in my life. I beat myself up every day about walking out. Why did I do it? I would love to turn the clock back to that day and reverse my decision. I had moved out a couple of times before to give us some space, but I loved her and missed her so much and when I came back, it was twice as good. However, this time when I left, I left Karen to cope with two children, Shea was only one year old. How could I do it and why did I do it? I used to think I was a good dad, but a good dad wouldn't walk out on his wife and kids and break up his family. I had let my ego get out of control. Karen never went with anybody else, so who knows.

My faith in God is growing every day and I would go to Mass two or three times a week. I would go to Holy Hour on the Glen Road every Tuesday, where we would say a rosary and the blessed sacrament would be exposed. I would go to adoration also and sometimes to divine mercy on a Friday in the Sacred Heart chapel on the Oldpark Road. I would pray daily. I am also big into cursillo and I first did a cursillo in 1995, and that was in St Clements on the Antrim Road. You can only do it as a candidate once, but through time you can work (serve God) on as many as you want (as long as you are picked). While I really enjoyed it, as a candidate, I then drifted back into the ways of the world for seventeen years, but I still would have gone to Mass every Sunday. It was my friend, Mickey Stevenson, that first got me involved in cursillo and it was Mickey that talked me into coming back to work on one. as my faith had lapsed and I was becoming what is called a mechanical Catholic (just going to Mass by habit and not really listening or participating). Well, when I went back to serve God on a cursillo weekend, I was well and truly blown away. I have worked on about twenty weekends since, including being a rector. There is a vow that no one can speak about what goes on in this three-day retreat, 'What you see here, what you hear here, let it stay here.' And this is only because you don't want to spoil it for anybody (nothing sinister). It is perfectly designed by God and I hope to be part of cursillo until the day I die. The Pope has done a cursillo and I would strongly recommend it to everyone and I can promise you one thing, you won't regret it (**De Colores** my cursillo friends).

I remember being up in Derry a few years ago, and the 1970 Eurovision song contest winner, Dana, gave a witness, which was one of the best I ever heard. Later, we all joined hands and formed a circle around her and as she stood in the middle, we sang the cursillo anthem 'Lady of Knock' to her as she stood there crying her eyes out. Dana had written that song. We were all stood there around her and some of us were crying our eyes out also. Not me though.

A miracle happened one cursillo weekend in Crossgar in October 2017, but I will go back four months before that, when a fella from West Belfast called Steven Ferguson collapsed during the weekend in Benburb and had to be rushed to hospital. The fella had been a heavy drinker and a sponsor called Steven McCloskey had convinced him to do the weekend only the previous day when he had bumped into him by chance (Steven McCloskey had never previously met this other guy). To be honest, the fella should never have been on the weekend, as he was not fit or prepared mentally, physically or spiritually. The fella looked sick and gaunt (skinny as a rake) the first time I set eyes on him. I do recall him saying that he had done a bit of boxing and had boxed while he was out in America. The thing though was that being on a cursillo weekend had saved his life. He had lived in a flat on his own and the hospital even told him if he had have been in the flat then he would have died. He collapsed on the second day of the cursillo (Friday) right in front of us. We had put him in the recovery position, as he was unconscious and an ambulance was quick to arrive and duly brought him to hospital, where he was quickly attended to. Steven was prayed for the whole weekend and I heard no more until the October weekend in Crossgar, when this athletic, well-built fella came over to me and started talking as if he knew me. It was Steven. I didn't recognise him, as he was unrecognisable from the last weekend and it took a while for the penny to drop with me, but when it did, then I was absolutely gobsmacked. He told me that God was working that weekend and he had saved him from certain death and hell. And he told me that he hadn't touched a drop of alcohol from the day he had collapsed, four months previously. He had also started training and had put on some weight and to be honest, he looked a million dolars. I couldn't believe it and to me this was a miracle. Throughout the whole weekend (which he loved), I would look over at him, shake my head and whisper, 'Praise the Lord'.

You can be saved right up until the last breath you take. Remember the story of the good robber who was crucified beside Jesus. He rebuked the other robber who was mocking our Lord. He then turned to Jesus and said, 'Jesus remember me when you come into your kingdom.' And Jesus then told him, 'Believe me, today you will be with me in paradise.' He is called the good robber because he stole his way into heaven.

I also love doing the Knock Walk pilgrimage every July. It is closely linked to cursillo and we walk from Blessington (just outside Armagh) to Knock, which is over 130 miles away. We walk over five days (Wednesday to Sunday) and you would get about 70–90 people on the walk. You have the walkers, the food people, the music ministry (who keeps our spirits up with uplifting music at every water stop) and the rubbers (who take the pain away from our feet, knees, backs etc.). Also, people who would bring their cars along to be used at water stops and to be at key points to make sure that we were going in the right direction. There would be spiritual people like Fr Seán Kelly, who is on the walk most years and who did his cursillo the same time I did (St Clements 1995). We walk along the roads with our rosary beads praying or just chatting (many great friendships are made on the walk) and the cars would toot at us or when we walk through towns, people would stop us and ask us to pray for them or for some intention. We walk, we talk, we pray and we sing. It's so spiritual. We have built up many friendships down the years and people would put some of us up in their houses, or we would be in a town hall or a community centre. The first overnight stop is in Clones (just over the border), and we stay in this big hall and at the back of the hall, is a boxing gym where Barry McGuigan used to train and some of us actually sleep inside the ring (there are sleeping bags and some makeshift beds).

We have built a good reputation down the years and people love to see us and they smile and wave, but we will always be on our guard as there are always wolves among the sheep and we have had a few wee incidents down the years, but very few, thank God. Michael Stevenson told me a lovely wee story about the walk, that just sums up the people on it. Michael said that they were walking past a wee chapel on the road from Boyle to Gorteen and a funeral was taking place. Michael said that there was fewer than a dozen people at this funeral, as the fella who died (an elderly man) had died in England but wanted to be buried in the place of his birth. Michael was there, but it was his friend, Tony McNally, who said to one of the relatives as they were going into the chapel, 'Would you mind if we attend the funeral Mass and pay our respects to your brother?' And the fella said, 'You're all more than welcome to attend.' And Tony shouted, 'Get everyone down here, the music people, the walkers, everyone.' This was the late 1980s and the Knock Walk was getting big, big numbers and in no time at all, the wee chapel was busting with over 100 people there (instead of ten) and the music people played, everybody sang and the deceased had the best send-off ever. The fella's family all wept for joy and couldn't thank the Knock Walkers enough and if that's not God working, then I don't know what is. The Knock Walk was started by a Derry man called Thomas Gallagher and I am proud to say I know Thomas and he is always on the Knock Walk.

Thomas had a vision when he was in Medjugorje. In the middle of the night our holy mother told Thomas (in a dream) to start a peace walk from Derry to Knock. Our holy mother told him that she would guide him and that this walk (and rosaries on the walk) would bring peace to Ireland and that one day, they would walk from the four corners of Ireland to meet in Knock. And in 2015, pilgrims walked from Derry, Belfast, Dublin and Cork to meet up in Knock and I was one of the walkers. Also, the IRA announced their ceasefire in 1994 and it just happened to be during the five-day Knock Walk. Our holy mother was true to her word. Moreover, I remember giving Thomas Gallagher a big hug, amazing. The Derry men are very special. I heard that on their walk from Derry to Knock, a lot of them will walk in their bare feet and they would ask God for more pain as they struggle along with blisters, shin-splits, exhaustion etc. and they would be shouting, 'More pain Lord, give me more pain,' as they are offering their pain up for the holy souls in purgatory. Amazing. I have run the Belfast Marathon, but in my opinion, the Knock Walk is much tougher. I have also been to Medjugorje a few times and the peace out there is incredible. A little piece of heaven is how some people describe it.

I am a hopeless sinner. I fall a hundred times a day, but I pick myself up, dust myself down and get back on the road (the road to everlasting life). St Augustine said, 'The just man falls seven times a day.' I am anything but a just man, but God sees that I am trying, and I will die trying. 'The desire to please God, pleases God' (Thomas Merton, Jesuit). My faith hasn't been a road to Damascus one, but a very slow inch-by-inch one (yard-by-yard it's too hard, but inch-by-inch it's a cinch). I was the most reluctant Christian and I ran away from God for years. I put everything in front of God, but God kept putting these amazing people in my path. God wanted me, but I didn't want him, not yet. He's got me now though. I have surrendered. I still have to put God at the centre of my life though. It's God first, family second, and Eamon third.

I went to Krakow, Poland, for a friend's stag in June 2018. Eighteen of us went. The friend who was getting married was Ciarán Healy, whom I coached for his first five professional fights (all wins). I was to go to Auschwitz on the Wednesday and had gone to the shooting range that morning, where we had the opportunity to fire handguns, pump action shotguns, AKs, the lot. Not all of the lads wanted to go to the shooting range and I was to meet some of them at 1 p.m. to go to Auschwitz, but the taxi driver who took us back from the shooting range, told me that it was too late to go to Auschwitz as they would be long gone and he said that you had to leave early for Auschwitz as it's a long journey there and back (three hours to get there). I said to the taxi driver that a few of us had gone the night before to check out the Auschwitz tour and I'm sure the girl told us that the bus would pick us up at the hotel at 1 p.m., but the taxi driver said, 'No, long gone.' I was disappointed, but Tommy Tolan said to me to come along with him and Gerard McCafferty to view the house and tomb of sister Faustina Kowaiska. Incidentally, the taxi driver was wrong, as the boys did get picked up at the hotel at 1 p.m. for Auschwitz, but I think that it was meant to be, as I had a wonderful time at Sister Faustina's and have no regrets. In fact, all the ones who went to the Auschwitz tour came back thoroughly miserable and depressed and Tommy, Gerard and I came back on a high.

I had been expecting a wee house where her room would be (and her tomb), but the place was absolutely massive and we were there three or four hours, just getting around it and seeing everything. We went to Sister Faustina's tomb and we said the divine mercy there along with 30–40 people and there were hundreds of pilgrims walking around the grounds outside, it was amazing. After we had visited the tomb, and said the divine mercy, we went to see her bedroom and possessions. Jesus had told Sister Faustina to spread the divine mercy to the world and she wrote her dairy in this room, where she also died at 32 years of age. When we left the room, I walked outside and I saw Tommy Tolan talking to a nun and they went into this building and Gerard McCafferty and I followed. Gerard, Tommy and I had a lovely talk with this nun. She was beautiful, with a lovely smile and an infectious laugh and she seemed graceful and saintly. We asked her what her name is and she smiled and said, 'Faustina.' And we all laughed at the coincidence then she said, 'I have come down from heaven,' and she giggled. We had tried to talk to other nuns that day, but they were surly and didn't want to engage in conversation with us. Sister Faustina was the only one that was friendly and happy to chat.

As it was approaching 3 p.m., we went over to where sister Faustina Kowaiskas's tomb was interned and the young nun came with us. During the short walk, Tommy asked this young nun how old she was (Tommy can be direct) and she giggled and said 32 (the same age sister Faustina Kowaiskas died) and as we were entering the building she said, 'I am going upstairs to pray for you.' Then she was gone and we never saw her again. I have been told that sister Faustina Kowaiskas is known to appear in Krakow, I wonder, I just wonder. 2018 is the eightieth anniversary of sister Faustina's death and Gerard, Tommy and I were left gobsmacked, but it had been a truly wonderful day. One more thing, Tommy rang our friend from Liverpool, Robbie Ross, two days later and before Tommy had the chance to say anything, Robbie asked, 'Did you meet sister Faustina?' Robbie claimed that he had a dream about us meeting sister Faustina Kowaiskas!

A lot of boxers have faith. I remember one of my heroes, Evander Holyfield, boxing Mike Tyson in 1996 and he pulled off one of the biggest upsets in boxing history, when he stopped Tyson in eleven rounds in Las Vegas. I remember I watched the fight on Sky sports in Karen's and my house in Cranbrook Gardens with my dad and my friend, Brendan 'Moe' Toal. What amazed me in the fight, was that between rounds, when the coach usually gives advice and instructions on how to attack and defend, Holyfield's coach was simply saying to Evander, 'Concentrate on Jesus.' And Holyfield would be sitting in his stool in his corner, with his eyes closed, taking deep breaths and concentrating on Jesus. Holyfield was drawing strength from concentrating on Jesus.

At the end of the fight, when Evander was victorious, he was interviewed by American TV and he didn't want to talk about Tyson or how great a fight he (Evander) had fought, he just wanted to give thanks to God and praise God for giving him the strength and the will to win. Evander said, 'All praise be to God and not me, because if I was to take the glory, then I would be taking it away from God and that would be unjust' (I might not be quoting the exact words, but it was along those lines). The guy who was interviewing Evander tried to move him away from talking about God and tried to get him to talk about the fight, but Holyfield wouldn't be moved. Pretty inspiring stuff, eh. I would have pinned holy medals to my boxing boots and my mum would have lit holy candles and when I boxed as a professional, I would have gone to confession on the day of the fight (I got this idea from *Rocky*). I also lit holy candles and prayed, so I always had some faith. Some nights as I'm lying in bed, I would be getting attacked by the devil and I would think to myself, 'Concentrate on Jesus, Eamon.'

Rinty Monaghan

On 20 Thursday August 2015, a bronze statue was unveiled in the Cathedral gardens in Belfast city centre of North Belfast boxer John Joseph Monaghan. His nickname was Rinty. My great-uncle, Rinty was flyweight boxing champion of the world (1948–1950) and has the distinction of being the only 'home based' undisputed world boxing champion ever to come out of Ireland. Rinty held six belts all at the one time, he was a Northern Ireland champion (knocking out the great Bunty Doran), he was an all-Ireland champion beating Dublin's, Joe Collins. He was a European champion, beating Maurice Sandeyron, and he won the Empire, the British and the undisputed world title against Scotsman, Jackie Patterson.

Rinty retired in 1950 due to ill health, but was the undisputed and undefeated world boxing champion (it doesn't get any better than that). Rinty was known as the singing boxer, as he would always sing a song in the ring after his fights (win or lose). One of his favourites was 'When Irish Eyes Are Smiling'. And Irish eyes were certainly smiling as Lord Mayor Arder Carson, along with Rinty's brother, Tommy, sister, Marie, and daughters, Retta and Collette, pulled the cover away to reveal the 10ft. bronze statue (including plinth) of Rinty Monaghan which was made by Edinburgh man Alan Herriot Beattie. It was a great victory for the working class to have one of our own immortalised in a bronze statue and on display in the middle of Belfast city centre. This process started in 2010, when I went to see Sinn Féin councillor Margaret McClenaghan (who lived on my street) to see if she could get me a meeting with Sinn Féin MLA Alex Maskey, himself a former amateur boxer.

Well, Margaret McClenaghan did indeed get me the meeting (unfortunately Margaret died of cancer shortly after this and didn't live to see the statue). I brought my great-uncle Tommy (Rinty's brother) along to the meeting which was on the Ormeau Road in Alex's office. I had asked specifically for Alex, because his family is steeped in boxing and Alex's dad was a boxing historian and a good friend of Rinty's. Alex told us that a fella called Barry Flynn had called to see him regarding getting a statue erected of Falls Road boxer John Caldwell, and it was Alex who suggested not only to go for statues of these two great boxers, but also to include the contribution that boxers from the Shankill area have made in putting Belfast on the map. 'Don't forget,' said Alex, 'that it was Rinty and Shankill man Jimmy Warnock who started the whole thing off down at Ma Copey's 'chapel fields' in the 1930s and 1940s.' So that's what we did, we went for three statues.

We met regularly over a five-year period and Belfast city council put up £240,000 for three statues. Sculptor Alan Herriot Beattie was chosen to do the Rinty statue. Well, there must have been at least 200 people who came along for the unveiling and the whole story was covered extensively by the media. Speeches were made by the Lord Mayor, the sculptor, Alan Herriot Beattie, and some of Rinty's family (including me). Then Rinty's voice came over the PA system as he sang 'When Irish Eyes Are Smiling', and there wasn't a dry eye in the place. There was a big party in the Balmoral Hotel later that night, and many of Rinty's relatives had come over from the USA for the unveiling (and what a party we had).

Rinty's parents, Martha and Ta, lived in Highbury Gardens in Ardoyne for over twenty years and his eldest sister, Sarah (my granny), lived in Brompton Park, Ardoyne with her husband, Harry McAuley (my grandad), who was one of Rinty's main sparring partners and they lived out their remaining years there. So even though Rinty was not from Ardoyne (he was from Sailortown), there was indeed a big Ardoyne connection.

Rinty Monaghan's dad was my great-grandad, he was called Ta and was the seventh son of a seventh son, and allegedly had healing powers. Ta and his wife, Martha Wilson, from the Shankill Road, were wed in 1913 when Martha converted to the Catholic faith. My great-granny became a devout Catholic, practicing her faith daily. Ta and Martha, had all their pregnancies been successful, would have had fifteen kids instead of nine. Ta taught all his kids to sing and there was always music in the house (Ta played the accordion) and they were tough, but happy days. Ta worked in the merchant navy and earned up to £2 a week (a decent wage in those days). All the Monaghan boys went to sea and Rinty got the nickname

Sinbad, as his ship was found ship wrecked off Ballyholme Bay off the County Down coast. Ta taught his son Rinty how to box and encouraged him to drink raw eggs and goats milk. Rinty was born in Lancaster Street, then the family moved to Thomas Street, then to Concorde Street where the family's home was bombed by the Germans during the Second World War and reduced to rubble. Ta and his family were very lucky to survive. Ta's son Patsy, who was thirteen at the time, lost his best friend, Joseph McAuley, as he died that day along with many others. The Monaghans then moved to 61 Highbury Gardens, Ardoyne (five doors up from where I now live) and they lived there for many years (Rinty had gotten married and lived elsewhere, so Ardoyne can't claim him). Martha and Thomas lived well into their eighties.

I remember my mum telling me that her and my dad were once in their house, and my mum accidently stood on Ta's toe and he lashed her with a torrent of profanity and she said that he was a grumpy so and so anyway. I am not sure if I met my great-granny and great-grandad, but I clearly remember being at their funerals in the late seventies. I was great mates with Martha and Ta's youngest son, Tommy, and while I loved and respected Tommy, he could also be cantankerous at times. Uncle Tommy lived most of his life in Texas and Florida, but lived in Belfast in later years. I loved Tommy's craic and I loved to wind him up at times, as we had many intense debates about politics and boxing. At times, Tommy would get frustrated (exasperated even) and the, 'God damns' would be flying out of his mouth (God damn this and God damn that) and I would be killing myself laughing (there's a badness in me). I remember being in a cafe in Castle Street with Tommy, and the waitress approached to take our order and Tommy would be looking at me as he was saying, 'I will have soda bread with sausage on top and a pot of tea.' And I said, 'What are you telling me for? Tell the girl.' And he cracked up. 'God damn it Eamon, don't you get fucking fresh with me!' I would always just laugh. But I loved Tommy, I did. I loved meeting up with him. Tommy went to my pro-fights, including one in England. Tommy did a bit off boxing when he was young and one time, he had to box his brother, Patsy. Rinty did Tommy's corner and Ta did Patsy's (or vice-versa). Patsy won, but couldn't go to the All Irelands and Tommy took his place. Tommy lived to 87 years of age and lived to see the statue of his brother Rinty unveiled in Cathedral Gardens (just a stone's throw from where Rinty lived out his remaining years in Little Corporation Street) in 2015. Tommy went back to America shortly after that, and one day I received a phone call from him and as we were saying goodbye, he said, 'Eamon I love you.' And

I replied, 'I love you too Tommy.' That was the last time I spoke to him, as he died very shortly after that.

I wouldn't claim to have known Rinty with any great intimacy, I didn't. But I do have some great memories of him. I remember my dad bringing me down to see him just before Christmas in 1982 in his house in Little Corporation Street, as I had been back to Belfast (from Manchester) to spend time with my family at Christmas and had reached the NABC finals. I had blossomed into one of the best junior boxers in Britain and Ireland. I remember being shocked when Rinty told me that he hadn't even had one amateur fight. He told me that he learnt how to box at Ma Copey's chapel fields and had his first fight there at fourteen. Rinty's real passion was singing though, and he would also entertain the crowd with his song and dance act. I was sixteen in 1982, and I remember Rinty being in my face showing me combinations. He was very intense and passionate in what he said and did. My dad brought a camera along (an instant one) and we took some photos and I still have one today.

I also remember Rinty coming up to my uncle Seán's boxing show in Ligoniel in 1981. Seán was my dad's brother and Rinty's nephew. There was what seemed like hundreds packed into the gym (mostly kids), as there were boxing contests taking place and during the interval, Rinty took the opportunity to jump into the ring and he sang and danced, he did his Popeye and Olive Oil impressions and played his harmonica and he brought the house down (he loved to entertain). The problem was getting him out of the ring, to let the boxing contests continue (that took some time). But he was brilliant and had us all in stitches. My uncle Seán said that all he asked for in order to come up and entertain us, was a packet of cigarettes. When I was at the Cavendish club in Manchester, the top guy was a man called Bill Nedley and he asked my uncle Gerard and I if Rinty would be prepared to come over to be the guest of honour at one of their big shows at Maine Road (home of Manchester City football team). I was boxing in the show, but I remember Rinty being keen to come over and he was not asking for a penny. He was doing this for my uncle Gerard and I (whom I lived with then). There was a series of phone calls between Rinty and Gerard before Gerard and I pulled the plug on it.

Bill Nedley wanted to do this on the cheap, as he wanted Rinty to stay with Gerard in Gerard's house and was not prepared to put Rinty up in a basic hotel. Gerard only had a two-bedroom house and there was six of us living there as it was. Where was Rinty going to sleep, on the settee? Rinty was not in great health then and he died the following year. I felt that

Bill was not giving a legendary ex-world champion the respect he should have been afforded. So we pulled the plug on it. It was Bill and Cavendish boxing club's loss. I was grateful to Rinty though, he was prepared to come over. On 3 March 1984, Gerard and I were getting ready to go to Liverpool, as it was the final of 'Henry Cooper's Golden Belt' and it was Manchester v. Liverpool and we were the defending champions. I was down to box a guy that I had clearly beaten the previous year, Neil Foran. Before we left the house, my granny rang (Gerard's mum) and she told us that Rinty had died that morning. We were just heading out the door when she rang. I lost my fight on a close decision. After that loss to Foran in March 1984, I wasn't to lose again until 3 December 1987 and that was in my seventh professional contest. Between March 1984 to December 1987, I had nineteen amateur contests and six pro-contests without a loss. A 25 fight unbeaten streak.

I actually had a relative, a member of the Monaghan family, who died in the terrorist attack on the World Trade Center on 11 September 2001. His name was Brian Monaghan and he was only 21. His grandad was called Barney Monaghan and he was my granny Sarah's full cousin. Brian was in the Twin Towers when the planes struck the buildings. May he rest in peace.

The second statue is of Falls Road man, John Caldwell. John won an Olympic bronze medal in Melbourne in 1956, was a British and Empire flyweight boxing champion and he beat Frenchman, Alphonse Halimi, for the EBU version of the world bantamweight title (he also defended against Halimi in a rematch). Caldwell then travelled to Brazil to box Eder Jofre for the undisputed world bantamweight title, but was stopped in ten rounds by probably the greatest bantamweight ever. Caldwell then boxed fellow Belfast man, Ardoyne's, Freddie Gilroy, for the British, Empire and European titles (also world title eliminator) at a packed King's Hall in October 1962 and was stopped on cuts, as the ref wouldn't let him come out for the tenth round with the fight hanging in the balance (too close to call). John Caldwell's statue is on display at Dunville Park on the Falls Road

The third and last statue, is an anonymous statue to recognise the contribution boxers from the Shankill/Woodvale area made in putting Belfast on the map in sporting terms. Boxers like the four Warnock brothers least of all, Jimmy, who beat the great Benny Lynch twice (one of those wins was when Benny was the reigning world boxing champion). Unfortunately, they were non-title fights. You also had the Briers brothers, the Mekle brothers, Tommy Armour, who stopped the great Eric Boon in five rounds at Solitude (home of my beloved Cliftonville football club), in front of 30.000 fans. Davy Larmour won a Commonwealth gold in Christcurch in 1974 and won the British professional title in 1983. Davy also went to the 1976 Montreal Olympics, losing a split verdict against the eventual gold medal winner, Leo Randolph. Wayne McCullough won a Commonwealth gold, Olympic silver and won the WBC world bantamweight title in Japan in 1995. There were lots of other great boxers from the Shankill and I beat two of them, Davy Mitchell (RIP) and Alan McCullough (Wayne's brother).

I've a wee story now about the Shankill Boxing statue. Davy Larmour and I were brought on board to give an insight and an opinion on the statues and the sculptor, Englishman Mark Richards, initially came over to Belfast to meet us and he brought some sketches he had drawn, on how the statue might look. However, Davy and I told him that the sketches he had done were all wrong and out of proportion. I rose from my chair to explain to him and show him how a boxer throws a straight right and Mark asked could he take photos of me and I said, 'No problem, go right ahead'. And he took loads of photos of me standing posing, while pretending to throw a straight right hand and he walked around me snapping away from every angle. I swear to God, I can definitely see myself in that statue. That's me throwing a straight right, honest. Everybody laughs at me when I tell them there's a statue of me in Woodvale Park.

To Finish

I was in Albufeira (Portugal) in March 2017, and I was with a stag party consisting of about fourteen lads from North Belfast. This trip was during the Six Nations Rugby final match between Ireland and England and many of us brought our green Irish rugby tops along for the occasion. We were looking for a good bar to watch the match in and after trying a few different places, we walked into a bar full of English rugby supporters, many of whom were wearing their white England rugby tops. If this had have been a soccer match, then we would have gone nowhere near it, but the rugby crowds are a different kettle of fish and the English fans (consisting of many women and children), welcomed us with open arms. The craic and the banter was amazing during the match, with the English cheering and singing as they were going for the grand slam and also a world record for successive unbeaten matches, and the Irish were out to spoil it.

At half time, we had a giant scrum in the middle of the bar, which involved all fourteen of us against the English and it was hilarious. Even the owners and bar staff got involved and at the end of the giant scrum, we were all hugging and I remember stepping back with tears in my eyes, as I can get very emotional and I thought that it was just a beautiful thing, as I felt so much love in the room. There were English and Irish, Catholic and Protestant, black and white but more importantly, brother and sister. In the second half, we started singing rebel songs and the English sang with us. There was no offence intended and there was no offence taken and I thought, 'Why can't it always be like this?' I was so proud of my lads, as we were great ambassadors for our country and the same goes for the English.

One of the English girls was having a fiftieth birthday party the following day, and they begged us to come along and we finally relented and said we would (we didn't go). Ireland ended up winning the match, but that wasn't so important. Incidentally, one of our lads was called Blakey, and he had once been the victim of a freak accident that had caused him a brain bleed that nearly killed him. My brother-in law, Sam McBurney, who is married to my sister, Tanya, was playing golf and as he teed off, he whacked Blakey on the head with the golf ball. Thank God Blakey made a full and complete recovery. I didn't previously know Blakey, but I remember praying for him when it happened and I will tell you what, he really knows his boxing. Sam McBurney's cousin is married to former Liverpool, Celtic and now Leicester manager, Brendan Rodgers' brother, Conn Rodgers. Sam is a fanatical Celtic supporter and hasn't spoken to Brendan since he left Celtic. So I'm related (through marriage) to Brendan Rodgers.

Also, while I was in Albufeira, the boxing author and historian Gerry Callan, who lives there, came down one night to meet me and I was proud as punch that the lads stayed on to listen to him, and they were enthralled as he told boxing stories and they fired question after question at him. Gerry and I went head to head answering questions and in the end, they held up both our arms and called it a draw. It was another great night.

On Saturday 18 August 2018, Tommy Tucker Kelly from the New Lodge rang me and said that there was a guy in the Europa Hotel that wanted to meet me and could I get down to the Europa at 1 p.m. Tommy wouldn't tell me who this guy was and I got dressed and headed down to the Europa (which was the most bombed hotel in western Europe and the place where Karen had a stroke in 1999). I knew all the overseas boxers were staying in the Europa and that very night, Carl Frampton would be topping the bill at Windsor Park against Aussie, Luke Jackson, but I was intrigued to know why Tommy had invited me down. When I got there, I rang Tommy and he told me to come into the bar area of the Europa. When I arrived, Tucker was sitting down with Ricky Hatton and he shouted over, 'Eamon come over here, Ricky wants to meet you and have lunch with you.'

I had never met Ricky before although, I had been to his show *An audience with*', where he was on stage and talked to the crowd for over an hour, telling many funny stories about his life and terrific boxing career. Tommy had arranged this in the Europa for me, as a surprise, and I was thrilled. Also in the room were Billy Joe Saunders, Josh Warrington, Carl

Frampton and big Tyson Fury. They all knew Tucker and he introduced me to them all and I have the photos to prove it. I spent about an hour in Ricky's company and he was very down to earth and we had a right old chat. The next day, I bumped into Tommy in the town and I thanked him again and I remembered that Tommy had ordered us tea and sandwiches in the Europa (which wouldn't have been cheap). I said to Tommy to let me treat him to a coffee and some sandwiches and Tommy said, 'Eamon, don't worry about it. I told the staff in the Europa to put it on Ricky's hotel bill.' Then as we are having our coffee, Tommy rang somebody and during the course of the conversation, he turns around to me and says, 'Eamon, Glen McCrory wants to say hello to you.' (Glen McCrory is a former IBF world cruiserweight boxing champion from Newcastle and a pundit/commentator for Sky sports). Thank you Tommy, ya legend ye. The following Saturday (25) I went down to Dublin to see Pope Francis at Phoenix Park.

One boxer I would love to meet is Iron Mike Tyson and I came oh so close about a decade or so ago. Tyson was appearing at the Waterfront Hall in Belfast and my friend, Gerard McNulty, had three free tickets for me. Gerard is one of the managers of Clear Channel (who post events on the big advertising boards) and he would sometimes get free tickets for various events. The other two tickets I gave to my brother, Paul, and friend, Paul Mulvenna. Tyson would be talking about his life and, at the end, would do a question-and-answer session. Barry McGuigan was doing the warm-up (main supporting bout). I rang Barry the night before the event, and asked him could he get us backstage to meet mighty Mike and to get a photo with him. Barry told me that wouldn't be a problem, but warned me that Tyson and him had not been paid for the previous night in Scotland and they hadn't been able to contact the promoter, who Barry thought had done a runner and Barry warned me that the Belfast show was now in serious doubt. He was correct. When I woke up the next morning and turned my phone on, the first text that came though (sent at 6 a.m.) was from Barry who typed that the Belfast show was cancelled and neither Barry nor Tyson would be coming to Belfast. I was heartbroken. Tyson has never been to the north of Ireland. When Barry managed Carl Frampton sometimes, Barry would leave me free ringside tickets to be collected at the venue. Barry was my hero when I started boxing in 1978 and we are still in contact today. I consider him to be a friend.

It was truly amazing being in Phoenix Park on Sunday 26 August 2018, when Pope Francis said closing Mass after two days in Ireland, during the world meeting of families. It is mind-boggling to think that the pope turned bread and wine (with the power of God) into the body and blood of Christ, which I then received in me. For a Catholic, it doesn't get any better than that. There was around 300–400,000 pilgrims in attendance and as he was driving around in his Pope mobile, waving and smiling at everyone, he passed by my section, green route north circular section B (14B), and I was within touching distance of him (and I was able to film it). It was only the second time in history that a pope had come to Ireland and the first was 39 years earlier, when Pope John Paul II came in 1979.

I must admit that I was buzzing with excitement all day, but what a day. It had been a long day, as I had to be at St Patrick's Chapel at 6.45 a.m. as a bus was leaving from there and the night before, I had been working at a rave on the Holy Cross school pitch in Ardoyne. At the rave, up to 500 young men and women were off their heads on drink and drugs as the devil's music went boom, boom, boom. I just looked at them and I remember thinking that the devil had them in the palm of his hand. Then the violence broke out. Brawls started to break out all over the place (they were in a giant tent) and I remember, as I was putting someone out, looking over to the entrance/exit place and seeing a brawl involving the doormen. Instinctively, I rushed over and grabbed a guy who was throwing punches at the doormen and I wrestled with him and physically threw him out. I thought that he was going to come back at me and I was ready as I stood my ground, but he started shouting that he had been shot and he pulled up his trouser leg to show a wound that was bleeding. I thought this guy was just high on drink and drugs and had hit his leg against something during the brawl he had with the doormen.

I went back to the tent and there was a guy who earlier had gotten someone to take a photo of him and I, and he had said, 'Pretend you're throwing me out', so I pretended to grab him by the neck and we got the photo taken (I knew him). About an hour later, I really had him by the neck as I was dragging him out. Fights were breaking out all over the place and the organisers decided to close the place down, as the music stopped and the lights came on. As I was clearing them out, I could see the empty drug prescription packets all over the place, along with unopened carry outs. Also, handbags and phones that had been left behind. I went and got my wages, left and went straight to bed.

It was not until I got home from Dublin the next day after the Pope's visit, that I learnt that there was indeed a fella who had been shot in the leg. The police had confirmed it on Facebook. It must have been a flesh wound (just grazed his leg) as if he had had been shot through the leg then he would have been crippled. Also on Facebook was a photo of the fella I had thrown out and in the photo, he had his belly bare and was wielding a big machete. The photo was took minutes after I threw him out and it said on the Facebook post that he was out for revenge (two people were injured disarming him). I could have walked right into him as I left the venue. The next morning when I woke up, my neck, shoulders and back were hurting and I had blood on my coat and a nick on my eye. The guy with the machete recently got sentenced to six months for the incident.

I am a massive fan of my local soccer team, Cliftonville football club, and I have been supporting them since 1979. I was thirteen when the 'reds' won the Bass Irish cup at Windsor Park. Tony Bell scored the winning goal in the final minute, to beat Portadown 3–2. 1979 was the start of the reds revival. We had made red and white rattlers in Mr McCaffery's woodwork class in school for the occasion. I will never forget walking down the Boucher Road to Windsor Park Football Stadium that day, in a sea of red and white and standing in Spion Kop on one of the greatest days of my life. I remember the Cliftonville (1979) cup winning team coming to Ardoyne Youth Club and they were mobbed by the children. The club was situated in the Brookfield Street mill then, and it seemed like there were hundreds of kids shouting and screaming and getting the footballers to sign scraps of paper, cigarette papers, anything. I remember being right in the middle of it, and shaking hands with the players and I swear to God, I didn't wash my right hand for days. The Cliftonville players got a small taste of what The Beatles had to endure daily in the early 1960s. There have been barren years though, from 1980 up to 1998. We fought a relegation battle, season after season, and we might have had a half decent cup run or maybe won the odd County Antrim shield, but the big prizes eluded us. But in 1998, we won the league for the first time in 70 something years.

It went right down to an unforgettable day at Solitude, against Glentoran football club and we got the point that we needed, as Linfield (our nearest rivals) drew at Coleraine football club and I am not ashamed to say I shed a tear that day. Then we won the Gibson Cup again in 2013 (Geordie McMullan's last minute penalty winner against Linfield at Solitude) and we won the league again, the following year (two in a row). We also won four League cups in a row and drew the mighty Celtic in the Champions League (all recent). I don't support English or Scottish soccer teams. Why should I? I am not from England, Scotland or Spain. I am from North Belfast and there is only one team for me – Cliftonville – end of. When I used to go to Solitude in the late 1970s/early 80s, it was a shithole and up until the last six years, it was still a shithole. However in the last six years, we have got a new away stand, a new home stand, new floodlights and even a new pitch and within the next two years, we will be getting a new (modern) main stand. Then it will be practically a new ground. It's an exciting time for Cliftonville supporters.

I bring Karen's nephew, Daniel, and my brother Paul's grandson, Cole, to support the reds. They love it. My son, Shea, went for a couple of seasons but he doesn't want to go now, but the door is always open for him to come back to the red army. I can honestly say that sport is my life. I live for sport and my life would be so much sadder if they banned sport tomorrow.

As I mentioned earlier in the book, I am a veggie and the reason for that is simple, I love animals! I am amazed at people who say they love animals and I say, 'Oh, you're a veggie then?' And this puzzles them and they say, 'Well, no.' I have been a veggie for 30 years and will be until the day I die. Becoming veggie finished my boxing career but I don't regret becoming veggie. I love being veggie and I love veggie food. It was tough 30 years ago, as I was on a bit of a one-man crusade, but I read books and magazines and I learnt what to avoid, and that they use animal derivatives in most things including beer etc. Most places cater for veggies now. From March 2019, I have gone vegan, and I am now doing my bit for climate change and global warming.

I am also very proud to say I am a blood donor and have been for many years. There aren't many things more important than giving blood to save lives and if, by giving a small amount of my blood every three months, then it's a joy, an honour and a privilege to do this. I am in and out of the blood donor place in under twenty or thirty minutes (plus you get tea, juice, biscuits etc.). You get the green badge after giving blood ten times, you get the red badge after 25 visits and you get the gold badge after 50 donations, I am getting close to the gold badge.

When you give blood (which is under a pint) it replenishes in a few weeks. My four heroes throughout my life were former middleweight boxing champion, Harry Greb (who died in 1926), Ronnie Barker (comedy genius), Prince (musical genius) and Muhammad Ali (a man who transcended boxing). The four of them have passed now, but three were alive for most of my life. Prince and Ali passed within a few months of each other and I really took it bad (I am still not over Prince). I cried for days. I am also very proud that I boxed in the same hall as Harry Greb (Royal Albert Hall).

I have also made a documentary on boxers from my area (Ardoyne/ Bone). It is on YouTube and is 90 minutes long and boxers like Steve Collins, Barry McGuigan, Carl Frampton and many more contribute to it by talking about their experience of boxing or sparring someone from this very small area that has produced many great boxers and hard men. It's simply called **Ardoyne/Bone Boxers**. To view this, just go on YouTube and type that in. I also love doing interviews with local guys who didn't quite reach the dizzy heights of their chosen sport. You will find many of those interviews on YouTube, so check them out. Just type my name in and many videos will pop up. One video leads to many others. I interview people who have largely been forgotten and I love giving them a heads up.

I am 54 now and instead of slowing down and taking my foot off the pedal, I am determined to speed up and I still have drive, ambition and ideals, that's what gets me out of bed in the morning. I have never lost sight of the positive impact boxing can have in socially disadvantaged communities. I'm back coaching kids in the St John Bosco boxing club and loving it, I run over to Conway Mill on the Falls Road and after working with the kids (and when I say kids, these days I mean from ten years to thirty-five years), I then run home to Ardoyne. There are three coaches at St John Bosco (SJB), Gerard McCafferty, Stevie Martin and me, and we have all lost brothers to suicide (Gerard has lost two brothers). The club is a fantastic outlet for young people to keep fit and healthy and build up their confidence, as well as learning boxing skills. The gym isn't just for young people, as we have people in their 30s and 40s keeping fit at SJB. The craic and banter is always great, but we are training in third world conditions as we have no showers, no changing facilities for the girls and when it rains, the roof leaks and we have to put a wheelie bin in the middle of the gym to catch the water.

The SJB is one of the oldest boxing clubs in Ireland, and has produced many champions down the years, including four guys who went to the Olympic games: Freddy Gilroy (who got a bronze medal in Melbourne in 1956), Marty Quinn (Mexico 1968), Gerard McCafferty's own dad, Seán McCafferty (Tokyo 1964), and Michael Conlan (who went to two Olympic Games, winning a bronze in one). Freddie Gilroy went on to win the British, Empire (Commonwealth) and European professional bantamweight titles. Many of our girls and boys have experienced suicide, either in their family or in the community. In fact, Northern Ireland has the highest suicide rate than any other region in the UK or Ireland. Organisations such as PIPS (Public Initiative for Prevention of Suicide and Self-Harm) do great work to support those at risk of suicide or families affected by suicide, offering support and counselling throughout Belfast and Northern Ireland. Tackling suicide and addressing mental health, is an area which definitely needs more funding. As I write this, there has been ten deaths to suicide in West Belfast in the last two weeks. I was taking a girl on the pads just the other day, when she suddenly burst out crying. I brought her into the weights room, which was empty, and she broke down and told me she had just lost her friend to suicide lately. I wanted to console her by hugging her but I can't under the new child protection guidelines, so I called head coach, McCafferty, in and we talked to her and told her how proud we were that she has told us and got it off her chest and we told her how good it is to talk. Boxing coaches are sometimes like social workers or councillors. We are voluntary and we do it for the love of boxing and the communities that we come from. But it's time consuming and a big responsibility. So praise the Lord for all the boxing coaches down the years. Many of them are unsung heroes.

I was just looking at my amateur boxing medical card from when I moved to London and my professional boxing record also and I discovered that I won 29 out of my last 30 fights (and that's not bad!). Look for yourself:

P. Fitzgerald Lpts, B. McGarrigle Wrsc1, S. Summervile Wpts, A. Keogh Wpts, C. O'Brien Wpts, D. Cooper Wpts, P. Day WKo3, T. Reynolds Wpts, D. Grainger Wko1, A. Staples Wrsc3 (NABC final), O. Sidenko (Israel) Wko1, D. Murphy Wpts, B. Jenkins Wpts, T. Craham WKo1, M. O'Brien Wpts, L. Amass Wrsc3, R. Smyth Wrsc3, C. Crook Wrsc2 (ABA final), E. McArdle (Aus) Wpts, D. Bramald (pro debut) Wpts6, L. Remickie Wrsc2, L. Remickie Wrtd2, G. Jones Wpts6, T. Borg WKo4, N. Lucas Wrsc3, A. Furlong Lrtd3, G. Egbuniwie Wpts6, R. Bushell WRsc4, R. Davidson Wpts, P. Buckley Wpts, C. McAuley Wpts.

As mentioned, I also got two murals commissioned in Ardoyne/Bone of all the great boxers that came out of my area. I made the point that there were too many paramilitary murals looking back at the past. Too many murals of gunmen with guns and rifles in their hands. I told the people who commission the murals that we need positive, uplifting images to inspire kids and celebrate something positive in the area. We needed to move on from the past and look to the future. Now, as well as having the two boxing murals, we also have murals of GAA and local footballers, Joe Gormley and Rory Donnelly. They are now getting the message and I am grateful.

I am content with my life today, as I have my health and my faith. So many boys that I went to school with are dead and in their graves today. Others are addicted to alcohol or drugs, which were a byproduct of the

Troubles. People often drank trying to cope with the horror. So I don't feel sorry for myself, as I have a lot to be grateful for. I didn't fulfil my potential as a boxer, but I really enjoyed the ten years I spent boxing. If I had been a world champion and rich and famous, then I believe that it would have taken me down a different road and I might have been far away from God. At the end of the day, I simply wasn't good enough. On reflection, I know that now. I can make all the excuses I want, but a world champion will always find a way to the top, despite setbacks. That's what makes them special. I couldn't and I didn't.

Today, I do voluntary work delivering bread and food parcels to the old and needy in and around Belfast. My pals Mark Toal, Sam McBurney, Paddy 'the legend' Larkin, Eanes Keenan, Stevie Arthurs and I go out in Paddy and Eanes' vans, bringing hot meals and food parcels to both Catholic and Protestant areas. We also do outreach work, going into Belfast city centre to look for homeless and vulnerable people, bringing with us hot food and drinks as well as, thermal hats, socks and gloves to hand out. We chat with them, we listen to them and we try to get them fixed up with somewhere to stay. Some of them have been on the streets for ten or fifteen years. I feel so blessed to be doing this type of work. We operate out of the People's Kitchen at Farset on the Springfield Road. This project was once a vision of Paul McCusker and Sineád McKinney. A vision that has now became a reality.

When I get some free time, I go into the town (Belfast city centre) where I meet up with my friends and ex-pugs, Davy Larmour (an ex-Olympian, Commonwealth gold and a former British bantamweight champion), Paddy Maguire (a Commonwealth silver and former British bantamweight champion), Sammy Vernon (who beat Larmour and Maguire in the amateurs twice each) (Sammy was also an ex-professional), Neil Sinclair (a Common- wealth gold and a British welterweight champion) and Colin Holmes. Colin wasn't a boxer but he is a Christian, who I clearly see the light of Christ shine out of. He is a generous and kind-hearted fella who has helped and inspired me on my journey with Christ.

Karen, Shea and I went on a Mediterranean cruise in December 2019 to celebrate Karen's fiftieth birthday. I planned to get down on one knee and ask her to marry me. I hoped she would accept my proposal, as she has knocked me back a few times already. Either way, I'm content with my lot. 'Paul had learned to be content in all things,' (Philippians, chapter 4, verse 11–13). So at this point, I'll conclude my story.

On 6 December 2019 at 8.50 p.m., in La Palma, Gran Canaria, I had arranged with the head of entertainment, Giovanni from Costa Rica, that before the big show starts in the theatre, could he tell the 300 people in attendance that it was Karen's fiftieth birthday that day. Giovanni told us to arrive early and to sit in the front row. After the crowd had given Karen a round of applause, Giovanni handed the microphone to me, after saying Eamon wants to say something to you. I then said, 'Karen, you know the way I have spent all this money to bring you here for your fiftieth birthday, well, I'm about to make you the luckiest woman in the world...' And I got down on one knee after saying, 'Will you marry me?' and she said, 'Yes!'

This book got a happy ending after all. Praise God for that. God bless you all and thank you for letting me keep you company. Maybe, just maybe, I have finally found peace?

Healing Prayer

Lord Jesus through the power of the Holy Spirit go back into my memory as I sleep. Every hurt that has ever been done to me, heal that hurt. Every hurt that I have ever caused another person, heal that hurt. All the relationships that have been damaged in my whole life that I am not aware of, heal those relationships. But O Lord, if there is anything that I need to do; if I need to go to a person because he or she is still suffering from my hand, bring to my awareness that person. I choose to forgive and I ask to be forgiven. Remove whatever bitterness may be in my heart, Lord, and fill the empty spaces with your love. Amen.

References

Adams, Gerry (1994) *Selected Writings*, Dublin: Brandon Press.

Ardoyne Commemoration Project (2003) *Ardoyne: The Untold Truth*, Belfast: Beyond the Pale Publications.

The Bible, Christian Community Bible, Catholic Pastoral Edition.

Buchanan, Ken (2000) *The Tartan Legend: The Autobiography*, London: Headline Book Publishing.

Dillon, Martin (1990) *The Shankill Butchers: A Case Study of Mass Murder*, London: Arrow Books.

Egan, Joe (2006) *Big Joe Egan: The Toughest White Man on the Planet*, London: Pennant Books.

Fair, James (1946) *Give Him to the Angels: The Story of Harry Greb*, West Sussex: Summersdale Publishers.

Gibson, Paul and Magee, Eamonn (2018) *The Lost Soul of Eamonn Magee*, Cork: Mercier Press.

Holmes, Larry (1999) *Larry Holmes: Against the Odds*, New York: St Martin's Press.

Madden, Brian (2006) *Yesterday's Glovemen: The Golden Days of Ulster Boxing*, Belfast: Brehon Press Ltd.

Morrison, Ian (1986) *Boxing: The Records*, London: Guinness Publishing.